The
Resurrected
Skeleton

TRANSLATIONS FROM THE ASIAN CLASSICS

Translations from the Asian Classics

The
Resurrected
Skeleton

FROM ZHUANGZI TO LU XUN

Wilt L. Idema

COLUMBIA UNIVERSITY PRESS NEW YORK

COLUMBIA UNIVERSITY PRESS
Publishers Since 1893
New York   Chichester, West Sussex
cup.columbia.edu

Library of Congress Cataloging-in-Publication Data
Idema, W. L. (Wilt L.)
The Resurrected Skeleton : from Zhuangzi to Lu Xun / Wilt L. Idema.
pages cm. — (Translations from the Asian Classics)
Includes bibliographical references and index.
ISBN 978-0-231-16504-4 (cloth : acid-free paper)
ISBN 978-0-231-53651-6 (e-book)
1. Chinese literature—History and criticism.
2. Resurrection in literature. 3. Zhuangzi—In literature.
I. Title.

PL2275.R47134   2014
895.109'351—dc23   2013027557

Columbia University Press books are printed on permanent
and durable acid-free paper.
This book is printed on paper with recycled content.
Printed in the United States of America

c 10 9 8 7 6 5 4 3 2 1

COVER IMAGE: Li Song, *Kulou huanxi* (*A Magical Performance
of Skeletons*) (Reproduced with permission of Palace Museum,
Beijing [photograph by Zhou Yaoqing])
COVER DESIGN: Misha Beletsky

CONTENTS

ACKNOWLEDGMENTS

This book has had a relatively long time of gestation. I first became interested in Daoist storytelling and the legend of Master Zhuang's encounter with the skeleton more than twenty years ago when I was doing some research on Li Song's painting of the skeleton marionetteer. I became intrigued by references to *Master Zhuang Sighs over the Skeleton in Northern and Southern Lyrics and Songs*, a text that survived, it seemed, only in a single copy kept in the library of Yamagata University in Japan. This institution eventually provided me with a photocopy of (its own photocopy of) that text through the good offices of the then librarian of the Library of the Sinological Institute at Leiden University, John T. Ma. With generous funding from the Netherlands Organization for Scientific Research, I was able to invite Professor Tseng Yong-yih of Taiwan National University to Leiden in the summer of 1998 to spend a number of weeks reading the text with me, but unfortunately the photocopy was of such a quality that many passages were not legible, and I had to lay aside my plans for a translation of this text.

Over the years, I continually asked many colleagues for references to skulls and skeletons in premodern Chinese culture, and many of them obliged. These notes and materials languished in increasingly fatter folders. Only quite recently did I become aware that a complete and highly readable version of the *Master Zhuang Sighs over the Skeleton in Northern and Southern Lyrics and Songs* is available to all at the Web site of the University of Tokyo Library. This discovery provided the stimulus for me to return to the legend of Master Zhuang's encounter with the skeleton. The result is the following study and its accompanying translations.

A special word of thanks is due to Professor Wang Xiaoyun of the Institute for Chinese Literature of the Academy of Social Sciences in Beijing, who provided me with photographs of *The Precious Scroll of Master Zhuang's Butterfly Dream and Skeleton*, which is available only in a single manuscript copy in the institute's library. Professor Oki Yasushi of the University of Tokyo kindly provided me with photographs of the edition of Wang Yinglin's play preserved in the Naikaku Bunko and also assisted me in securing permission for the reproduction of the illustrations in *Master Zhuang Sighs over the Skeleton*. Professor Jeehee Hong of Syracuse University assisted me for the other illustrations. The Beijing Palace Museum kindly granted permission to use Li Song's painting of the skeleton marionetteer for the cover illustration. My student Sun Xiaosu alerted me to the popularity of Guo Degang's *Skeleton Lament*. The staffs of the Harvard-Yenching Library at Harvard and the East Asian Library at Leiden University have been extremely helpful, as always, in locating various secondary materials used for this study.

Last but not least I would like to express my gratitude to Columbia University Press for its willingness to publish this work in its series Translations from the Asian Classics.

The
Resurrected
Skeleton

Introduction

Once upon a time, the story tells us, the Daoist philosopher Master Zhuang, while traveling to the capital of the state of Chu, came across a skull by the roadside. After wondering aloud how the deceased may have come to his end, he laid himself down to sleep, using the skull as his headrest. The deceased thereupon appeared to him in a dream, praising the untrammeled pleasures of death over life. For all his vaunted relativism, Master Zhuang was not convinced and offered to bring him back to life, only to see his suggestion rudely rejected by the skull. We first encounter this little story in chapter 18 of the *Master Zhuang* (*Zhuangzi*), a collection of writings by Zhuang Zhou (ca. 300 B.C.E.), writings about him, and writings of other ancient philosophers that struck later Chinese scholars as equally extravagant. The text of the *Master Zhuang*, with its many fictive anecdotes and fanciful parables, has provided Chinese literature with an almost unlimited supply of allusions for over two thousand years, but few of the numerous dialogues and stories have successfully been taken up by later writers and developed into full-length poems, tales, dramas, or ballads. The story about Master Zhuang most popular from the early seventeenth century onward—how Master Zhuang tested his wife's fidelity by faking his own death, a test she miserably failed—has no clear source in the *Master Zhuang* at all. The only story from the *Master Zhuang* itself that continued to inspire poets, dramatists, and storytellers was the anecdote of Master Zhuang's meeting with the skull. This anecdote was taken up by the leading poets of the second and third centuries (Zhang Heng, Cao Zhi, and Lü An), each of whom developed the short account of the *Master Zhuang* into a full-length rhapsody. The theme was then abandoned for almost a thousand years, and when it made its comeback, the skull had expanded into a full skeleton. This skeleton does not appear to Master Zhuang in a dream but is brought back to life by him fully fleshed (three missing ribs are replaced by willow twigs). It is this later legend of Master Zhuang's resurrection of a skeleton and its consequences in its various manifestations in traditional Chinese literature of late imperial China and in modern Chinese literature that is the focus of this book.

The emergence of the tale of Master Zhuang's meeting with the skeleton is closely linked to the proselytizing activities of Wang Chongyang, the twelfth-century founder of Quanzhen Daoism. In the poems and lyrics that Wang used to preach his teaching, we encounter two images of the skeleton. On the one hand, the abandoned skeleton by the roadside stimulates the passing observer to lament the brevity of human life and the foolishness of those who do not timely seek salvation. On the other hand, every one who neglects to pursue enlightenment can be compared to a walking corpse, a living skeleton. It is the first image, however, that soon becomes connected to the anecdote of Master Zhuang's coming across a skull and develops into the tale of Master Zhuang lamenting the skeleton. In the later versions of this tale, Master Zhuang proceeds to bring the skeleton back to life, only to be accused by the resurrected skeleton of having stolen its belongings! In a confrontation before a district magistrate, Master Zhuang is forced to turn his opponent into a skeleton once again to prove his innocence. In fiction of the seventeenth century, the tale of Master Zhuang's lamenting the skeleton is portrayed as the tale typically told by preaching Quanzhen priests, and in the preserved adaptations of the tale, Master Zhuang himself is anachronistically identified as a Quanzhen priest. Over the centuries, the tale found appeal with moralists and mystics, cynics and satirists, and, among this range of writers, with anonymous authors of popular literature to elite writers such as Wang Yinglin (d. 1644), Ding Yaokang (1599–1671), and Lu Xun (1881–1936).

Popular as the tale of Master Zhuang's meeting with the skeleton may have been in the sixteenth and seventeenth centuries, it was largely supplanted by the tale of Master Zhuang testing his wife's fidelity. This tale was first printed in 1624, by Feng Menglong (1574–1646), as one of the forty vernacular stories making up *Stories to Caution the World* (*Jingshi tongyan*). In this story, Master Zhuang, while strolling through the fields, comes across a young widow who is fanning a grave. When Master Zhuang asks her why she is doing so, she replies that her husband had, before his death, given her permission to remarry as soon as the earth of his grave had dried. Master Zhuang helps her by using his magic power to dry the grave. When he arrives home and tells his wife what had happened, she curses the widow for her lack of fidelity and swears eternal loyalty to her husband. In order to test her, Master Zhuang then feigns his own death and takes on the shape of a handsome prince. His wife immediately falls in love with the prince and insists on marrying him; when the prince slips into a coma on their wedding night, she prepares to split open her former husband's coffin and remove Master Zhuang's brains in order to save her new husband's life. When Master Zhuang revives that very instant, his wife is so mortified by shame that she commits suicide. Chapter 18 of the *Master Zhuang* contains an anecdote describing Master Zhuang's equanimity following his wife's death, but it provides no information on the manner of her death. As Master Zhuang is reproved for his lack of feeling by his friends, who praise her behavior, there is no suggestion in the *Master Zhuang* that the deceased wife ever acted inappropriately. Whatever the origins of this tale, it was widely adapted in many performative genres over the next three centuries. Some of these adaptations include Master Zhuang's meeting with the skeleton, either preceding or following the episode of Master Zhuang's testing his wife; in some of those in which the meeting with the skeleton is included, the resurrection of the skeleton is omitted. At the same time, adaptations of Master Zhuang's meeting with the skeleton continued to circulate as independent texts.

Following a detailed study of the development of the legend of Master Zhuang's meeting with the skeleton through two thousand years of imperial Chinese history, this volume presents full and extensively annotated translations of its major adaptations. The core of these translations is constituted by three texts of the seventeenth century—by Du Hui, Ding Yaokang, and Wang Yinglin, respectively—each of which presents its own idiosyncratic take on the legend. These seventeenth-century texts are followed by two relatively short ballads from the nineteenth century or even later that combine in one way or another the legend of Master Zhuang's encounter with the skeleton with the tale of Master Zhuang's meeting with the widow who is fanning her husband's grave and its consequences. This series is concluded by one modern adaptation of the legend, by Lu Xun, whose Master Zhuang fails to turn the resurrected skeleton into a skeleton once again—his Master Zhuang becomes the emblem for all grandiloquent and power-hungry but ultimately ineffectual intellectuals of his own day and of all times. The three appendixes provide translations of a number of closely related texts.

The *Master Zhuang*

If we can trust the stories in the *Master Zhuang* in which a certain Zhuang Zhou declines the offers of kings to make him prime minister of their kingdoms, Master Zhuang must have lived at the end of the fourth century B.C.E. The great historian Sima Qian (145–87? B.C.E.) informs us in *Records of the Historian* (*Shiji*) that "Master Zhuang hailed from Meng, and his personal name was Zhou. He served at one time as the administrator of the Lacquer Grove in Meng and lived at the time of King Hui of Liang and King Xuan of Qi." Meng is said to have been located within the borders of the kingdom of Liang, but Master Zhuang is usually associated with the southern state of Chu, and while his office as administrator (*li*) may well seem lowly to later eyes, it probably held great economic importance, since the Lacquer Grove was the source of lacquer used in the production of the increasingly popular lacquerware. Sima Qian's very brief notice on Master Zhuang would appear to be based on the writings transmitted under his name, from which he quotes Master Zhuang's rejection of King Wei of Chu's invitation to join his court as chancellor.[1]

External references to Master Zhuang from the third century B.C.E. are very rare. His writings may have been compiled for the first time in the second century B.C.E., but the text would acquire its present shape only in the third century C.E., when an earlier compilation in fifty-two "sections" was edited by Guo Xiang (252–312) into thirty-three chapters.[2] This edition is subdivided into three sections: seven "inner chapters," fifteen "outer chapters," and eleven "mixed chapters." Only the seven inner chapters are commonly believed to be the writings of Zhuang Zhou.[3] The other chapters contain anecdotes about Zhuang Zhou (some of which show him in conversation with the logician Hui Shi) and writings deriving from other schools of thought. Despite the heterogeneity of the texts that make up the *Master Zhuang*, the work as a whole is unique among those of the ancient philosophers because of its dazzling style, its unbridled fantasy, and its eagerness to entertain the most extreme philosophical positions.[4] For generations of readers, Master Zhuang's absolute but playful relativism has been best represented by his butterfly dream, as narrated in chapter 2:

> Once upon a time Zhuang Zhou dreamed he was a butterfly, as happy as could be a butterfly! He knew he could follow his whim and didn't know he was Zhou. When a moment later he woke up, he was to his consternation Zhou, and he did not know whether he had been dreaming he was a butterfly or whether the butterfly was dreaming it was Zhou. Between Zhou and a butterfly there has to be a distinction. This is called the transformation of beings.

In characterizing the writings of Master Zhuang, Sima Qian stated that despite their broad diversity they in essence derived from "the words of the Old Master." This is somewhat surprising since despite its flights of mysticism, the *Book of the Way and Its Virtue* (*Daode jing*) is in many ways a handbook of rulership, whereas the *Master Zhuang* stresses the dangers of administrative service and praises the joys of retirement and uselessness. But whereas Confucius may be portrayed alternatively as a sage and as an ineffective pedant in the *Master Zhuang*, the Old Master is always held up for praise. The *Master Zhuang* was classified together with the *Book of the Way and Its Virtue* of the Old Master Li Dan as Daoist texts from as early as the late first century B.C.E., but while that short text and its author would play a central role in the Daoist religion as it developed from the second century on, the *Master Zhuang* remained primarily a philosophical text, even though it was eventually included in the Daoist Canon. And although the Old Master was deified and became one of the highest divinities in the Daoist pantheon, Master Zhuang never became the object of a cult, despite his being ranked as an immortal in later legend. During the Tang dynasty (618–906), when the reigning family claimed to descend from Li Dan, Emperor Xuanzong (r. 712–756), a great patron of Daoism, in 751 bestowed on the *Master Zhuang* the title of the *True Classic of Southern Florescence* (*Nanhua zhenjing*). This title was probably inspired by the conventional association of the *Master Zhuang* with the southern state of Chu.

Chapters in the *Master Zhuang* in many cases start out with an extended essay or a long dialogue on a given topic, which is then followed by a number of more or less thematically related anecdotes and parables. Chapter 18 carries the title "Perfect Happiness" and starts with a disquisition on the impossibility of defining perfect happiness, ending in praise of inaction—that is, the inaction of Heaven and Earth by which everything originated. The issue of perfect happiness is linked to the issue of eternal life, which is rejected in favor of constant transformation. This disquisition is then followed by anecdotes that teach how each living being has its own nature and is subject to an endless chain of change. The first anecdote to follow this disquisition is the anecdote that shows Master Zhuang pounding a tub and singing following the death of his wife. To his reproving friends, Master Zhuang explains that his wife has rejoined the unending process of change and that weeping would show a lack of understanding:

> Master Zhuang's wife died and Master Hui offered his condolences. But he found Master Zhuang singing while sitting with widespread legs and drumming on a tub. Master Hui said, "You lived with her and raised children. Now she has died of old age. It would already be too bad if you didn't weep, but now you even sing while drumming a tub—isn't that way too extreme?" Master Zhuang replied, "Not at all! When she had just died, I too of course was deeply moved. But then I considered that originally she had had no life. And not only did she originally have no life, she originally did not have a body. And not only did she have no body, she originally did

not have any energy. She was all mixed up with the unfathomable. Following a transformation there was energy; following a transformation of that energy there was a shape, and following a transformation of that shape there was a life. Now, following yet another transformation she has gone to death. This is the mutual sequence of the four seasons of spring and autumn, winter and summer. She is sleeping peacefully in this grand room. If I thereupon, sobbing and bawling, would weep over her, I would be of the opinion that I had no understanding of fate. And that's why I stopped."

Following yet another anecdote on the process of transformation, we encounter the anecdote of Master Zhuang's meeting with the skull. But whereas the anecdote of the death of Master Zhuang's wife would seem to urge us to confront life and death with equanimity, we now encounter a skull who praises the joys of death over the pleasures of life:

When Master Zhuang went to Chu, he saw an empty skull, clearly manifesting the shape of the bare bones. He touched it with his horsewhip, and then questioned it as follows: "Did this come to pass because you made a mistake in your desire for life? Or did this come to pass because of the destruction of your state or an execution by the axe? Or did this come to pass because you committed some foul crime, a shameful scandal that made you abandon father and mother, wife and children? Or did this come to pass because you suffered from cold and hunger? Or did this come about because of the number of your years?" When he was finished speaking, he took the skull and went to sleep, using it as a headrest.

At midnight the skull appeared in his dream and said, "By your way of talking you seem to be a rhetorician. When I observe your words, they all concern the troubles of the living, but in death we are free of them. Would you like to hear a description of death?" "Certainly," Master Zhuang replied, and the skull said, "In death you have no lord above you and no servants under you. There's also not the business of the four seasons even if you have the age of heaven and earth. Even the pleasures of a southward-facing king cannot surpass this."

Master Zhuang was not convinced and said, "I will have the master of fate[5] give you back your shape, provide you with bones and flesh, tendons and skin, and bring back your father and mother, wife and children, neighbors and friends. Would you be interested?" The skull looked extremely sad and said, "How could I abandon the joys of a southward-facing king for the toil of a human existence?"

Of the three remaining anecdotes, one depicts a certain Master Lie encountering a skull and equating life and death.[6]

Since Master Zhuang's encounter with a skull is one of the many anecdotes intended to illustrate the outrageous nature of his opinions, the story could have come into being at any time between the third century B.C.E. and the second century C.E., when the theme was taken up by Zhang Heng (78–139). This may well make Master Zhuang's dialogue with the skull the first recorded instance of a theme that is encountered widely throughout Eurasia and northern Africa. Probably the best-known instance of a meditation on a skull from Western literature is Hamlet's monologue occasioned by the discovery of the skull of the former court jester Yorick in Shakespeare's *Hamlet* at the beginning of act 5.[7] There the point is that the skull cannot speak anymore ("That skull had a tongue in it and could sing once"), but as much as a century before Shakespeare, Robert Henryson (ca. 1425–1508) had allowed three skulls to have their say in *The Thre Deid Pollis*. These literary works fit in with the greatly increased visibility of skulls and skeletons in the visual arts of western Europe from the fifteenth century on, spurred on by the great strides in the development of anatomy in the sixteenth century.[8] But in medieval times, the confrontation with death—for instance, in the legend of the three living and the three dead[9]—was usually a confrontation with a decaying corpse. In the Islamic world of the Middle East, however, legends of encounters with a speaking or revived skull were widely circulating at least as early as the ninth century. Most often, the central figure in these stories is Jesus (Isa), who in his wanderings encounters a skull. When he questions the skull as to his identity in life, the skull usually reveals himself to have been a king and brags about his powers and pleasures while alive before continuing with an accounting of his sufferings upon death, providing a detailed description of hell.[10] In many versions, the king is allowed to be reborn in order to embrace the true religion of Islam and be saved. As Islam spread, this legend became widely popular from Morocco to Java in both oral and written versions. It was also widely popular in Central Asia. One of its best-known versions is a short narrative poem attributed to the famous twelfth-century Persian poet Farid od-Din Attar. In some early versions of the legend, it is the Prophet's nephew Ali who encounters the skull, and in eastern Christianity some saints—for example, Saint Macarius—are credited with similar experiences.[11]

Modern experts on the *Master Zhuang* rarely discuss chapter 18.[12] One of the very few critics to have taken up the anecdote of Master Zhuang's meeting with the skull is Stephen Owen:

> The skull that frowns and knits the brows it does not have, to express a repugnance it cannot feel is one of those touches of Chuang-tzu's humor (or the humor of his spiritual progeny) that reminds us of the distance between the world of parable and the truth that eludes direct words. "The happiness of a king on his throne" is a happiness Chuang-tzu knows too well to be no happiness, yet the metaphor is given to persuade us and an unenlightened Chuang-tzu of death's absolute liberty. At the moment we doubt the metaphor and the expressive mobility of the rigid bone, we realize that in death there is no will to delight in the exercise of such liberty nor any inclination to disabuse those of us who might misunderstand death. The parable, and even the motive for offering it to us, dissolve in understanding its message.[13]

To fully understand the outrageous nature of the anecdote of Master Zhuang's meeting with the skull, we should perhaps take into account traditional Chinese concepts of death. Anything that had to do with death was classified as *xiong* (unlucky) and was avoided as far as possible, and the extremely detailed rules for funerals and mourning probably originated as much in fear of the ghost of the deceased as in love for the person of the departed. Contact with the physical remains was avoided as much as possible, and the unexpected encounter with human bones would have filled many with horror. The *Expounded Meaning of the Exceptional Writings of Master Zhuang* (*Zhuangzi qiwen yanyi*), a selective vernacular retelling of the *Master Zhuang* of the earliest years of the twentieth century that otherwise offers a straightforward translation, still finds it necessary to insert lines that stress Master Zhuang's exceptional curiosity and his total lack of fear in sleeping with a skull as headrest.[14]

In this connection, we should also note that throughout the centuries of late imperial China, the skull was often associated with black magic. Vixens that were a thousand years old and determined to increase their store of vital power by seducing men were believed to turn themselves into charming wenches by placing a skull over their head. When sixteenth-century novels describe the black magic employed by the Khitan Liao against the Chinese generals of the Yang family, their most potent weapon is a naked barbarian princess holding a skull, the ultimate concentration of the power of yin (women, foreigners, and death).[15] It is the act of a barbarian chieftain to turn the skull of a slain enemy into a drinking vessel. The use of ritual implements made of human bones by Tibetan and Mongol clerics could only have emphasized the barbarian nature of these monks in Chinese eyes.[16]

Rhapsodies on Skulls

Encyclopedias and anthologies compiled in the early Tang preserve more or less complete versions of three poetic adaptations in the shape of a rhapsody (*fu*) on the theme of a meeting with a skull.[17] These three works are ascribed to some of the most famous literary names of the second and third centuries. The shortest fragment is attributed to Lü An (d. 263).[18] Lü An was renowned for his noble and unbridled character. He was one of the best friends of the famous Ji Kang (223–263). When Lü An's wife engaged in an adulterous affair with his elder brother, that brother accused Lü An of a lack of filial piety, and when Ji Kang tried to intervene to save him, both were executed. Lü An's poem opens with a vision of a lonely traveler who comes across a skull. The traveler offers to properly bury the skull, whereupon the deceased appears to him and informs him that death is inevitable. Perhaps the traveler offered to bring him back to life,[19] whereupon the deceased may have vaunted the superior pleasures of death, but in what appear to have been the final lines of the rhapsody, the traveler clearly rejects that standpoint:

> Thereupon I
> Was moved by his bitter suffering,
>   But sneered at what he expounded.
> "Because of your terrible hardship
>   As shape and spirit are torn apart,
>   I now
> Will house you in the solid earth,
>   So it may be your eternal location:
> We will have to go our different ways,
>   From now on we will be separated."

It is tempting to read this poem as Lü An's meditation on death on the eve of his execution, also because the deceased mentions having "transgressed against Highest Heaven." In view of the existence of two other poems on the same topic by earlier writers, however, it may be safer to treat the poem as an exercise on a well-established theme.

The adaptation that seems to hew most closely to the anecdote as recounted in the *Master Zhuang* is the version ascribed to Cao Zhi (192–232).[20] Cao Zhi was the fourth son of the warlord Cao Cao (155–220), whose power in the final years of his life extended over all of northern China. Upon the death of Cao Cao, his second son, Cao Pi (187–226), accepted the abdication of the last emperor of the Eastern Han and became the founding emperor of the Wei dynasty (220–264). Many believed that Cao Cao would have preferred to see Cao Zhi ascend the throne, but his elder brother, once established, banished him to his princedom and kept him far away from the central government. As a poet, Cao Zhi wrote both poems (*shi*) and rhapsodies. His rhapsody on the skull, which may have been preserved very much complete, is actually titled a discourse (*shuo*), which may reflect the fact that it includes some extended passages in prose. Even though Cao Zhi follows the outline of the anecdote in the *Master Zhuang*, he rejects in his conclusion the equivalence of life and death as expounded by the spirit of the deceased by invoking the authority of Confucius (Xuanni):

Now the different situations of existence and nonbeing
    Have been set out in detail by Xuanni,
So how can an empty reply, a spirit's manifestation,
    Declare the absolute equality of death and life?

Surprisingly, the most original adaptation of the theme would appear to have been the earliest of these works if we can trust the ascription to Zhang Heng (78–139). This is also the poem that has the best chance of having been transmitted in its entirety.[21] Zhang Heng was not only a high official but also probably the most learned man of his time. One of the inventions he is credited with is that of a seismograph. He was also an outstanding poet. His most famous poetic composition is "Rhapsody on the Two Capitals" (Liangjing fu), a long epideictic poem that compares the simplicity of Chang'an, the capital of the Western Han dynasty (206 B.C.E.–8 C.E.), with the extravagance of Luoyang, the capital of the Eastern Han (25–220). In his "Rhapsody on the Skull," a more modest work, the deceased who appears in his dream vaunting the joys of death at great length turns out to be none other than Master Zhuang himself, whose remains the poet has come across. Following Master Zhuang's ecstatic descriptions of his pleasures now that he has once again become united with the universe, the poet keeps silent and limits himself to burying the skull:

I looked around and decided to depart. I ordered
    my groom
To wrap the skull in a white scarf,
    And cover it with the dark earth.
Shedding tears for its sake,
    I poured out a libation by the side of the road.[22]

The disappearance of the theme of the skull from the poetry of the fourth century and later is somewhat puzzling.[23] One would expect that the introduction of Buddhism, widely known among the Chinese elite from the fourth century onward, would have stimulated an interest in a topic like this. The Buddha is said to have started on his long road to enlightenment following confrontations with poverty, sickness, and death, and the contemplation of corpses was an established practice in the training program of monks intended to convince them of the ephemerality and hence "emptiness" of life. To the extent that this practice was introduced into China,[24] it was probably never as widely practiced as in South Asia, but pictures of corpses and skeletons were considered proper adornment of monastic quarters in the Tang dynasty.[25] In the preserved Buddhist art of the Tang from Dunhuang or farther afield in Central Asia, one may indeed on occasion come across skulls or even skeletons, but only very rarely.[26]

In the meditation on bones as practiced in East Asia, the emphasis was not on the skull or the skeleton as the outcome of the process of decomposition but on the complete process of decomposition, from the first bloating and discoloration of the corpse until its final and total dissolution, when even the last bones had turned to dust.[27] Buddhist homiletic poetry, such as the poems ascribed to Wang Fanzhi and discovered at Dunhuang, refer ad nauseam to this final fate of the body, but it is a theme that was carefully avoided by the members of the cultural elite of the Tang and the Song (960–1279) in their poetry and prose, at least to the extent that their writings have been preserved. Two sets of nine poems each on the successive stages of decomposition, however, have been preserved in Japan. One of these sets is included in the collected works of the famous monk Kūkai (774–835), but it has long been suggested that he copied part or all of this set during his years of study in China.[28] The other set is ascribed to the famous Song-dynasty poet Su Shi (1036–1101); unlikely as this ascription is, it suggests that its Japanese readers believed these poems to have originated in China.[29] In both sets of poems, the decomposing body is that of a woman, bringing home the Buddhist point that even the most seductive temptresses are, in the final analysis, nothing but "charming cadavers."[30]

But if homiletic Buddhist literature dwells lovingly on each stage of decomposition of ordinary corpses, Buddhist hagiographic literature insists that bodhisattvas and other holy persons might manifest their divine nature by their indestructible, interlinked bones that might tinkle like metal.[31] This motif is encountered in many texts, but it would appear to be especially associated with the figure of the bodhisattva Guanyin—in her urge to convert the sinners of this world, one legend tells, she once, at Yanzhou, manifested herself as a common whore who upon her death turned out to possess interlinked bones.[32]

Skeletons in Quanzhen Daoism

The skull abandoned by the roadside, now developed into a full-length skeleton but still an object of pity, becomes a major motif once again in the writings of Wang Chongyang (1112–1170) and his immediate disciples. Wang was born near present-day Xi'an, in Shaanxi province. He enjoyed a sound traditional education but failed to pass the state examinations. After having spent some years in a grave pit as "a living dead," he achieved enlightenment and started to preach. In Wang's opinion, man was shackled by his four passions for wine, sex, money, and honor (*jiu se cai qi*). In order to achieve enlightenment, one had therefore to divest oneself of all earthly possessions, break with one's wife and children, and live by begging for food in the streets. Enlightenment was to be achieved through the practice of religious exercises and self-cultivation; these meditational exercises were described in the terminology of "inner alchemy."[33] Soon after achieving enlightenment, Wang traveled to Shandong province, where he made a number of devoted converts. Due to their active proselytizing, the movement quickly expanded. One of Wang's disciples, Qiu Chuji, greatly impressed Genghis Khan, and in the wake of the Mongol conquest of northern China the movement enjoyed the patronage of the Yuan (1279–1368) court. In modern scholarship, the movement is referred to as Quanzhen Daoism. Quanzhen is variously translated as "Complete Truth," "Completion of Authenticity," "Complete Reality," and "Complete Perfection."[34]

Wang Chongyang and his disciples made a great use of songs and poems in their teachings.[35] One of the images frequently encountered in their poems is that of the skeleton.[36] This image is used basically in two ways. First, one encounters lyrics and poems in which the skeleton by the wayside is a warning that we all die and that if we want to pursue eternal life, we should turn around immediately. A typical example from the works of Wang Chongyang is the following lyric to the tune "Mo yu'er":

I lament the skeleton
Lying in the open fields:
So sad the white bones, so forlorn!
A traveler from an unknown place,
No way to know whether a woman or a man—
No one took care of him
Because he did not cultivate himself in former lives
But fooled around as if a monkey,
And in this life now he collapsed.
Blown by the wind, drenched by the rain, bleached by the sun,
And beaten by the senseless herding boys.

I still would like to ask you for the reasons,
But sadness wounds my heart
For how could you now speak?
Your mouth is filled with mud, your eyes are full of sand—
This is the way you will decay.
Forever, day and night,
You count the yearly change of autumn, winter,
Of spring and summer too,
Through all four seasons lonely and alone.
Come to your senses, people old and young,
Don't flaunt your smartness, flash your charms![37]

The following lyric, to the tune "Mantingfang," on the same theme was written by Ma Yu (Ma Danyang, 1123–1183), who was Wang's first disciple in Shandong:

Leaning on my staff and walking about
I was leisurely walking through the fields
When by the side of the road I suddenly saw a skeleton.
The eyes were filled with mud
And from its mouth were growing stinking weeds.
So sad! I cannot bring myself to tell this tale again—
How could he now again
Flash his smart charms?

In former days, I am quite sure,
When he was urged to study the Way,
He refused to turn around.

He was ashamed to go out begging in the streets,
But now
He shows his white bones without shame.
If he only would have realized that living we dwell in a burning
    house
And upon death fall into a dark dungeon,
He would have ripped the ash of his emotions,
Have left the family,
And free of any fetters practiced his austerities.
Oh luster of the hallowed radiance!
Walking steadily on auspicious clouds
I go straightaway to the Isle of the Immortals.[38]

If the early Quanzhen masters allowed the skeleton to speak out, it was not to praise the pleasures of death but to bewail its own stupidity while alive:

In a dream I was strolling through the fields
When a skeleton spoke to me.
The wailing sound was a piercing sound, the piercing sound
    was a wail:
"Oh how I regret in former days
My lust for wine and women, my anger and avarice!"[39]

The second common use of the image of the skeleton is as a symbol of those who refuse to turn around and pursue salvation. As long as a human being has not been made new by the experience of enlightenment, he or she, Wang Chongyang and his followers argue, is as good as dead and nothing more than a walking corpse, a running skeleton, a manipulated marionette. This idea is clearly expressed in the first stanza of another lyric, again to the tune "Mantingfang," by Ma Yu:

The typical skeleton
Is an expert in trading in his bones
As his karma goes on and on.
He flaunts his cunning
But refuses to rest his mind but for a while.
Turning and turning without any pause or stop
Throughout the present and the past,
He changes and renews his set of bones.
In vain he covets longevity
As even after myriad kalpas
He still will be subjected to the wheel of transmigration.[40]

An anonymous Quanzhen lyric, once again to the popular tune "Mantingfang," even envisions a world completely populated by skeletons:

He is a walking corpse,
She is just running bones:
Husband and wife are both skeletons.
Their children and grandchildren
Through all later generations are little skeletons.
When after many days and years these have grown up,
Money is expended to mate these skeletons:
The whole house is filled by living ghosts
And all day long you play with skeletons!

The skeleton fellow who is head of the household
Is busy all day raising skeletons.
When one day you die, who will replace your skeleton?
When you have breathed your final breath,
The living skeletons will bury your dead skeleton.
But don't be sad at heart:
I urge you to come to your senses quickly
And to take care of your own skeleton![41]

Many of these poems and lyrics end with an appeal to their audiences to convert as soon as possible. Wang and his disciples enhanced the emotional appeal of their words by showing their audiences paintings of skeletons. When Wang was living with Ma Yu, he converted him by showing him a painting of a skeleton accompanied by the following quatrain:

> How sad it is that everyone lives in pain and sorrow,
> So now I've had to go as far as painting this skeleton:
> During their lifetime only lusting after sins,
> They will not stop until they are like this![42]

Ma Yu recorded his conversion in a lyric to the tune "Mantingfang," the first stanza of which might be rendered as follows:

> The Mad Immortal instructed me
> By verses without number,
> But still I had a doubting mind.
> Seeing this painted skeleton, I achieve enlightenment
> And decide to follow the Master.
> If one wishes to study the Way next year,
> I am afraid one may suddenly die this year.
> If I wish to do so tomorrow,
> Tonight I may die
> And I'll lose this great sign.[43]

Wang Chongyang's conversion of Ma Yu by showing him a painting of a skeleton is one of the scenes of the life of the master depicted on the inner walls of the Chunyang Hall of the Yonglegong at Ruicheng, which originally dates from the thirteenth century. The fresco portrays a seated Wang Chongyang showing a picture of a standing skeleton to Ma Yu and his wife.[44]

One of Wang's other early disciples was Tan Chuduan (1123–1185). Tan's most famous work is "Song of the Skeleton"; the final lines of the poem reveal that he, too, preached while showing his audiences a painting of a skeleton:

Skeleton, O skeleton, your face is oh so ugly,
All because in life you loved women and wine.
Cunningly smiling you took your fill of meats and furs,
So your blood and flesh gradually wasted away.
    Gradually wasted away—but still you continued to lust,
Lusting for riches, spending your semen you reaped no rewards.
Your desires were without limit but your life had its term,
And now today you have become this skeleton.
    Become a skeleton—you now listen to me:
It's not easy to acquire this precious human body.
Understand that the life force is like pulling strings,[45]
So do not blindly follow your emotions.
    That's why I have painted his form to show to you,
To see whether today you will become enlightened![46]

It is not clear how long the Quanzhen preachers used this kind of
visual aid in their proselytizing activities, but we can perhaps detect
a sign of its lasting influence on the Chinese imagination in chapter
12 of the famous eighteenth-century novel *Dream of the Red Chamber*
(*Honglou meng*; also known as *Story of the Stone*), in which a Daoist
priest presents Jia Rui, who has fallen madly in love with Wang Xifeng,
with a "Mirror for the Romantic": one side shows a seductive female,
while the reverse side shows an erect skeleton.[47] The teachers of sectar-
ian religions of the Ming (1368–1644) and Qing (1644–1911) dynasties
also used the image of the skeleton in their preaching. For instance, *The
Book of Nonactivism in Lamentation for the World* (*Tanshi wuwei juan*)
of Luo Qing (second half of fifteenth century) is followed in some
printed editions (but apparently not in the presumably earliest pre-
served printing) by a set of twenty-one songs lamenting the skeleton,[48]
and a set of songs lamenting the ten (actually eight) kinds of skeleton is
appended to the anonymous *Precious Scroll on the Emperor of the Liang*
(*Liang huang baojuan*) as printed in 1899.[49] The early Qing poet Jin
Bao left us a set of seven lyrics to the tune "Qinyuanchun" titled "On a
Painting of a Skeleton" (Ti kulou tu).[50] Funeral rituals as recorded from
the nineteenth and twentieth centuries from various parts of China
also often include a "Lament over the Skeleton" (Tan kulou), also

known as "Skeleton Song" (Kulou ge) or "True Words on the Skeleton" (Kulou zhenyan).[51]

The frequent use of the image of the skeleton by the early Quanzhen masters in their poems and paintings should be understood in the context of the greater visibility of images of skulls and skeletons in Song and Yuan culture. When in early-twelfth-century Kaifeng, actors performed the role of the demon queller Zhong Kui, he might be accompanied by "two or three lean and skinny characters who have plastered their body with powder; with golden eyes and white faces they looked like skulls."[52] Medical works started to include more or less detailed pictures of the human skeleton;[53] one also finds a picture of the skeleton in the standard handbook of forensic medicine.[54] Captions (*zan* and *song*) for paintings of skulls or skeletons in the works of Su Shi, Huang Tingjian (1045–1105), and others prove the circulation of paintings of skulls in the eleventh and twelfth centuries.[55] From the thirteenth century, we have the lyric "On a Female Skull en Face" (Fu banmian nü kulou [to the tune "Si jiake"]), by the well-known lyricist Wu Wenying (ca. 1200–ca. 1260), while from the fourteenth century we have the lyric "On a Painted Skeleton" (Ti hua kulou [to the tune "Qinyuanchun"]), by the well-known painter Wu Zhen (1280–1354).[56]

The Southern Song painter Li Song (fl. 1190–1230), otherwise perhaps best known for his paintings of peddlers, appears to have specialized to some degree in paintings of skeletons. Three paintings by him on the theme of skeletons are known, but only one of them, *A Magic Performance of Skeletons* (Kulou huanxi tu), showing a skeleton puppet master performing with a small skeleton marionette in front of a nursing mother and some young children, has been preserved (most likely as a later copy).[57] This copy carries as an inscription a song to the tune "Zuizhongtian" by the well-known Daoist and painter Huang Gongwang (1269–1354):

> Without half a speck of skin or flesh
> But carrying a load of grief and sorrow:
> A marionette himself he still is pulling strings,
> Manipulating a small model of himself in order to entice
>   his love.
> Having seen through this, should one not be ashamed?
> Dumbfounded at the first milestone on the road.[58]

Li Song, *A Magic Performance of Skeletons*, as reproduced as a woodblock print in *Master Gu's Painting Album* (*Gushi huapu*, 1603).

Li Song's two lost paintings on skeletons were *Skeleton Pulling a Cart* (*Kulou yeche tu*)[59] and *A Skeleton Sitting in [the Square Hole of] a Copper Coin* (*Qianyan zhong zuo kulou*).[60] Li Song's paintings of peddlers also show skeleton marionettes among their offerings.[61]

From the period 1250 to 1450, we also have vernacular stories that feature skeletons in their cast of characters, such as "The White Falcon of Master Cui Summons Monsters" (Cui yanei baiyao zhaoyao).[62] The early Ming playwright Lu Jinzhi is said to have written the play *A Bloodied Skeleton Creates Havoc in the Hundred Flowers Pavilion* (*Xue kulou danao Baihuating*), but this play has unfortunately been lost.[63] The most famous skeleton in the vernacular literature of later centuries may well be the White Bone Demon. She is one of the terrible monsters who confront the holy monk Xuanzang and his companions in the sixteenth-century novel *Journey to the West* (*Xiyou ji*). But she appears first in the shape of "a girl with a face like the moon and features like flowers," next as "a woman eighty years old," and eventually in the shape of "an old man."[64] It is only when she has been killed by Monkey once and for all that she shows her true shape as a skeleton—her identity is conveniently indicated by the inscription on her spine.

Master Zhuang and the Skeleton

While the early Quanzhen masters wrote poems and lyrics about their encounters with a skeleton, later Quanzhen priests told the story of Master Zhuang's encounter with a skeleton and his lament over its fate.[65] This change may have occurred at a relatively early date, considering that the playwright Li Shouqing (late thirteenth century) is credited with a *zaju* bearing the title *Singing While Drumming on a Tub: Master Zhuang Laments the Skeleton* (*Gupen ge Zhuangzi tan kulou*).[66] Unfortunately, only the songs of act 1 of the play have been transmitted.[67] These songs make no mention of a skeleton. The act seems to have dramatized Master Zhuang's rejection of an invitation to join the court bureaucracy.[68] Throughout this set of songs, the character of Master Zhuang vaunts the pleasures of a life of retirement in contrast to the constant dangers of a life at court. To judge from the title (and also considering some later versions of the legend), act 2 then most likely would have been devoted to Master Zhuang's reaction to the death of his wife. The encounter with the skeleton most likely would have been treated in act 3. The commonly used mode for the third set of songs would have allowed Li Shouqing to write a number of arias to the tune "Shuahai'er" in which Master Zhuang questions the skeleton as to his identity and manner of death, but we have no way of knowing whether he did so. We also do not know whether at this moment the story included the episode of Master Zhuang's resurrection of the skeleton. Act 4, the final act of the play, most likely would have depicted Master Zhuang's departure for the Isles of the Immortals in the Eastern Ocean or to the paradises atop the Kun-lun Mountains to join the other immortals at a banquet hosted by the Queen Mother of the West.[69]

Li Shouqing was not the only Yuan-dynasty playwright to be inspired by Master Zhuang, but to judge from the titles of their works, these other playwrights focused on the famous butterfly dream of Master Zhuang.[70] There is, for example, the preserved *zaju The Dream of Zhuang Zhou* (*Zhuang Zhou meng*). While it is usually ascribed to Shi Jiu Jingxian, it is most likely at best only a heavily rewritten version of his work. Although the first modern editor of the text greatly praised the play's arias[71] and although another scholar has hailed this play as "one of the most inter-esting plays in the whole corpus of Yüan drama,"[72] the play may best be characterized, in my opinion, as a lame and elaborate deliverance play, which makes one regret even more the loss of the play by Li Shouqing. The play's greatest claim to originality may be that it sports among its roles a man-size butterfly. The Maiwangguan collection originally also included the play *Zhuang Zhou at the Middle of His Life: The Butterfly Dream* (*Zhuang Zhou banshi Hudie meng*), but this anonymous play has not been preserved.[73]

The *Selected Charms from the Forest of Lyrics* (*Cilin zhaiyan*), an early-sixteenth-century anthology of arias compiled by Zhang Lu and printed in 1525, provides us with the text of a set of songs in the Banshe mode under the title *Master Zhuang Laments the Skeleton* (*Zhuangzi tan kulou*). It authorship is ascribed to a certain Lü Jingru, about whom no other information is available.[74] Apart from an introductory song and a coda, the set consists of eleven songs to the tune "Shuahai'er." Clearly, this set of songs is sung in the voice of Master Zhuang, who in his opening songs praises the pleasures of his untrammeled existence:

> The heroes of the Warring States[75] are caught up in a fight,
> All because of their desire for fame and struggle for profit.
> How can they compare to me, whose joys can be compared to
> 　　the swimming fishes,
> Who with a smile discusses the roc's transformations,[76]
> And in his dreams pursues the butterfly's delusion.
> The clear sky is my curtain, and the earth is my mat;
> Brown grasses give me clothes, the trees provide food.
> I have jumped out of the barred cage;
> I travel through the famous mountains,
> I always observe the living streams!

In the first song to the tune "Shuahai'er," he then describes how he has been traveling since the death of his wife and has come upon a skeleton. The next song describes the skeleton very much in the manner of the lyrics of the Quanzhen masters, with the remaining nine songs posing questions to the skeleton. The first of these nine songs runs as follows:

> You must have left your hometown to make a fortune,
> You must have come to this place for merit and fame,
> You must have had the bad luck to run into evil villains.
> 　　You must have been poisoned and bewitched beyond recovery,
> You must have suffered from heat and cold without any medicine,
> And who today can substitute for your own deeds?
> 　　As a result you cohabit in one busy crowd with ants during
> 　　　　the day
> And shivering for cold, sleep with foxes at night.

These suggestions and questions, continued for another eight songs, all remain unanswered, and the coda relates Master Zhuang's decision to provide the skeleton with a proper funeral:

Skeleton,

> All the bamboo of the southern hills cannot fully describe your
> stupidity and wisdom;
> All the waves of the northern sea cannot wash away your rights
> and wrongs.
> I now will dig a deep hole to bury you at the Yellow Springs,[77]
> So freed from death and birth you'll be a free and easy ghost!

The eleven songs in this set formed the backbone of many later adaptations of the legend of the meeting of Master Zhuang and the skeleton, whether as a narrative or as a play. Each of the later versions expands on the original number of "Shuahai'er" songs.[78] At the same time, these later versions change the story by including the episode of Master Zhuang's resurrection of the skeleton.

The earliest preserved dramatic version that includes this twist is the scene "Master Zhuang of the Zhou Laments the Skeleton" (Zhou Zhuangzi tan kulou) from the otherwise unrecorded play *The Skin Sack* (*Pinang ji*), included in the *Marvelous Sounds from Selected Brocades* (*Zhaijin qiyin*), an anonymous song and drama anthology printed in 1611.[79] In this scene, the extra (*wai*) who plays the part of Master Zhuang informs us in his first two songs that he has arrived in his wanderings outside Luoyang, where he discovers a skeleton by the side of the road. In the next eighteen songs, to the tune "Shuahai'er," Master Zhuang proceeds to question the skeleton as to sex, name, origin, profession, morality, manner of death, and other details of his or her former life. The scene concludes in the following manner:

[MASTER ZHUANG:] Come to think of it, to save the life of a single person is better than building a seven-story pagoda. I would like to deliver you. But what to do about the fact that you're missing four bones? I will have to substitute them with willow twigs. I put this immortal elixir in his mouth. Now wake up quickly! [(*Sings:*)]
> [To the tune "Langtaosha"]
> In the Third Month this is Clear and Bright,[80]
> When one sacrifices at swept grave tombs.

I see a pile of bleached bones lying in the dust:
With one immortal pill I will deliver you
So you can be reborn as a human being.

Suddenly I see that this skeleton has revived. Let me ask you: What is your name and where are you from?

Skeleton, now that you have revived,
Let me ask you what happened.
What is your name and where are you from?
Now out of compassion I have delivered you,
Please don't forget the favor I've shown you.

(*From backstage*:) My name is Zhang Cong and I hail from Xiangyang. I was murdered, and now you, Master, have been so kind as to revive me. I had some luggage and an umbrella with me. Please return them to me so I can set out on the way back home. If you refuse to return those goods, I will take you to the district office and lodge an accusation against you.

Master, you have been exceedingly kind to me
In saving my poor life,
But if you do not return to me
The pack, and the umbrella and money I had with me,
I will seek justice from the district magistrate!

[(]*After* DISTRICT MAGISTRATE LIANG *has accepted the deposition, he questions* MASTER ZHUANG. MASTER ZHUANG *declares*:[)] After I had shown him the favor of resurrecting him, he deployed his treacherous mind. I used willow twigs to make up for his missing bones. Now let me use another magic pill and spit a mouthful of water on him so his original shape will once again be turned into a skeleton.

This fellow has a criminal mind!

Let's forget my favor of saving his life!
He has to claim he had luggage and money
And pays me back with enmity,
So I have to suffer his deception.
All my life I've loved to deliver people;
You were beyond deliverance,
So I had to display this supernatural power.
(*Repeat*)

As for his life, Zhang Cong is sent back to the shades;
Master Zhuang in broad daylight ascends on the clouds,
And once Magistrate Liang sees this, he bows down,
Since he wants to abandon his job and practice religion!
A poem reads:
Human life is like a dream, passing through spring and fall;
With light and shade like an arrow[81] one quickly turns white.
As long as you have three inches of breath, use it in a thousand
ways,
But as soon as one day Impermanence arrives, all business is
finished.[82]

The summary way in which the resurrection of the skeleton, the law-suit, and the execution of the skeleton are described strongly suggests that the story was widely known by the time this version for the stage was put on paper, quite possibly on the basis of a narrative version.[83] Various seventeenth-century works of fiction do indeed strongly suggest that the story of Master Zhuang's resurrection of the skeleton was the typical subject of Daoist storytelling (*daoqing*).[84] It is mentioned as such in the vernacular story "Daoist Li Enters Cloud Gate Cave Alone" (Li Daoren dubu Yunmen), included by Feng Menglong in his third col-lection of forty vernacular stories, *Stories to Awaken the World* (*Xingshi hengyan*, 1627). In this case, the *daoqing* performer is a blind old man who performs his songs and tales outside the local Eastern Marchmount temple while playing the fisherman's drum and bamboo clappers:

Beating his fisherman's drum and bamboo clappers [the old man] first recited four lines of verse:

Summer heat is followed by winter, spring by autumn;
In the evening sun the river flows east below the bridge.
The general and his battle horse—where are they now?
Wild grasses and flowers fill the field with their sorrow.

After he had recited this four-line poem, he in good order devel-oped his main story, which was the tale of *Master Zhuang Laments the Skeleton.* . . . The old man would speak for a while and then sing for a while, until he had reached the point where the skeleton once again had grown skin and flesh, come back to life, and jumped up from the ground, so some people there were laughing and some people gaped in amazement. This was exactly the midpoint of his story, so the blind man stopped playing his drum and clappers in order to collect some money before he would resume his tale, as is the normal rule with storytellers.[85]

A generation later, Ding Yaokang (1599–1661) included an abbreviated but sill quite extensive narrative version of the legend as told by a Daoist priest in chapter 48 of his novel *A Sequel to Plum in the Golden Vase* (*Xu Jinpingmei*).[86] The "Shuahai'er" songs sung by Master Zhuang in this version derive from the same sets discussed in the foregoing. In contrast to other adaptations, however, Ding Yaokang's version allows the resurrected skeleton to sing a number of songs, to the tune "Shuahai'er," when arguing his case before the district magistrate.

The library of the Institute of Oriental Culture (Tōyō Bunka Kenkyūjo), University of Tokyo, has a manuscript copy of the *Newly Composed, Enlarged, and Expanded, with a Forest of Appreciative Comments: Master Zhuang Sighs over the Skeleton in Northern and Southern Lyrics and Songs* (*Xinbian zengbu pinglin: Zhuangzi tan kulou nanbei ciqu*). This text originally belonged to the famous Japanese bibliographer and bibliophile Nagasawa Kikuya (1902–1980) and formed part of his Shōkōdō Bunko.[87] This text appears to have been copied from a printed edition of the late Ming.[88] The editor of the text is given as the "Shunyi Mountain Recluse" Du Hui, about whom no information is available beyond the fact that he hailed from Changshu, and that applies also to Chen Kui, who is listed as the printer. The text must have been in circulation by the 1620s because Wang Yinglin mentions in the preface to his play on the legend of Master Zhuang and the skeleton that he read "Sighs over the Skeleton by the Shunyi Mountain Recluse" in 1626.[89] The text comes with four illustrations. This prosimetric text, in which short prose passages alternate with poems and songs to a variety of tunes, most likely is the only surviving complete example of a Ming-dynasty narrative *daoqing*. The core of the story is still the (once again expanded) series of

"Shuahai'er" songs in which Master Zhuang laments the skeleton's fate and questions him as to his identity and morality.[90] Once the revived skeleton has shown his ingratitude and again has been reduced to a pile of bones, the text spends considerable space on Master Zhuang's instructions to the district magistrate, who now wants to abandon his position in order to seek eternal life.[91]

It is difficult to describe the general characteristics of a genre of Ming-dynasty prosimetric literature on the basis of a single example.[92] The best-known prosimetric genres of the Ming are ballad stories (*cihua*) and precious scrolls (*baojuan*). In the ballad stories, passages in prose alternate with passages in ballad verse. Such verse passages are basically composed in lines of seven-syllable verse (*ci*); passages in ten-syllable verse (*zan*) are encountered only very rarely (such lines tend to have a very strongly emphasized tripartite structure of three, three, and four syllables). Ballad stories are not subdivided into chapters, but longer texts may be presented as two "scrolls" (*juan*). Narrative *baojuan* tend to follow the same format, with the exception that prose passages are often followed by a couplet and the formula *Namo Guanshiyin pusa* (Hail Bodhisattva Guanyin) or *Namo Amituo fo* (Hail Amitabha Buddha) to be recited by the pious audience. The "sectarian" *baojuan* tend to be divided into a number of chapters (*pin*); following an alternation of verse and prose, such chapters are often concluded by a number of songs that summarize the contents of the chapter. In the *Master Zhuang Sighs over the Skeleton in Northern and Southern Lyrics and Songs*, the prose passages are usually very short. For the verse sections, it only rarely employs the ballad-style seven-syllable line; as a rule, the verse sections consist of a sequence of lyrics, arias, and poems. This preponderance of lyrics and songs, which is already suggested in the title, goes so far that one almost has the impression that the main function of the narrative is providing a frame for these lyrics and songs.[93] While the preponderance of lyrics and songs in the text invites a comparison with the earlier genre of "all keys and modes" (*zhugongdiao*), that genre organized its songs in mode-specific sets and placed a much greater emphasis on plot and characterization in stories full of unexpected twists and turns. And whereas the "all keys and modes" was accompanied by stringed instruments in performance, the *daoqing* was accompanied in performance by only the fisherman's drum and bamboo clappers and could do without such a complicated organization. The great number of lyrics and songs in narrative *daoqing* also invites a comparison with the genre of rustic songs (*liqu*) as practiced in Shandong in the early Qing dynasty by Pu Songling (1640–1715). But in that genre, songs to the same tune could be repeated, separated by one or two lines in prose, for tens if not hundreds of times. The variety of tunes in our *daoqing*, together with the occasional use of poems and ballad verse, must have made for a far more exciting musical entertainment.

A few words should be said about the "Shuahai'er" songs that are so central to the various versions of the story of Master Zhuang's meeting with the skeleton discussed so far. Songs to the tune "Shuahai'er" consist of eight lines divided into three groups of three, three, and two lines, respectively. The first two lines of the first group of three lines are each made up of two groups of three syllables and are followed by a regular seven-syllable line with a caesura following the fourth syllable. The next threesome consists of three regular seven-syllable lines, which are often parallel in structure. Each of the final two lines consists of a four-syllable phrase, which as a rule is preceded by an extrametrical three-syllable phrase. These final two lines often summarize the song in a pithy or satiric fashion. Songs to the tune "Shuahai'er" can be repeated any number of times, which made them the perfect vehicle for extended descriptions or narrative.[94] Some local genres of narrative *daoqing* came to rely exclusively on "Shuahai'er" songs for their verse sections.

In their combination of the motif of the skeleton and the cataloguing of social and moral types, the various versions of the legend of Master Zhuang's meeting with the skeleton show, despite all obvious differences, a remarkable affinity with the theme of the danse macabre, which enjoyed a remarkable popularity in western Europe during roughly the same period.[95] In the many versions of the danse macabre, death, represented first as a corpse and later as a skeleton, confronts all manner of people in order to take them to their graves, telling them that despite all their present riches and beauty they will soon be like him. In the legend of Master Zhuang's meeting with the skeleton, however, the deceased has already turned into a pile of bones and Master Zhuang catalogues his or her possible identities. Another major difference is that the heyday of the danse macabre in European literature coincided with the period of great strides in anatomy, resulting in an increasingly naturalistic depiction of the skeletons in the illustrations accompanying the songs that made up the texts of the various versions of the danse macabre. The prints of Hans Holbein the Younger, in particular, stand out for their inventive rendering of skeletons. In China, however, the heyday of the precise depiction of the skeleton preceded the popularity of the fully developed legend of Master Zhuang's meeting with the skeleton by a few centuries, and the theme of the skull and the skeleton appears to have almost completely disappeared from the Chinese art of the Ming dynasty until its reintroduction by Jesuit missionaries in the seventeenth century. The second and the fourth illustrations that accompany our copy of the *Master Zhuang Sighs over the Skeleton in Northern and Southern Lyrics and Songs* show a skeleton, but one has to conclude that these two skeletons are very ineptly drawn.[96] The ineptitude is more glaring when these pictures are compared with Li Song's painting of the skeleton marionetteer.

By the early seventeenth century, when Wang Yinglin wrote his dramatic adaptation of the legend of Master Zhuang's encounter with the skeleton, Master Zhuang's lament was so well known that Wang chose not to include it at all.[97] Wang was an erudite scholar from Shaoxing who never passed the highest examinations, but because of recommendations he was eventually employed in minor positions in the metropolitan bureaucracy. During the Tianqi reign (1621–1627), his public opposition against the growing power of the eunuch Wei Zhongxian earned him a public beating in court, and he barely escaped with his life. Wang later wrote a *chuanqi* play on Wei's reign of terror, but this work, *A Clear and Cool Fan* (*Qingliangshan*), has not been preserved, despite the high praise of contemporaries.[98] Early in the Chongzhen reign (1628–1644), Wang was reinstated to his post. He committed suicide following the capture of Beijing by rebels in the spring of 1644.

When Wang's play about the philosopher and the skeleton was first printed as part of the *Miscellaneous Works of Wang Yinglin* (*Wang Yinglin zaji*), it bore the title *Master Zhuang on Stage: A New Tune* (*Yan Zhuang xindiao*).[99] The only known copy of this edition is preserved in the Cabinet Library (Naikaku Bunko) in Tokyo. Unfortunately, this edition is missing its final pages and so is incomplete. When the play was included by Shen Tai in *A Second Collection of Short Plays of the*

Glorious Ming (*Sheng Ming zaju erji*), it was given the title *Free and Easy Roaming* (*Xiaoyao you*),[100] and it is this edition that has served as the basis of the translation included in this volume. Even though the play is called a *zaju*, it does not follow the formal rules of the genre in its early days, when plays were made up of four suites of songs. By the last century of the Ming, *zaju* had come to designate any kind of short play (in contrast, *chuanqi*, the popular plays of the day, could have more than forty scenes). *Zaju* from the last century of the Ming show a remarkable propensity to experimentation in formal matters such as musical organization, and Wang Yinglin's play is no exception. Even though it is presented as a one-act play, it opens with a short introductory scene in the manner of a *chuanqi*. The main action of the play occurs over three sections: Master Zhuang's discussion with his acolyte, who tries to pry a coin from the skull's clenched jaws; following the resurrection of the skeleton, Master Zhuang's encounter with the district magistrate, who is obsessed about his fame; and a final section in which Master Zhuang answers the questions put to him by his two disciples. The songs in this play do not constitute a formal suite made up of different tunes. The songs in the first section are all sung to the tune "Langtaosha," the songs in the second section are all sung to the tune "Huangying'er," and the final section contains eight songs to the tune "Shuahai'er."[101]

Zaju of this time also show a strong tendency to explore novel and daring topics, often indulging in explicit social criticism. In Wang Yinglin's adaptation of the legend, it is no longer the resurrected skeleton and his greed that are the main butt of satire. The skeleton's role is very much reduced as the emphasis shifts to Master Zhuang's acolyte and the district magistrate. The acolyte, who in other versions often has only a minor role, now plays a much more prominent part as he is shown to be obsessed with money. The district magistrate, who in other versions is often an exceedingly bland character, is revealed as obsessed by a desire for fame—without a spectacular law case on his record, he will not be able to obtain a promotion in rank now that his three-year term of office is coming to an end! Wang's play was highly praised by the Ming critic Qi Biaojia (1602–1645): "In the space of one square foot of silk [the author] delivers us from samsara and has us transcend fame and profit. This is the enthusiasm of the author's enlightenment. He even manages to outdo Master Zhuang himself!"[102] The originality of Wang's adaptation is underscored when later in their extensive discussion on money and fame, the district magistrate asks Master Zhuang for more background information on the skeleton, and Master Zhuang replies simply, "The skeleton's occupation and sex have been exhaustively dealt with by those texts in the world that lament the skeleton."

A further element of originality in Wang's version is its ending. Whereas Du Hui's version culminates in a summary of inner alchemy teaching as the highest truth, Wang's Master Zhuang is eventually forced to admit the superiority of Buddhist no-birth over Daoist life eternal, since even the eternal longevity of the Daoist immortals will come to an end with the conclusion of the current kalpa, which, like all kalpas, will end, after an unimaginably long period, in a total annihilation of the current world system (after which, following an equally unimaginably long period, a new world system will originate from the residue of karma from the previous kalpa). In the final lines Wang shows himself an adherent of the strong syncretistic tendency in late Ming thought, which held that all three teachings (Confucianism, Daoism, and Buddhism), in the final analysis, agree on a single truth:

> Don't harbor doubts because the teachings are different;
> You have to know that the three teachings all converge.

Fanning the Grave

At about the same time that Wang Yinglin dismissed the many versions of Master Zhuang's lament over the skeleton as already known to all, Feng Menglong (1574–1646) provided the late Ming reading public with a new tale of Master Zhuang that would quickly acquire great popularity. This tale was included in his second collection of forty vernacular stories, which he published in 1624 as *Stories to Caution the World* (*Jingshi tongyan*), and had the title "Zhuang Zixiu Drums on the Tub and Achieves the Great Way" (Zhuang Zixiu gupen cheng dadao). As its title indicates, this story deals with the death of Master Zhuang's wife. Whereas the

Master Zhuang suggests that she served him well, this story turns her into a fickle creature whose utter lack of fidelity is the final impulse for her husband to retire to the mountains and pursue religion.[103]

In this new tale, Master Zhuang, who is living with his wife in the countryside, one day while walking comes across a young widow who is fanning a grave mound. When he asks her why, she tells him that her husband, whom she loved dearly, had told her to remarry following his death as soon as the earth of his grave had dried. Seeing her eagerness to remarry, Master Zhuang helps her by using his magic powers, whereupon she gives him her fan as a token of her gratitude. When Master Zhuang returns home and tells the story to his wife, she tears the fan to pieces, curses the widow as a slut, and swears that she will stay loyal to her husband forever. A few days later, Master Zhuang falls ill and dies, but soon after he has been placed in his coffin, a prince arrives who had hoped to study with him. Once Master Zhuang's wife sees the handsome young man, she immediately falls in love with him, and her passion is so strong that she pressures the prince to marry her. On their wedding night, however, the prince collapses, and when his servant informs her that he can be saved only by the brains of a living or recently deceased person, she promptly gets out an ax to open the coffin and extract her husband's brains.[104] But as soon as the coffin lid is removed, Master Zhuang comes back to life: he had only feigned his death in order to test his wife's loyalty. She then commits suicide out of shame, and Master Zhuang drums on the tub and sings and later leaves for the hills to pursue religion.

When *Stories to Caution the World* had dropped out of circulation by the end of the seventeenth century, the continued popularity of this vernacular story was nonetheless ensured by its inclusion, in the final years of the Ming dynasty, in the anonymous *Extraordinary Sights from Present and Past (Jingu qiguan)*, an anthology of once again forty stories from the collections put out by Feng Menglong and his contemporary Ling Mengchu (1580–1644). *Extraordinary Sights from Present and Past* continued to circulate widely throughout the nearly three centuries of the Qing dynasty. It was also eagerly read by the early generations of European sinologists, and the first translation in a Western language (French) of "Zhuang Zixiu Drums on the Tub and Achieves the Great Way" appeared as early as 1735.[105] Many other translations would follow over the years.

The editor of the French translation noted the resemblance of the story to the tale of the Matron of Ephesus. This story of a loving widow who is willing to have the corpse of her dear husband nailed to a cross once she has fallen in love with a common soldier is known from the work of the classical author Petronius and has many analogues in premodern European literature and folklore. In East Asia, however, the story type is known only from "Zhuang Zixiu Drums on the Tub and Achieves the Great Way," to the great perplexity of folktale specialists.[106] Whatever the story's origin, it was published by Feng at a moment of fervid veneration of female chastity and fidelity throughout society in combination with a popularity (at least in vernacular fiction) of the figure of the sexually insatiable woman and jealous shrew.

Feng Menglong's misogynistic story of female fickleness was soon adapted for the stage. The earliest stage adaptation appears to be the short play included in the *Four Great Stupidities* (*Si da chi*), compiled and printed during the Chongzhen reign. It is the only anonymous play in this collection of four *zaju*. The adaptation limits itself to the story as presented in Feng's tale; its only addition is a final scene in which the ghost of the young widow and that of Master Zhuang's wife confront each other in the underworld.[107] Other adaptations of Feng's tale, however, tried to incorporate the story of Master Zhuang's meeting with the skeleton. This is the case in Xie Guo's *Butterfly Dream* (*Hudie meng*), for example, a full-length *chuanqi* play about the life of Master Zhuang.[108] This play returns to the account of Master Zhuang's dream dialogue with the skull in the *Master Zhuang*, which it dramatizes in scene 11 as "Dream Miracle" (Mengyi). Xie Guo's *Butterfly Dream*, which seems not to have made a major impact on the stage, should be distinguished from a play of the same title included in the eighteenth-century drama anthology *Zhuibaiqiu*. That play includes scene 11 of Xie Guo's play but combines it with scenes from yet another *chuanqi* play, also called *The Butterfly Dream* (*Hudie meng*), by the early Qing playwright Shi Pang, which also dramatizes the story of Master Zhuang testing his wife. This became the popular Kunqu version of the legend.[109] Later stage adaptations may drop the episode of Master Zhuang's meeting with the skull or skeleton but emphasize the karmic enmity of Master Zhuang and his wife and expand the role of the bodhisattva Guanyin as the story's mastermind.[110]

Feng Menglong's tale of fickle widows was not only adapted for the stage but also taken up in many genres of prosimetric storytelling.[111] We have, for instance, four independent adaptations of Feng's tale as a youth book (*zidishu*; also known as bannermen tales). Most of these limit themselves to a retelling of the story of Master Zhuang's meeting with the young widow fanning her husband's grave, but the adaptation translated in this volume, *The Butterfly Dream* (*Hudie meng*), by Chunshuzhai, includes the episode of Master Zhuang's meeting with the skeleton.[112] Youth books were popular with Manchu amateur performers in eighteenth- and nineteenth-century Beijing and Shenyang. Many of their authors were highly literate and well read in both classical and popular literature, which makes youth books the most literary genre of traditional performative literature. Youth books are as a rule made up of one or more chapters of up to two hundred lines of verse. The basic length of each line is seven syllables, but since the music to which youth books were sung was rather slow, many lines were extended by additional syllables. Chapters are often preceded by an eight-line poem. In our case, *The Butterfly Dream* is made up of four chapters. Chunshuzhai was a Manchu who belonged to the imperial Aisin Gioro clan; he lived in the second half of the nineteenth century and was well acquainted with some other youth book authors, but *The Butterfly Dream* is his only surviving work in the genre.

One also finds prosimetric adaptations of Feng Menglong's tale that follow the sequence suggested by chapter 18 of the *Master Zhuang*, in which the account of the death of Master Zhuang's wife precedes the account of Master Zhuang's meeting with the skull. An example of this arrangement is provided by the anonymous *Precious Scroll of Master Zhuang's Butterfly Dream and Skeleton* (*Zhuangzi diemeng kulou baojuan*). This text is preserved in only a single manuscript and probably dates from the late nineteenth or even early twentieth century. The basic narrative is told in an alternation of prose and seven-syllable ballad verse. Following a quite spirited retelling of the testing of Master Zhuang's wife, we read a very short summary of Master's Zhuang's resurrection of the skeleton and its return to dust. This latter episode, however, sets the scene for two extensive sermons in ten-syllable verse directed, respectively, at the district magistrate and his wife. In Du Hui's *Master Zhuang Sighs over the*

Skeleton in Northern and Southern Lyrics and Songs, the magistrate's wife, it might be pointed out, very much tries to dissuade her husband from following Master Zhuang's advice, but in this text she is just as eager as her husband to be instructed. This is, of course, related to the teachings dispensed by Master Zhuang. If the earlier text instructed the magistrate to leave the household in order to pursue his religious quest, the sermon addressed to him in this precious scroll sings the praises of filial piety; the sermon addressed to his wife accordingly teaches her to behave in a filial way toward her parents-in-law. Both sermons hold out the promise that a virtuous life in family and society will result in uncounted blessings and is an absolute precondition for any kind of religious pursuit.

These versified sermons also circulated (and continue to circulate) as independent poems.[113] As the precious scroll informs us, they were revealed to us mortals through the process of spirit writing by the immortal Liu Qi. The message of Liu Qi very much conforms to the tenor of lay piety in late imperial times.[114] Liu Qi, who has his own temple in several places, is said to have been a disciple of the immortal Lü Dongbin. According to some accounts of his legend, Liu Qi had been a willow tree ("willow" and "Liu," written with the same character, are pronounced the same in Chinese) outside Yueyang Tower, and the sermon to the magistrate's wife starts out with an account of this legend.[115] The same sermon concludes with a summary of the legend of the earthly life of the bodhisattva Guanyin as the princess Miaoshan as a model of filial piety for women, reflecting the eminent role of Guanyin in all forms of popular religion in late imperial China.[116] In the youth books discussed in the preceding, the widow fanning the grave is described as an apparition conjured up by Guanyin in order to enlighten Master Zhuang and free him from any remaining attachments and illusions.

The Resurrected Skeleton in Modern Times

Despite the popularity of the story of Master Zhuang's encounter with the widow fanning the grave and his subsequent testing of his wife, ballads and plays devoted exclusively to Master Zhuang's lament over the skeleton also continued to circulate in various parts of China in late imperial and early

Republican times. In the repertoire of Peking opera of those decades, one encounters, for example, the play *Hitting the Bone to Seek the Cash* (*Qiaogu qiujin*), which dramatizes once again the legend of Master Zhuang's encounter with the skeleton but provides the story with its own twist.[117] This time, the skeleton belongs to a traveling merchant named Zhang Cong. When he is killed and robbed, two coins end up in his mouth. When later two travelers who pass by want to break his skull to get at the coins, they are berated by Master Zhuang, who promises them two coins. When these men then ask for ten coins each, Master Zhuang scares them away with his divine tiger. He next proceeds to revive the skeleton, replacing his missing organs with those of a dog. When the revived Zhang Cong subsequently takes him to see the magistrate of Nanhua district, Bai Jin, and accuses him of robbery, Master Zhuang turns him back into a skeleton using his yin-yang fan. Bai Jin is converted and chooses a life of religion. In 1920, the famous *laosheng* actor Liu Hongsheng (1875–1921) recorded the following arias sung by Master Zhuang during the confrontation in court:

ZHUANG ZHOU (*sings*):

> I saw those white bones between heaven and earth illuminated by the three lights;[118]
> For one who has left the family compassion is happily the root, good deeds are the gate.
> If I would have abandoned the bones of this drifting corpse in that spot,
> It would have filled me with pain and hurt my heart.
> With my yin-yang fan I fixated a dog—
> In order to save your life I had to kill an animal.
> Made out of loam you had the heart of a dog,
> So how could your heart be like a human heart!

ZHUANG:

> From birth this little Zhang Cong was unfortunate.
> Once he had eaten his fill, he demanded clothes to wear.
> Once he was dressed in fine silks and satin,
> His mind was set on marrying a beautiful wife.
> Once a pretty girl of sixteen was sitting next to you,
> Your mind was all set on becoming an official.
> When you were a district magistrate of the seventh rank,

You were afraid that as a low official you would be cheated
    by a high official.
When you had become the prime minister at court of the
    first rank,
Your mind was set on becoming emperor and ascending the
    throne.
When the golden carriage and palace hall had been ceded to
    you,
You had a high ladder set up to climb up to high heaven.
And when you arrived beyond the ninth welkin's clouds,
The ninth welkin beyond the clouds, you despised heaven as
    too low.
But the fate of little Zhang Cong had to be like this:
His flesh turned to a gust of air, his bones turned to mud.
With my yin-yang fan I have now transformed you again,
DISTRICT MAGISTRATE:
And this same instant the hall is filled by white bones.[119]

    The story might be taken up also in the context of stories that in origin
had little to do with either Zhuangzi or Daoism. For instance, Master
Zhuang makes an appearance in the nineteenth-century *Precious Scroll
of Good-in-Talent and Dragon Girl* (*Shancai Longnü baojuan*), in which
he narrates the story of his resurrection of the skeleton as proof of the
assertion that in this world a favor will be repaid by ingratitude. In that
version, too, the three willow twigs have been replaced by the guts of a
dog to explain the ingratitude of the resurrected skeleton.[120]
    In the twentieth century, the leading modern writer Lu Xun (1881–
1936) provided his own rewrite of the story as "Raising the Dead" (Qisi)
in his final collection of stories, *Old Tales Retold* (*Gushi xinbian*).[121] This
slim collection consists of ancient Chinese legends retold from a critical
perspective, often resulting in the subversion of the original meaning.
In Lu Xun's version of the legend of Master Zhuang's meeting with the
skull, he weaves together elements from the original *Master Zhuang* anec-
dote and from the later legends. The lofty philosopher Master Zhuang
is on his way to see the king of Chu when he finds a skull. After first
chiding ghosts for their insufficient understanding of death, he insists on
resurrecting the skeleton, despite the sage advice to the contrary of the

arbiter of fate. The resurrected skeleton, a local peasant, insistently asks Master Zhuang for some clothes and his possessions so he can get on with his life. When Master Zhuang fails to turn the bothersome peasant into a skeleton once again, he blows his whistle and appeals to the police, and an easily impressed police officer allows the philosopher to continue his journey and sends the resurrected skeleton packing. In this way, Lu Xun turned the old tale of Master Zhuang lamenting the skeleton into a biting satire of the state and of the intellectuals who, despite all their lofty talk, fail to be of any benefit to the poor—even worse, by their self-righteous meddling in their affairs, they only increase their misery.[122] Lu Xun wrote his adaptation of the legend in dramatic form, but since the resurrected skeleton is described as stark naked, it is not likely that he envisioned any performance.[123]

Even in the early years of the twenty-first century, the legend of Master Zhuang's encounter with the skeleton has not been forgotten. One of the items in the repertoire of Guo Degang, one of the most popular *xiangsheng* performers of the moment,[124] is the following *Taiping geci* rap[125] "Skeleton Lament" (Kulou tan):

> Master Zhuang came down the hillside on his horse,
> And so encountered a skeleton, lying there in the muck.
> As soon as he saw it, he was filled with compassion
> And reached for the gourd he carried on his back.
>   From that gourd he took one pill of gold—
> One-half of his pills were red, one-half white.
> The red pills he used to cure the men, the real guys;
> The white pills he used to cure girls in their finery.
>   He prised the clenched jaws open, poured in the drug,
> And the skeleton, once revived, jumped to its feet.
> He stretched out his hand and grabbed the horse,
> And shouted, "Master, now listen clearly!
> What happened to my golden saddle and jade stirrups and
>   my free and easy horse?
>   What happened to my zither and sword and chest of
>   books and that small infant?
> All those other things I don't care about at all,

But hurry up and give me back my money!"
    When Master Zhuang heard this, he heaved a heavy sigh:
"As soon as some petty fellow comes alive, he wants cash!"
One word is not enough to sing through this skeleton lament,
    I only wish all of you all together all happiness, free from
        harm and disaster![126]

It would appear that the changed conditions of contemporary Chinese society have made an old-fashioned jab at financial greed highly topical once again!

NOTES

1. Sima Qian, *Shiji* (Beijing: Zhonghua shuju, 1959), 9:2143–45. Translations are my own unless noted differently. Most commentators place Meng in the state of Liang, but some place it in Song. For a general introduction to the *Master Zhuang*, see Victor Mair, "The *Zhuangzi* and Its Impact," in *Daoism Handbook*, ed. Livia Kohn (Leiden: Brill, 2000), 30–52.

2. It is often suggested that many of the materials excluded by Guo made their way into the *Liezi*.

3. For a recent article questioning this assumption, see Esther Klein, "Were There 'Inner Chapters' in the Warring States? A New Examination of Evidence About the *Zhuangzi*," *T'oung Pao* 96 (2010): 299–369.

4. For a concise account of the textual history of the *Zhuangzi*, see H. D. Roth, "*Chuang tzu*," in *Early Chinese Texts: A Bibliographical Guide*, ed. Michael Loewe (Berkeley: Society for the Study of Early China and Institute of East Asian Studies, University of California, 1993), 56–59. The *Zhuangzi* has repeatedly been rendered into English. A highly readable translation is Zhuangzi, *The Complete Works of Chuang Tzu*, trans. Burton Watson (New York: Columbia University Press, 1970). Zhuangzi, *Chuang-tzu: The Seven Inner Chapters and Other Writings from the Book of Chuang-tzu*, trans. A. C. Graham (London: Allen & Unwin, 1981), is not complete, but renders the rhymed portions of the text as verse.

5. In later imperial China, master of fate (*siming*) was one of the titles of the lowly kitchen god, but in ancient centuries the title must have referred to (a) far more august and powerful god(s). The *Songs of the South* (*Chuci*), which includes a number of hymns from the southern regions of preimperial China,

contains in its *Nine Songs* (*Jiuge*) two hymns to, respectively, the greater master of fate and the smaller master of fate. An early twentieth-century recasting of the anecdote of Master Zhuang's meeting with the skull in the vernacular in the *Expounded Meaning of the Exceptional Writings of Master Zhuang* (*Zhuangzi qiwen yanyi*) replaces the master(s) of fate with the figure of King Yama, the ruler of the underworld and the highest judge in its ten courts. See Xiangmeng Ciren, *Zhuangzi qiwen yanyi* (Shanghai: Dadong shuju, 1918), 3:6b–7a.

6. This anecdote is also included in the *Liezi*. For a translation of that version, see Liezi, *The Book of Lieh-tzu*, trans. A. C. Graham (London: Murray, 1960), 20–22.

7. Marjorie Garber, *Shakespeare After All* (New York: Anchor Books, 2005), 503–4.

8. Folke Henschen, *The Human Skull: A Cultural History* (London: Thames & Hudson, 1965), 128–34; Patrizia Nitti, ed., *C'est la vie! Vanités de Pompéi à Damien Hirst* (Paris: Flammarion, 2010). The tradition of representing death and the dead by skulls and skeletons of the first and second centuries c.e. was not continued in medieval times.

9. Léonard P. Kurtz, *The Dance of Death and the Macabre Spirit in European Literature* (1934; repr., Geneva: Slatkine, 1975), 12–13; James M. Clark, *The Dance of Death in the Middle Ages and the Renaissance* (Glasgow: Jackson, 1950), 95–99.

10. In one of the earliest recorded versions, however, the revived skull is an old man on his way to the market.

11. R. Tottoli, "The Story of Jesus and the Skull in Arabic Literature: The Emergence and Growth of a Religious Tradition," *Jerusalem Studies in Arabic and Islam* 28 (2003): 225–59. See also Fabrizio A. Pennacchietti, *Three Mirrors for Two Biblical Ladies: Susanna and the Queen of Sheba in the Eyes of Jews, Christians, and Muslims* (Piscataway, N.J.: Gorgias Press, 2006), 27–77; and C. Brakel-Papenhuyzen, "The Tale of the Skull: An Islamic Description of Hell in Javanese," *Bijdragen tot de Taal-, Land- en Volkenkunde* 158, no. 1 (2002): 1–19.

12. For a short discussion of the *Zhuangzi* on death, see A. C. Graham, *Disputers of the Tao: Philosophical Argument in Ancient China* (Chicago: Open Court, 1989), 202–4; for a more detailed discussion, see Mark Berkson, "Death in the *Zhuangzi*: Mind, Nature, and the Art of Forgetting," in *Mortality in Traditional Chinese Thought*, ed. Amy Olberding and Philip J. Ivanhoe (Albany: State University of New York Press, 2012), 191–224.

13. Stephen Owen, *Remembrances: The Experience of the Past in Classical Chinese Literature* (Cambridge, Mass.: Harvard University Press, 1986), 33–34.

14. Xiangmeng, *Zhuangzi qiwen yanyi*, 3:7a.

15. *Yangjiafu yanyi* (Shanghai: Shanghai guji chubanshe, 1980), 134; *Yangjia-jiang yanyi* (Beijing: Baowentang, 1980), 174.

16. Berthold Laufer, *Use of Human Skulls and Bones in Tibet* (Chicago: Museum of Natural History, 1923). The Japanese heretical Tachikawa sect, which, according to its enemies, used skulls to work magic, appears to have had no counterpart in Chinese Buddhism. See James H. Sanford, "The Abominable Tachikawa Skull Ritual," *Monumenta Nipponica* 46, no. 1 (1991): 1–20.

17. Ouyang Xun, comp., *Yiwen leiju*, ed. Wang Shaoying (Beijing: Zhonghua shuju, 1965), 320–22. See also Qian Zhongshu, *Guanzhui bian* (Beijing: Zhonghua shuju, 1979), 3:1011–13. Of the "Rhapsody on the Skull" by the third-century writer Li Kang, only two uninformative lines survive. For complete translations of the rhapsodies by Zhang Heng, Cao Zhi, and Lü An, see appendix 1.

18. Ji Kang, *Ji Kang ji jiaozhu*, annot. Dai Mingyang (Beijing: Renmin wenxue chubanshe, 1962), 431.

19. One source quotes two lines as being from Lü An's poem ("Above I will appeal to the Primordial Spirit, / Below I will speak to the August Divinities") (ibid., 431), but it is unclear where these two lines would fit in the poem, if they are indeed from the poem.

20. Cao Zhi, *Cao Zhi ji jiaozhu*, annot. Zhao Youwen (repr., Taipei: Ming wen, 1985), 524–28.

21. Zhang Heng, *Zhang Heng shiwenji jiaozhu*, annot. Zhang Zhenze (Shanghai: Shanghai guji chubanshe, 1986), 247–52. For an English translation of this poem by Arthur Waley as "The Bones of Chuang-tzu," see *Chinese Poems* (London: Unwin Paperbacks, 1982), 59–62.

22. For a brief discussion of Zhang Heng's poem, see Owen, *Remembrances*, 35–38. Zhang Shasha wishes to read both Cao Zhi's and Zhang Heng's works as political fables, in which the skull becomes a spokesperson for the author, in "'Kulou' yixiang zhong de zhengzhi yuyan: 'Zhuangzi tan kulou' yu Zhang Heng *Kulou fu*, Cao Zhi *Kuloushuo* de bijiao," *Leshan shifan xueyuan xuebao* 27, no. 4 (2012): 38–39. She dates Cao Zhi's work to the last years of his life and reads it as a manifestation of his dejection and frustration over his alienation from political power. She dates Zhang Heng's work to the autumn of 137 and reads it as a spirited attack against his political opponents.

23. Continuing his discussion of the theme of the encounter with unidentified bones, Owen translates and analyzes texts by Xie Huilian (379–433) and Wang Shouren (1472–1528) on the (re)burial of accidentally encountered human remains of unknown origins, in *Remembrances*, 38–49.

24. The most extensive study of the topic to date is Eric Matthew Green, "Of Bones and Buddhas: Contemplation of the Corpse and Its Connection to Meditations on Purity as Evidenced by 5th Century Chinese Meditation Manuals" (master's thesis, University of California, Berkeley, 2006). The disgust of physicality manifested in the texts concerned may go so far as describing living human beings as sacks of skin, filled with pus and shit, or even "walking shithouses."

25. Erik Zürcher, "Buddhist Art in Medieval China: The Ecclesiastical View," in *Function and Meaning in Buddhist Art*, ed. K. R. van der Kooij and H. van der Veere (Groningen: Forsten, 1995), 6–7.

26. For an early example of a full-length lying skeleton, see the Lotus Sutra tableau in Cave 217 at Mogaoku, Dunhuang, in Eugene Wang, *Shaping the Lotus Sutra: Buddhist Visual Culture in Medieval China* (Seattle: University of Washington Press, 2005), 94, fig. 2.11. See also Jacques Giès, *Les arts de l'Asie centrale: La collection Paul Pelliot du Musée national des arts asiatiques; Guimet* (Paris: Réunion des Musées Nationaux, 1995), 1:no. 5 (MG 17655).

27. The Tantric *Dafo dingguangju tuoluoni jing*, however, describes a form of magic that makes it possible for the practitioner to bring skeletons back to life. See Kang Baocheng, "'Gulou ge' de zhenwei yu yuanyuan xintan," *Wenxue yichan*, no. 2 (2003): 99–103.

28. "*Henjō hakki seireishū* (The Spirit and Mind Collection: The Revelations of the Priest Henjō [Kūkai])," in *Dance of the Butterflies: Chinese Poetry from the Japanese Court Tradition*, trans. and ed. Judith N. Rabinovitch and Timothy R. Bradstock (Ithaca, N.Y.: East Asia Program, Cornell University, 2005), 99–105.

29. James H. Sanford, "The Nine Faces of Death: 'Su Tung-po's' *Kuzō-shi*," *Eastern Buddhist* 22, no. 2 (1988): 54–77.

30. Liz Wilson, *Charming Cadavers: Horrific Figurations of the Feminine in Indian Buddhist Hagiographic Literature* (Chicago: University of Chicago Press, 1996). In this connection, it should cause no surprise that in the sixteenth-century novel *Journey to the West* (*Xiyou ji*), the White Bone Demon encountered on the monk Xuanzang's pilgrimage to the Western Paradise is a female character. See [Wu Cheng'en,] *The Journey to the West*, trans. Anthony Yu (Chicago: University of Chicago Press, 1977–1983), 2:16–32. One of Xuanzang's companions on his pilgrimage in the *Xiyouji* is Sha Heshang, who carries a necklace of nine skulls. See Kang Baocheng, "Sha Heshang de kulou xianglian: Cong toulu chongbai dao mizong yishi," *Henan daxue xuebao*, no. 1 (2004): 75–78.

31. Bernard Faure, *The Rhetoric of Immediacy: A Cultural Critique of Chan/Zen Buddhism* (Princeton, N.J.: Princeton University Press, 1991), 140.

32. Chün-fang Yü, *Kuanyin: The Chinese Transformation of Avalokiteśvara*

(New York: Columbia University Press, 2001), 421–27. Xu Jingbo illustrates and discusses an anonymous Yuan-dynasty painting showing Guanyin's interconnected bones, in "Guanshiyin pusa kaoshu," in *Guanyin pusa quanshu* (Shenyang: Chunfeng wenyi chubanshe, 1987), 251.

33. Inner alchemy uses the language of outer alchemy, which seeks to produce the elixir of life by physical means, to envision the fusion of all contradictory energies within the human body and the creation of an immortal embryo. For a concise introduction to the subject of inner alchemy, see Fabrizio Pregadio and Lowell Skarr, "Inner Alchemy," in *Daoism Handbook*, ed. Kohn, 464–97.

34. For general introductions to Quanzhen Daoism, see Stephen Eskildsen, *The Teachings and Practices of the Early Quanzhen Taoist Masters* (Albany: State University of New York Press, 2004); Louis Komjathy, *Cultivating Perfection: Mysticism and Self-Transformation in Early Quanzhen Daoism* (Leiden: Brill, 2007); and Pierre Marsone, *Wang Chongyang (1113–1170) et la fondation du Quanzhen: Ascètes taoïstes et alchimie intérieure* (Paris: Collège de France, Institut des hautes études chinoises, 2010). See also Ted Yao, "Quanzhen—Complete Perfection," in *Daoism Handbook*, ed. Kohn, 567–93; and Vincent Goossaert, "Quanzhen," in *Encyclopedia of Taoism*, ed. Fabrizio Pregadio (London: Routledge, 2008), 2:814–20.

35. For biographical sketches of the early Quanzhen masters and characterizations of their voluminous writings, see Judith Magee Boltz, *A Survey of Taoist Literature, Tenth to Seventeenth Centuries* (Berkeley: Institute of East Asian Studies and Center for Chinese Studies, University of California, 1987), 143–90.

36. On the use of the image of the skeleton by early Quanzhen masters, see Eskildsen, *Teachings and Practices*, 167–168; Komjathy, *Cultivating Perfection*, 100–104; and Marsone, *Wang Chongyang*, 204–5.

37. Wang Zhe, *Chongyang quanzhen ji* (*Daozang*, vols. 793–96), 3:8.

38. Ma Yu, *Danyang shenguangcan* (*Daozang*, vol. 791), 27.

39. This is the first stanza of a lyric to the tune "Nankezi" by Ma Yu, in *Jianwu ji* (*Daozang*, vol. 786), 2:3.

40. Ma Yu, *Dongxuan jinyu ji* (*Daozang*, vols. 789–90), 21.

41. *Minghe yuyin* (*Daozang*, vols. 744–45), 3:3. One wonders whether perhaps songs like this may have found their way to Japan and influenced the visions of cavorting skeletons in the writings and sketches of the Zen monk Ikkyū Sōjun (1394–1481). For translations of the essay and reproductions of the sketches, see Ikkyū Sōjun, "Ikkyu's Skeletons," trans. R. H. Blyth, *Eastern Buddhist* 6, no. 1 (1973): 111–25; and James H. Sanford, *Zen-Man Ikkyū* (Chico, Calif.: Scholars Press, 1981), 201–16. (It is not clear to what extent the transmitted sketches are indeed the handiwork of Ikkyū.)

42. Wang Zhe, *Chongyang quanzhen ji*, 10:14.

43. Ma, *Danyang shenguangcan*, 31. The "Mad Immortal" of the opening line is Wang Chongyang.

44. For a black-and-white reproduction of this fresco, see *Yongle gong* (Beijing: Renmin meishu chubanshe, 1964), pl. 191. For a color reproduction, see *Eirakukyū hekiga* (Kyoto: Binobi, 1981), pl. 101. See also Zhu, "Yongle gong bihua tiji luwen," *Wenwu*, August 1963, 61–78. When I visited the Yongle gong in 1991, the standing skeleton had been effaced.

45. The strings of a marionette.

46. Tan Chuduan, *Shuiyun ji* (*Daozang*, vol. 798), 2:18. For a reproduction of a rubbing of an 1183 stele from Luoyang depicting a Daoist master accompanied by his acolyte coming across a skeleton in the fields, see Chen Yuan, comp., *Daojia jinshi lüe* (Beijing: Wenwu chubanshe, 1988), 432. Below the picture is inscribed another poem by Tan Chuduan lamenting a skeleton. The poem, "White Bones" (Baigu), can be translated as follows:

> Deeply wounded and affected, I now lament this skeleton:
> A gorgeous girl or cute boy who never stopped loving.
> With all your mind you slaved away, coveting riches and money;
> You never had any inclination to practice religious cultivation.
>   During your lifetime you created sins without any limit—
> Who will substitute for you after your death for your evil karma?
> Your seed and blood have all gone with your passion and lust,
> Leaving behind only your bones lying on this overgrown hill.

47. Cao Xueqin and Gao E, *Honglou meng* (Beijing: Renmin wenxue chubanshe, 1982), 171. David Hawkes turns the standing skeleton into "a grinning skull," in his translation of Cao Xueqin, *The Story of the Stone*, vol. 1, *The Golden Days* (Harmondsworth: Penguin, 1973), 252. See also Xu Zhenhui, "*Honglou meng* de xing yu ai," *Shuwu*, no. 4 (2002): 42–44. In discussing this passage, Qian Zhongshu draws attention to the parallel with French mirrors of the seventeenth century that showed a skull on the back, in *Guanzhui bian*, 1:33–34. See Monika Motsch, *Mit Bambusrohr und Ahle: Von Qian Zhongshus "Guanzhuibian" zu einer neubetrachtung Du Fus* (Frankfurt: Lang, 1994), 148–49, 165–66.

48. The edition I have used is the one reprinted in Zhang Xishun, ed., *Baojuan chuji* (Taiyuan: Shanxi renmin chubanshe, 1994), 1:543–72. For a full translation of this set of songs, see appendix 2. Che Xilun lists a *Kulou baojuan*, which so far seems not to have been reprinted and which I have not seen, in *Zhongguo baojuan zongmu* (Beijing: Beijing Yanshan chubanshe, 2000), 135.

Perhaps the title refers to this set of songs as an independent text? On Luo Qing and his writings, see Daniel L. Overmyer, *Precious Volumes: An Introduction to Chinese Sectarian Scriptures from the Sixteenth and Seventeenth Centuries* (Cambridge, Mass.: Harvard University Asia Center, 1999), 92–135. While I treat the set of appended songs as the work of Luo Qing, it is, of course, also possible that the songs are not by him and have to be credited to an anonymous author. In theme and language, however, these songs seem to be consistent with the *Tanshi wuwei juan.*

49. Pu Wenqi, ed., *Zhongguo zongjiao lishi wenxian jicheng: Minjian baojuan* (Hefei: Huangshan shushe, 2005), vol. 1. For a full translation of this poem, see appendix 3.

50. *Quan Qing ci* (Beijing: Zhonghua shuju, 1994), 990–91. It should be kept in mind that in the late Ming and early Qing Jesuit missionaries introduced Western prints of skeletons and skulls to the Chinese public. One of the rare Qing-dynasty painters influenced by such paintings appears to have been Luo Pin (1733–1799), one of the "Eight Yangzhou Eccentrics." See Zhuang Shen, "Luo Pin yu qi *Guiqu tu*—jian lun Zhongguo guihua zhi yuanliu," *Zhongyang yanjiusuo Lishi yuyan yanjiusuo jikan* 44, no. 3 (1972): 403–34.

51. Judith Magee Boltz, "Singing to the Spirits of the Dead: A Daoist Ritual of Salvation," in *Harmony and Counterpoint: Ritual Music in Chinese Context*, ed. Evelyn S. Rawski and Rubie S. Watson (Stanford, Calif.: Stanford University Press, 1996), 209–10; François Picard, "Le chant du squelette (Kulou ge), " *Journal asiatique* 292 (2004): 382–412. See also Kang, " 'Gulou ge,' 100–102. A large number of texts from Sichuan for lamenting the skeleton can be found as "Ba Yu minjian fashi—kulou zhenyan (Tan kulou)," at http://blog.sina.com.cn/s/blog_60b676d8010000ms.html. One of the texts included is Ma Yu's lyric to the tune "Mantingfang" translated earlier.

52. Meng Yuanlao et al., *Dongjing menghua lu (wai si zhong)* (Beijing: Zhonghua shuju, 1962), 43; Meng Yuanlao, *Dongjing menghua lu*, annot. Deng Zhicheng (repr., Hong Kong: Shangwu yinshuguan, 1961), 202; Wilt Idema and Stephen H. West, *Chinese Theater, 1100–1450: A Source Book* (Wiesbaden: Steiner, 1982), 41–42. In 1281, under the Yuan dynasty, the wearing of skeleton heads was prohibited. See *Yuan dianzhang* (Taipei: Wenhai chubanshe, 1964), 57:50a (*xingbu* 19, "zajin"); and Wang Liqi, *Yuan Ming Qing sandai jinhui xiaoshuo xiqu shiliao*, rev. ed. (Shanghai: Shanghai guji chubanshe, 1981), 4–5. Dancers wearing skull-like white heads, however, are to this day included in the Wuyagu dance performed in Pingding county in eastern Shanxi. See the color photograph in Wu Xiaohong et al., eds., *Shanxi luogu* (Taiyuan: Shanxi renmin

chubanshe, 1991), 39. In the late nineteenth and early twentieth centuries, the dances performed by the Lamaist monks of Beijing's Yonghegong included performers wearing a skull mask and dressed as skeletons. See Berthold Laufer, "Origins of Our Dance of Death," *Open Court* 22 (1908): 599.

53. Detailed pictorial depictions of the internal body were included for example in the Song-period *Tongren yuxue zhenzhi tujing* by Wang Weiyi (d. after 1027). See *Tongren yuxue zhenzhi tujing*, in *Zhenzhi mingzhu jicheng*, ed. Huang Longxiang (Beijing: Huaxia chubanshe, 1997), 171. It should be noted that the edition in the modern edition is based on a Ming edition of the text. For a brief discussion of anatomical drawings of the Northern Song based on sections, see Jeehee Hong, "Theatricalizing Death and Society in *The Skeleton's Illusory Performance* by Li Song," *Art Bulletin* 93, no. 1 (2011): 76n.5.

54. Sung Tz'u [Song Ci], *The Washing Away of Wrongs: Forensic Medicine in Thirteenth-Century China*, trans. Brian E. McKnight (Ann Arbor: Center for Chinese Studies, University of Michigan, 1981), 95–106. The preface to the *Xiyuan lu* by the author Song Ci is dated 1247, but no Song edition has been preserved. McKnight based his translation on a reprint of a Yuan-dynasty edition. It is not clear whether the original edition carried illustrations, but the description of the human skeleton in the text is quite detailed.

55. The most detailed survey of references to paintings of or including skulls or skeletons for the Song and Yuan dynasties is Yi Ruofen, "Kulou huanxi: Zhongguo wenxue yu tuxiang zhong de shengming yishi," *Zhongguo wenzhe yanjiu jikan* 26 (2005): 90–94. The relatively large number of monks among the writers concerned indicates the continuing association of skulls and skeletons with Buddhism at this time.

56. Tang Guizhang, comp., *Quan Jin Yuan ci* (Beijing, Zhonghua shuju, 1979), 2:936. See also Ding Ruomu, "'Xingxing han, pinang chepo, bianshi kulou': Cong Wu Zhen hua kulou shuoqi," *Zongjiaoxue yanjiu* no. 1 (1996): 41–47. For a full translation of this lyric, see Wilt L. Idema, "Skulls and Skeletons in Art and on Stage," in *Conflict and Accommodation in Early Modern East Asia: Essays in Honour of Erik Zürcher*, ed. Leonard Blussé and Harriet T. Zurndorfer (Leiden: Brill, 1993), 209. The learned eighteenth-century editors of the *Siku quanshu* expressed their surprise that an eminent painter like Wu Zhen could have painted such a lugubrious subject. See Yi, "Kulou huanxi," 94.

57. For a color reproduction of this painting, see Wu Zhefu, ed., *Zhonghua wuqiannian wenwu jikan: Songhua pian* IV (Taipei: Zhonghua wuqiannian wenwu jikan bianji weiyuanhui, 1981), 26, illus. 24. This painting has generated a considerable body of scholarship. See Ellen Johnston Laing, "Li Sung and Some

Aspects of Southern Sung Figure Painting," *Artibus Asiae* 37, nos. 1–2 (1975): 5–38; Li Fushun, "Li Song he ta de 'Kulou huanxi tu,'" *Duoyun*, no. 3 (1981): 165–68, 150; Idema, "Skulls and Skeletons"; Kang Baocheng, "Bushuo 'Kulou huanxi tu'—jianshuo 'kulou,' 'kuilei' ji qi yu fojiao guanxi," *Xueshu yanjiu*, no. 11 (2003): 127–29; Shen Xiping, "Shixi daojiao dui Zhongguo huihua de yingxiang," *Yishu tansuo*, no. 4 (2004): 68–72; and Yi, "Kulou huanxi." For a meticulous visual analysis of this painting, see Hong, "Theatricalizing Death."

58. Sui Shusen, comp., *Quan Yuan sanqu* (Beijing: Zhonghua shuju, 1964), 2:1028.

59. Gu Fu, *Pingsheng zhuangguan* (Shanghai: Shanghai renmin meishu chubanshe, 1962), 8:48. The Art Museum of the Chinese University of Hong Kong includes a painting of 1874 by Ju Lian (1828–1904) with the title *Cart Puller* (*Qianche tu*). It shows a man tethered to a cart as an ox. The cart is loaded with the family's possessions. His wife and children are riding in the cart, and his wife spurs the husband on with her whip. Perhaps Li Song's painting had a similar composition.

60. Sun Feng, *Sunshi shuhua chao*, quoted in Yi "Kulou huanxi," 75. A Yuan-dynasty wall painting in the middle hall of the Green Dragon Temple (Qinglongsi) at Jishan in Shanxi shows among the denizens of hell a skeleton wrapped in strings of cash. See Shi Honglei and Yi Bao, "Shanxi Jishan Qinglongsi yaodian bihua de minsu fengge tezheng," *Meishu daguan*, no. 3 (2009): 77.

61. Since little is known to what extent the Quanzhen movement had made inroads in the territory of the Southern Song, it is difficult to ascertain whether Li Song's fascination with skeletons and marionettes was due to Quanzhen influence. It may be significant, however, that he has also been credited with the *Painting of the Four Delusions* (*Simi tu*), which depicts the four main vices as identified in Quanzhen thought. We are informed about the existence of this painting by a long poem by the fourteenth-century poet Yuan Hua, included in Li E, *Nan Song yuanhua lu*, in *Huashi congshu*, comp. Yu Anlan (Shanghai: Shanghai renmin meishu chubanshe, 1963), 8:48. A painting acquired by Zhang Daqian in Japan, showing four gentlemen in various states of drunkenness, may be the panel on "wine" from Li Song's otherwise lost painting, according to Yang Xiu, "Li Song 'Simi tu' chukao," *Sichuan wenwu*, no. 5 (2008): 69–71.

62. This story was included by Feng Menglong in *Jingshi tongyan* (1624). See Feng Menglong, comp., *Jingshi tongyan xinzhu quanben*, annot. Wu Shuyin (Beijing: Shiyue wenyi chubanshe, 1994), 269–81; and *Stories to Caution the World*, trans. Shuhui Yang and Yunqin Yang (Seattle: University of Washington

Press, 2005), 290–303. The date of composition of this *huaben* is discussed in Patrick Hanan, *The Chinese Short Story: Studies in Dating, Authorship, and Composition* (Cambridge, Mass.: Harvard University Press, 1973), 240.

63. Fu Xihua, *Mingdai zaju quanmu* (Beijing: Zuojia chubanshe, 1958), 38.

64. [Wu Cheng'en,] *Journey to the West*, 2:16–32. This episode from the novel enjoyed remarkable popularity in the first three decades of the People's Republic of China. See Rudolf G. Wagner, *The Contemporary Chinese Historical Drama: Four Studies* (Berkeley: University of California Press, 1990), 139–235. In the years of the Cultural Revolution, the story was also widely known outside China. One manifestation of this was the opera *Aap verslaat de knekelgeest* (*Monkey Subdues the White Bone Demon*, 1980), by the Dutch composer Peter Schat (1935–2003).

65. Zhang Zehong, "Daojiao chang daoqing suojian de Lao Zhuang sixiang: Yi *Zhuangzi tan kulou* daoqing wei zhongxin," in *Quanzhendao yu Lao-Zhuang xue guoji xueshu yantaohui lunwenji*, ed. Xiong Tieji and Mai Zifei (Wuhan: Huazhong shifan daxue chubanshe, 2009), and *Daojiao chang daoqing* (Beijing: Renmin chubanshe, 2011), 161–76; Jiang Kebin, "Shilun *Zhuangzi tan kulou* gushi zhi shanbian," *Beijing huagong daxue xuebao (shehui kexueban)*, no. 2 (2010): 29–33.

66. *Zaju* was the most popular type of drama in the period 1250 to 1450. *Zaju* plays usually consist of four acts built around four sets of songs that are all sung by a single performer.

67. Zhao Jingshen, *Yuanren zaju gouchen* (Shanghai: Shanghai guji chubanshe, 1956), 35–39. The set has been preserved in three sixteenth-century anthologies of arias. Li Shouqing (second part of the thirteenth century) hailed from Taiyuan; he is known to have written ten *zaju*, of which two have been preserved.

68. The full title of the play as provided in the earliest catalogue suggests that Li Shouqing had moved the setting of the play to the Song dynasty.

69. The story "Master Zhuang Lamenting the Skeleton" is also mentioned in one of the arias in act 1 of Zhang Guobin's *Luo Lilang*.

70. Among the known titles of *yuanben* of the Jin dynasty (1115–1234), we encounter a *Zhuang Zhou meng*.

71. Wang Jilie, "Tiyao," 7b–8a, no. 14, "*Zhuang Zhou meng*," in *Guben Yuan Ming zaju* (repr., Beijing: Zhongguo xiju chubanshe, 1958).

72. Helmut Wilhelm, "On Chuang-Tzu Plays from the Yüan Store," *Literature East and West* 17, nos. 2–4 (1973): 249.

73. Fu Xihua, *Yuandai zaju quanmu* (Beijing: Zuojia chubanshe, 1957), 363.

74. Xie Boyang, comp. *Quan Ming sanqu* (Jinan: Qi Lu shushe, 1993), 1:847–49. The original source mentions that two of the arias had been added by Ningzhai, a person about whom no additional information is available.

75. The period of the Warring States corresponds roughly to the fourth and third centuries B.C.E. and culminates in the unification of the Chinese world by the First Emperor of the Qin dynasty (221–206 B.C.E.).

76. The transformations of the huge roc are discussed in chapter 1 of the *Zhuangzi*.

77. The name Yellow Springs refers to the world of the dead.

78. In some versions of the legend of Jesus and the skeleton, too, Jesus's questions to the skeleton about his identity when alive are greatly expanded: "In the Arabic edition of *Jesus and the Skull* in Maghribi verse, the questions about the dead man's identity occupy no fewer than 24 of the 128 stanzas, one fifth of the poem, and review all the possible roles, professions and trades that the skull's owner may have fulfilled during his life" (Pennacchietti, *Three Mirrors*, 72).

79. *Zhaijin qiyin*, in *Shanben xiqu congkan*, ed. Wang Qiugui (Taipei: Xuesheng shuju, 1984), 3:17b–21a (pp. 160–67). On this play, see Wang Kui, "Mingkan xiqu sanchu *Zhou Zhuangzi tan kulou* xintan," *Anhui daxue xuebao*, no. 1 (2005): 121–25. Buddhist homiletic poetry often describes the human body as a sack of skin filled with pus and excrement. The *Yuefu wanxiangxin* (1:1b–8b), yet another late Ming drama anthology from Jiangxi, includes the same text but lists the otherwise unknown play *Xizi ji* as its source (pp. 90–104, upper register). Xizi is an alternative name for Xi Shi, the fifth-century B.C.E. woman who brought down the kingdom of Wu with her seductive charms.

80. Clear and Bright (Qingming) refers to the spring festival celebrated on the 105th day following the longest night. On that day, families visit the graves of their ancestors to clean and repair them.

81. That is, passing as quick as an arrow.

82. Impermanence is the name of the underworld representative who comes to fetch one when one's life has reached its end. The term may also indicate a twosome of such underworld runners, one tall and white and the other short and black, known respectively as White Impermanence and Black Impermanence.

83. The story of Master Zhuang's first resurrecting the skeleton and eventually killing him may well be indebted to the legend of Xu Jia, the ungrateful servant of the Old Master. In the earliest version of the legend, Xu Jia is an ungrateful servant who is seduced by his wife-to-be to demand his back pay, which runs into millions. When the Old Master takes away a talisman that he had given to him, Xu Jia collapses into a pile of bones and is revived only after others plead for mercy. By the tenth century, the legend had come to include the detail that Xu Jia had become the Old Master's servant after the Old Master had found him

as a pile of bones and revived him. See Livia Kohn, "Xu Jia," in *Encyclopedia of Taoism*, ed. Pregadio, 2:1122–23.

84. The term *daoqing* referred originally to songs giving expression to Daoist sentiments such as the joys of retirement and the desire for immortality. As such, it is frequently encountered in the titles of Yuan-dynasty *sanqu*—but the best-known example may well be Zheng Xie's (Banqiao; 1693–1765) *Daoqing shizhong*, which is made up of ten songs to the tune "Shuahai'er." For a translation of these songs, see Zheng Xie, *Chêng Pan-ch'iao: Selected Poems, Calligraphy, Paintings and Seal Engravings*, trans. Anthony Cheung and Paul Gurofsky (Hong Kong: Joint Publishing, 1987), 1–18. By the Ming dynasty at the latest, *daoqing* had also become the designation for stories told to the accompaniment of the fisherman's drum and bamboo clappers (the fisherman's drum [*yugu*], made from a piece of bamboo, was also called the simpleton's drum [*yugu*]). In later generations, the offshoots of *daoqing* storytelling might also be called *yugu* or *qinshu*. As the themes and music of *daoqing* were borrowed by the stage and the shadow theater, we also see the emergence of theater genres referred to as *daoqing*. In time, such genres frequently lost their exclusive focus on Daoist subjects. For a comprehensive study of *daoqing* literature, see Wu Yimin, *Zhongguo daoqing yishu gailun* (Taiyuan: Shanxi guji chubanshe, 1997); and Zhang Zehong, *Daojiao chang daoqing*. See also Sawada Mizuho, "Dōjō ni tsuite," *Chūgoku bungaku geppō* 44 (1938): 117–23; Ono Shihei, "Dōjō ni tsuite," in *Chūgoku kinsei ni okeru tampen shōsetsu no kenkyū* (Tokyo: Hyōronsha, 1979), 288–309; Zhan Renzhong, "Shitan daoqing," *Quyi yishu luncong* 7 (1988): 52–57; Sun Fuxuan, "Daoqing kaoshi," *Daojiao luntan*, no. 2 (2005): 17–22; and Che Xilun, "Daoqing kao," *Xiju yanjiu* 70 (2006): 218–38.

85. Feng Menglong, comp., *Xingshi hengyan xinzhu quanben*, annot. Zhang Minggao (Beijing: Shiyue wenyi chubanshe, 1994), 893–94. For a full translation of this story, see Feng Menglong, comp., *Stories to Awaken the World*, trans. Shuhui Yang and Yunqin Yang (Seattle: University of Washington Press, 2009), 886–914. This *huaben* was adapted from a prosimetric text. See Patrick Hanan, "The *Yün-men chuan*: From *Chantefable* to Short Story," *Bulletin of the School of Oriental and African Studies* 36, no. 2 (1973): 299–308. While the *Yunmen zhuan* features the character of the *daoqing* performer, it does not include the detailed description of a performance of a narrative *daoqing* on the legend of Master Zhuang's encountering the skeleton as provided by Feng Menglong. See *Yunmen zhuan*, 56b–59a, National Library of Peiping, Rare Books Collection, Microfilms, no. 2699.

86. Ding Yaokang, *Xu Junpingmei*, in *Guben xiaoshuo jicheng*, 43:1–4 (Shanghai: Shanghai guji chubanshe, 1990), 3:1302–15. For a typeset and annotated

edition of Ding Yaokang's *Master Zhuang Laments the Skeleton*, see Liu Guang-ming, *Gudai shuochang bianti* (Beijing: Shoudu shifan daxue chubanshe, 1996), 136–41. This text is retained in the two abbreviated versions of Ding's novel, *Flowers Behind the Curtain* (*Gelian huaying*) and *Golden House Dream* (*Jinwu meng*). Like some other seventeenth-century Shandong intellectuals, Ding Yao-kang showed an active interest in prosimetric literature. He not only included descriptions of performances in his novel but also is credited with the author-ship of some prosimetric texts himself. On Ding Yaokang and his novel, see Siao-chen Hu, "In the Name of Correctness: Ding Yaokang's *Xu Jin Ping Mei* as a Reading of *Jin Ping Mei*," in *Snakes' Legs: Sequels, Continuations, Rewritings, and Chinese Fiction*, ed. Martin W. Huang (Honolulu: University of Hawai'i Press, 2004), 75–97. On Ding Yaokang as a writer of prosimetric literature, see Ding Yaokang, "Southern Window Dream," trans. Wilt L. Idema, *Renditions* 69 (2008): 20–33.

87. The text has not been reprinted but is available at the Web site of the Institute of Oriental Culture, http://shanben.ioc.u-tokyo.ac.jp/index.html.

88. In its Kuraishi Collection, the Institute of Oriental Culture also holds a partial copy of a printed version, but it has not been made available on the Web. Various sources mention a work of the same title as a late Ming printed work at one time in the possession of the modern scholar Du Yingtao. References in Chinese scholarship to this text are often confusing, probably because the authors have not seen the original. Scholars not infrequently repeat the mistaken statement of Ye Dejun, *Song Yuan Ming jiangchang wenxue* (Shanghai: Gudian wenxue chubanshe, 1957), 68, that, despite its title, the verse sections consist mostly of seven-syllable and ten-syllable ballad verse. See, for instance, Zhao Jingshen, "Sichuan zhuqin *Sanguozhi* xu," in *Quyi luncong* (Beijing: Zhongguo quyi chubanshe, 1982), 229.

89. Wang Yinglin, *Yan Zhuang xindiao*, preface, 1a, in *Wang Yinglin zaji*, orig-inal woodblock ed. (ca. 1620), Naikaku Bunko, Tokyo.

90. Du Hui's adaptation and Ding Yaokang's adaptation are clearly related, but it seems more likely that they share a source than that either text derives directly from the other.

91. The only scholar to have described this text in some detail is Ono, "Dōjō ni tsuite," 300–304. He provides a summary of the narrative and stresses the ele-ments of social criticism in the text.

92. For an overview of prosimetric and verse narrative in Ming (and Qing) times, see Wilt L. Idema, "Prosimetric and Verse Narrative," in *The Cambridge History of Chinese Literature*, vol. 2, *From 1375*, ed. Kang-i Sun Chang and

Stephen Owen (Cambridge: Cambridge University Press, 2010), 350–61. Jiang Kun and Ni Zhongzhi discuss the Ming-dynasty narrative *daoqing* primarily on the basis of the *Han Xiangzi jiudu Wengong daoqing*, in *Zhongguo quyi tongshi* (Beijing: Renmin wenxue chubanshe, 2005), 382–87. But this work has been preserved only in Qing-dynasty printings of the nineteenth century or later. This is a much longer work than *Master Zhuang Sighs over the Skeleton in Northern and Southern Lyrics and Songs* and has a much more complicated plot. For its verse passages, it relies primarily on songs, many to the same tunes used in *Master Zhuang Sighs over the Skeleton in Northern and Southern Lyrics and Songs*. We also know from two Ming-dynasty sources that the legend of Han Xiangzi, one of the Eight Immortals, was performed as a narrative *daoqing* at the time. For an extensive discussion of the legend of Han Xiangzi and its *daoqing* adaptations, see Zhang Zehong, *Daojiao chang daoqing*, 147–60.

93. Even when the legend of Han Xiangzi was turned into a vernacular novel by Yang Erzeng as *Han Xiangzi zhuan*, the text was distinguished by the inclusion of a very large number of songs. For a translation of this novel, see Yang Erzeng, *The Story of Han Xiangzi: The Alchemical Adventures of a Daoist Immortal*, trans. Philip Clart (Seattle: University of Washington Press, 2007). Since a *daoqing* on the legend of Han Xiangzi is mentioned in chapter 64 of the sixteenth-century novel *Jinpingmei*, it is quite possible that the novel is a reworking of an earlier *daoqing* narrative.

94. Dale R. Johnson, *Yuan Music Dramas: Studies in Prosody and Structure and a Complete Catalogue of Northern Arias in the Dramatic Style* (Ann Arbor: Center for Chinese Studies, University of Michigan, 1980), 260–62; Zheng Qian, *Beiqu taoshi huilu xiangjie* (Taipei: Yiwen yinshuguan, 1973), 122–26. See also Ren Guangwei, "'Shuahai'er' zonghengkao," in *"Xiqu yishu" ershinian jinian wenji Xiqu wenxue, xiqushi yanjiu juan* (Beijing: Zhongguo xiju chubanshe, 2000), 395–418.

95. For general studies of the genre, see Kurtz, *Dance of Death*; Clark, *Dance of Death*; Elina Gertsman, *The Dance of Death in the Middle Ages: Image, Text, Performance* (Turnhout, Belgium: Brepols, 2010). For a study of a single example of the genre, see Ann Tukey Harrison, ed., *The Danse Macabre of Women: Ms. fr. 995 of the Bibliothèque Nationale* (Kent, Ohio: Kent State University Press, 1994). Jurgis Baltrušaitis argues for Asian influences in the late medieval obsession with decomposition and skeletons, in *Le moyen âge fantastique: Antiquités et exotismes dans l'art gothique* (Paris: Flammarion, 1981), 226–39. As early as 1908, Laufer had suggested a Tibetan and/or Mongol origin of the dance of death, in "Origins of Our Dance of Death," but on very flimsy grounds.

96. This also applies to the rare contemporary pictures of skeletons in illustrations of Meng Jiangnü bringing down the Great Wall by her weeping. The lack of experience of late imperial Chinese woodblock artists in rendering skeletons is clearly brought out in the reproduction of Li Song's famous painting of the skeleton marionetteer in the *Gushi huapu* (1603), a collection of high-quality woodblock reproductions of famous paintings. See Zheng Zhenduo, comp., *Zhongguo gudai banhua congkan* (Shanghai: Shanghai guji chubanshe, 1988), 3:49. It is also obvious in their reproductions of Western pictures of skeletons—for example, the reproduction of the famous print of a skeleton meditating on a skull from Andreas Vesalius's *De Humani Corporis Fabrica* (1543), in Andrea-Giovanni Lubelli's *Wanmin simo tu* (*Picture of the Four Last Things of All People*, ca. 1683). See Adrian Dudink, "Lubelli's *Wanmin simo tu* (*Picture of the Four Last Things of All People*), ca. 1683," *Sino-Western Cultural Relations Journal* 28 (2006): 1–17. The awkwardness of the skeletons in Chinese woodblock prints also contrasts sharply with the well-drawn skulls and skeletons in Japanese woodblock prints of the eighteenth and nineteenth centuries—for instance, in the works of Katsushika Hokusai (1760–1849), Utagawa Kunisada (1786–1864), and Utagawa Kuniyoshi (1797–1861). During the same period in Japan, skulls and skeletons were also a popular theme with netsuke carvers.

97. Wang Kui, "Mingkan xiqu," 121–22. Wang also points out the mistake of those scholars who identify Wang Yinglin's one-act play with the single scene "Zhou Zhuangzi tan kulou" from *Pinang ji*. Wang Yinglin was acquainted with *Master Zhuang Sighs over the Skeleton in Northern and Southern Lyrics and Songs.*

98. Fu Xihua, *Mingdai chuanqi quanmu* (Beijing: Renmin wenxue chubanshe, 1959), 311.

99. Wang's original title was a reference to an earlier play, now lost, called simply *Yan Zhuang*. The author of this prior play is known only under his pseudonym, Yecheng Laoren. Qi Biaojia describes its contents as follows: "The many songs of its long lament appear to have seen through the conundrum of life and death, but where is the Way of escape? For that, one has to consult Yunlai Daoren [that is, Wang Yinglin]" (*Yuanshan tang Ming qupin jupin jiaolu*, ed. Huang Shang [Shanghai: Shanghai chuban gongsi, 1955], 208). Qi's characterization might suggest that Yecheng Laoren's adaptation very much resembled the one act from *Pinang ji.*

100. Shen Tai, ed., *Sheng Ming zaju erji* (repr., Beijing: Zhongguo xiju chubanshe, 1958). Shen did not include the prefatory materials of the original edition in his printing of the play. The annotations in the upper margin of his text are

not found in the earlier edition and have not been included in the translation. The main text of the play is, for all practical purposes, identical in both editions.

101. These exceptional formal features were noted in Zeng Yongyi, *Ming zaju gailun* (Taipei: Xuehai chubanshe, 1979), 374–75.

102. Qi, *Yuanshan tang*, 184–85.

103. For an annotated modern edition of this tale, see Feng, *Jingshi tongyanxinzhu quanben*, 14–24. For a recent English translation, see Feng, *Stories to Caution the World*, 21–32. Hanan discusses the authorship of this story (and some others), and concludes, "There are some slight reasons for linking several of these stories to Feng Meng-lung, but they are not sufficient for even a tentative attribution" (*Chinese Short Story*, 85). See also André Lévy, *Inventaire analytique et critique du conte chinois en langue vulgaire*, part 1, vol. 1 (Paris: Collège de France, Institut de hautes études chinoises, 1979), 359–63. Although Feng Menglong provides us with the earliest text, the story must have circulated earlier, since we encounter an allusion to it in the *Gu mingjia zaju* edition (ca. 1588) of Guan Hanqing's (ca. 1230–ca. 1310) *Dou E yuan*. See Lan Liming, ed., *Huijiao xiangzhu Guan Hanqing ji* (Beijing: Zhonghua shuju, 2006), 1054. The allusion was removed when Zang Maoxun included the play in his *Yuanqu xuan* in 1616.

104. Human brains are not a common element in Chinese materia medica, but horror stories of black magic tell of the use of the brains of infants (as the repository of *jing* [essence/semen]) to increase longevity and achieve physical immortality. For a discussion of a late-sixteenth-century inventory of the pharmaceutical properties of human body parts (which is silent on human brains), see Carla Nappi, *The Monkey and the Inkpot: Natural History and Its Transformation in Early Modern China* (Cambridge, Mass.: Harvard University Press, 2009), 130–35.

105. This translation was included in *Description géographique, historique . . . de l'empire de la Chine et de la Tartarie chinoise*, edited by Jean-Baptiste Du Halde (1674–1743), and subsequently translated into many other European languages.

106. Ton Dekker, Jurjen van der Kooi, and Theo Meder. *Van Aladdin tot Zwaan kleef aan: Lexicon van sprookjes; Ontstaan, ontwikkeling, variaties* (Nijmegen: SUN, 1997), 165–68. In the global classification of folktale types devised by Antti Aarne and revised by Stith Thompson, stories of this type are classified as AT 1510. See Antii Aarne and Stith Thompson, *The Types of Folktales: A Classification and Bibliography*, 2nd rev. ed. (Helsinki: Suomalainen Tiedeakatemia, 1973); and Hans-Jörg Uther, *The Types of International Folktales: A Classification and Bibliography, Based on the System of Antti Aarne and Stith Thompson* (Helsinki: Suomalainen Tiedeakatemia, 2004). Actually, the story of Master

Zhuang's testing his wife's fidelity shows perhaps an even greater similarity to AT 823A, "Mother Dies of Fright When She Learns That She Was About to Commit Incest with Her Son." The basic plot of this story type is summarized as follows:

> Responding to an assertion that all women are faithless or that his own spouse is exceptionally virtuous, a man decides to test his wife (mother). He arranges for an accomplice to try to seduce her, and when she yields, she is convicted in the presence of her husband (son), which confirms for him the truth of the statement that women are ultimately faithless or at least that his own wife (mother) is no exception to the rule. The woman kills herself or dies from shame, and the man (or his accomplice) is profoundly changed by the experience. (William Hansen, *Ariadne's Thread: A Guide to International Tales Found in Classical Literature* [Ithaca, N.Y.: Cornell University Press, 2002], 284)

Wilhelm, "On Chuang-Tzu Plays," 244, claims that a Jataka tale translated as "Die betrogene Ehebrecherin" (The Cheated Adulteress) by Else Lüders (Else Lüders and Heinrich Lüders, *Buddhistische Märchen aus dem alten Indien* [Düsseldorf: Diederichs, 1981], 221–25) shows a great similarity to the tale of Master Zhuang and his wife. In the Jataka tale, however, the wife, who has suddenly fallen in love with her husband's enemy, allows that man to kill her husband in a fight, but her new lover, aware of her fickle nature, robs her of her belongings and abandons her at the first opportunity. Although the two tales may share the theme of a woman's fickleness, the story line of the former is quite different, and it takes considerable imagination to see the Jataka tale as the source of the story published by Feng Menglong.

107. Li Fengshi et al., *Si da chi*, late Ming woodblock edition, Harvard-Yenching Library, Harvard College Library, Cambridge, Mass.

108. This play must have been written during the period 1625 to 1633. A photographic reproduction of the original Chongzhen woodblock edition is available in *Guben xiqu congkan sanji*. For a summary of its contents and an inventory of other Zhuangzi plays, see Guo Yingde, *Ming Qing chuanqi zonglu* (Shijiazhuang: Hebei jiaoyu chubanshe, 1997), 376–79. Yet another full-length *chuanqi*, also with the title *Hudie meng*, by Chen Yiqiu, has survived only as a manuscript, kept in the Zhejiang Library. The *Quhai zongmu tiyao* includes the summary of still another anonymous *chuanqi*, with the title *Hudie meng*.

109. Qian Decang, comp., *Zhuibaiqiu* (Beijing: Zhonghua shuju, 2005), 6:131–68. See also Xu Fuming, "Kunqu *Hudie meng* de lailong qumai," *Yishu*

baijia, no. 4 (1993): 96–103. This play has recently been revived. See Lei Jingxuan, *Kunqu Hudiemeng: Yibu chuantongxi de zaixian* (Hong Kong: Oxford University Press, 2005). For a brief discussion of this play in comparison with *Hamlet*, see Chen Tsu-wen, "*Hamlet* and *The Butterfly Dream*." Chen focuses on two themes, the frailty of women and the discussion with the skull.

110. See, for example, the translation of the Peking opera *Hudiemeng* as *The Butterfly Dream* in A. C. Scott, *Traditional Chinese Plays* (Madison: University of Wisconsin Press, 1970), 93–146; and the translation of a *yangge* play from Dingxian, "Drying the Tomb with a Fan," in Sidney D. Gamble, *Chinese Village Plays from the Ting Hsien Region (Yang Ke Hsüan)* (Amsterdam: Philo Press, 1970), 683–702. The theme of Master Zhuang testing his wife has continued to inspire modern playwrights, including such luminaries as Gao Xingjian (b. 1940). In Gao's *Mingcheng* (1988), most of the play, however, is devoted to an elaborate description of the experiences of Master Zhuang's wife in the underworld following her suicide.

111. Zhao Jingshen mentions a *daoqing* text in his possession with the title *Zhuangzi daoqing: Piguan zhuan* (*A Daoqing Narrative on Master Zhuang: The Tale of Splitting the Coffin*) and lists the many song tunes employed in the narrative, in "Sichuan zhuqin," 228.

112. *Qing Menggu Che wangfu cang zidishu* (Beijing: Guoji wenhua chuban gongsi, 1994), 2:671–74. This text was also performed as a drum ballad (*guci*). Chunshuzhai's work should be distinguished from two other youth books, each in four chapters, also with the title *Hudie meng*. The *Che wangfu* collection of manuscripts contains three play manuscripts with the title *Hudie meng* starting with Master Zhuang's meeting with a young widow fanning a grave and ending with his wife's suicide, alongside a play, *Huanhua*, that dramatizes Master Zhuang's meeting with a skeleton that, in his dream, expounds on the pleasures of death. See Guo Jingrui et al., eds., *Che wangfu quben tiyao* (Guangzhou: Zhongshan daxue chubanshe, 1989), 177–79.

113. The Chinese texts of these two poems are presented as "Liuxian wenhua yichan—xiaoshun tongsu ge" on the Web site of Qinxian district, http://www .qinxian.gov.cn/typenews.asp?id=3230.

114. On spirit writing and spirit-writing cults, see David K. Jordan and Daniel L. Overmyer, *The Flying Phoenix: Aspects of Chinese Sectarianism in Taiwan* (Princeton, N.J.: Princeton University Press, 1986).

115. For a brief discussion of Yuan and early Ming deliverance plays featuring trees, see Wilt L. Idema, *The Dramatic Oeuvre of Chu Yu-tun (1379–1439)* (Leiden: Brill, 1985), 66. For a translation of one of these plays, see Ma Zhiyuan,

"The Yüeh-yang Tower," in *Four Plays of the Yuan Drama*, trans. Richard F. S. Yang (Taipei: China Post, 1972).

116. Chün-fang Yü, *Kuanyin*; Glen Dudbridge, *The Legend of Miaoshan* (Oxford: Oxford University Press, 2004); Wilt L. Idema, *Personal Salvation and Filial Piety: Two Precious Scroll Narratives of Guanyin and Her Acolytes* (Honolulu: University of Hawai'i Press, 2008).

117. Zeng Bairong, ed., *Jingju jumu cidian* (Beijing: Zhongguo xiju chubanshe, 1989), 71–72; Wang Senran, *Zhongguo jumu cidian* (Shijiazhuang: Hebei jiaoyu chubanshe, 1997), 833. Under a variety of titles, a comparable play can also be found in a number of other genres of local drama. *Hitting the Bone to Seek the Cash* is listed not only as an independent play but also as a section of more extensive plays on Master Zhuang's meeting with the young widow fanning her husband's grave and Master Zhuang's widow's passion for the prince. Performances of these latter plays were prohibited in the early decades of the People's Republic (the ban was officially lifted in 2007). See Siyuan Liu, "Theatre Reform as Censorship: Censoring Traditional Theatre in China in the Early 1950s," *Theatre Journal* 61, no. 3 (2009): 400.

118. The "three lights" are the sun, moon, and stars.

119. Chai Junwei, ed. *Jingju da xikao* (Shanghai: Xuelin chubanshe, 2004), 15. A *laosheng* (old male) specializes in performing positive male roles of a certain age.

120. Idema, *Personal Salvation*, 177–79.

121. Lu Xun, "Qisi," in *Lu Xun xiaoshuo ji* (Beijing: Renmin wenxue chubanshe, 1964), 441–52. This story has been translated into French as "Le mort ressuscité" (Lou Siun, *Contes anciens à notre manière*, trans. Li Tche-houa [Paris: Gallimard, 1959], 162–74) and into English as "Resurrecting the Dead" (Lu Hsun, *Old Tales Retold*, trans. Yang Hsien-yi and Gladys Yang [Beijing: Foreign Languages Press, 1961], 124–37). For a recent translation, see Lu Xun, "Bringing Back the Dead," in *The Real Story of Ah-Q and Other Tales of China: The Complete Fiction of Lu Xun*, trans. Julia Lovell (New York: Penguin, 2009), 393–402. None of these translations (or any of the Chinese editions or studies of this tale by specialists in modern Chinese literature that I have seen) alerts the reader to the existence of the many earlier adaptations of this theme, since they all appear to assume that Lu Xun based his story directly and exclusively on the anecdote in chapter 18 of the *Master Zhuang*. In *Zhongguo xiaoshuo shilüe*, however, Lu Xun discusses Ding Yaokang's *Xu Jinpingmei* at length, so he must at least have been acquainted with the brief version of the legend contained in that novel. See Lu Hsun, *A Brief History of Chinese Fiction*, trans. Yang Hsien-yi and

Gladys Yang (Beijing: Foreign Languages Press, 1959), 240–44. Lu Xun's indebtedness in writing "Qisi" to the legend of Master Zhuang's meeting the skeleton has been pointed out, however, in Jiang Kebin, "Shilun *Zhuangzi*," 29. Jiang Kebin, "Huangdan yu yinyu," provides a more detailed discussion of the relation between Lu Xun's story and the version of the legend in the *Xu Jinpingmei*, in "Huangdan yu yinyu de chonggou—lun *Gushi xinbian* 'Qisi,' " *Shenyang shifan daxue xuebao*, no. 4 (2010): 84–87. Another detailed comparison of Lu Xun's "Qisi" and the version of the legend in Ding Yaokang's *Xu Jinpingmei* is given in Zhao Guangya, "Lu Xun xiaoshuo *Qisi* de wenti xuanze yu chonggou," *Nanjing shifan daxue wenxueyuan xuebao*, no. 1 (2012): 62–67. See also Wilt L. Idema, "Free and Easy Wanderings: Lu Xun's 'Resurrecting the Dead' and Its Precursors," *Chinese Literature: Essays, Articles, Reviews* 34 (2012): 15–29.

122. Chinese studies of this tale link its topic to the intense political debates Lu Xun was involved in during the last year of his life and read the story as an all-out attack on those who refused to choose sides by embracing a more relativistic stance.

123. Lu Xun's collection of prose poems *Wild Grass* (*Yecao*, 1927) also contains one text that is written in dramatic form. Both this text and "Resurrecting the Dead" follow the conventions of "spoken drama" (*huaju*) as written in China since the 1920s. In contrast to earlier genres of Chinese theater (such as *zaju*, *chuanqi*, and Peking opera), spoken drama, following Western models, did not include songs.

124. *Xiangsheng* is the name of a genre of comic dialogue for two (or three) performers that enjoys considerable popularity in the People's Republic of China. The contents of the dialogues can vary from slapstick to satire.

125. *Taiping geci* songs are recited to a rapid rap-like beat. The genre enjoyed its greatest popularity in the early decades of the twentieth century. See Zhou Chunyi, "Taiping geci yanjiu, shang," *Minsu quyi*, no. 60 (1989): 102–27, and "Taiping geci yanjiu, xia," *Minsu quyi*, no. 61 (1989): 116–27.

126. The Chinese text can be found, for example, at http://www.underone .com/2008/05/21/kuloutan.

of song is obvious in our text, which contains a great number of such songs to a wide variety of popular melodies. These songs are interspersed with four-line and eight-line poems on comparable subjects. The narrative is carried forward mostly by the prose passages (and by a few passages in ballad verse). In the prose passages, we encounter many couplets made up of two lines of seven-syllable verse. Many of these couplets are from well-known poems, but I only rarely reference their origin since these couplets had often acquired the status of proverbs. Songs, poems, prose passages, and passages in ballad verse would have been delivered in performance each in its own characteristic manner, providing for a musically variegated entertainment. The reader, while enjoying the text in private, one assumes, would have been tempted to reproduce that variation if only by humming along. Performance directions in the original are set off from the main text with circles around them; in the translation, they are reproduced as italicized headings.

The text is organized in two parts. Part 1 describes Master Zhuang's happy life as a Daoist recluse and his decision to set out on a journey, which results in his encounter with the skeleton. It concludes with a long series of thirty-six songs, all to the tune "Shuahai'er," in which Master Zhuang questions the skeleton as to his identity, profession, and morality when alive. Part 2 begins with further lamentations over the skeleton and then narrates how Master Zhuang revives the skeleton and how the revived skeleton accuses Master Zhuang of having stolen his belongings and hauls him before the local magistrate. There Master Zhuang proves his version of events by turning the revived skeleton back into a skeleton and showing the three willow twigs that he had used to replace the missing ribs. The local magistrate is then convinced of the emptiness of an existence spent in the pursuit of ephemeral glory and riches and decides to abandon his career and his family in order to seek eternal life by following Master Zhuang's example. In a long speech that relies heavily on the technical language of internal alchemy, Master Zhuang instructs him in the techniques of meditation and self-cultivation that aim for the production of an indestructible embryo within the self through the coupling and merging of the contrasting elements that make up body and mind. After Master Zhuang has left, the magistrate ignores the pleas of his wife to continue his career and leaves for the Zhongnan Mountains. Eventually he, too, will join the immortals.

Master Zhuang loves the Way and practices self-cultivation.

DU HUI

Newly Composed, Enlarged, and Expanded, with a Forest of Appreciative Comments: Master Zhuang Sighs over the Skeleton in Northern and Southern Lyrics and Songs, Part 1

Composed by the Shunyi Mountain Recluse Du Hui of Kunling; Printed by Chen Kui (also known as Yangwen) of the same city.

Recite a poem:
> A hundred years are autumn dew and springtime flowers,
> But please unlock your frown, do not heave heavy sighs.
> Recite some poems and so dissipate your worldly worries,
> Pour out three cups of wine, enjoy these glorious days!
> When idle, play a game of go: your heart will feel happy;
> At leisure strum your zither and so pleasure will be yours.
> There is no need to care about matters that don't concern you,
> Just pursue the most enjoyable life in past and present!

Speak:
At present the sagely Ming occupies the throne and capable ministers display their loyalty; the whole world is at peace and the common people enjoy their occupations. This truly is a time of perfect order, an era of Great Peace. If we as human beings are alive at such a moment, we must open the jugs of Northern Ocean[1] and together drink to a longevity like the Southern Mountains.[2] Even though we may be only light dust and

---

1. The poet and free-thinking spirit Kong Rong (153–208) served for a while as chancellor of Beihai (Northern Ocean). He is credited with the saying "As long as guests fill the house and there is still wine in the jugs, I have no worry in the world."
2. The Southern Mountains are the hills and mountains to the south of the Han (and Tang) capital Chang'an (modern Xi'an). In poetry, these mountains often serve as a symbol of permanence in contrast to the ephemerality of human existence.

tender grasses, we should not ignore this fine scenery and great day. This wonderful scenery before our eyes cannot be fully described! With this sharp-pointed brush of a few inches I will entrust the greatest joy of my entire life to a few dashed-off lyrics on this sheet of paper and record the fable of Master Zhuang to admonish the people of this world to practice virtue. Assembling these brief lyrics, I present them to those who love such things.

Recite a lyric to the tune "Zhegutian" [Partridge Sky]:
　　The change of scenery startles the mind: time flees like a colt;[3]
　　A hundred years and overturned are both later and earlier carts.[4]
　　The cloudy hills that fill the eye are a true source of pleasure;
　　In the final analysis fame and profit turn out to be empty indeed.

　　Having bought myself a good drink,
　　I ask the woodcutters and fishermen:
　　What can compare to these majestic mountains and valleys?
　　At leisure I've adapted the few lines of Master Zhuang's tale
　　And written it up as this one book about the skeleton's fate.

Recite a poem:
　　Summer heat goes, winter cold comes; then spring and fall:
　　All of a sudden specks of gray appear in a young man's hair.
　　Where are now the palaces of the Qin, the gates of the Han?[5]
　　Those fierce fighters and cunning advisers are all long gone.

---

3. The passage of time is often compared to a running horse perceived through a crack in the wall.

4. The overturned cart is supposed to serve as a warning to all later cart drivers who pass by the same dangerous spot on the road. The line suggests that people tend to make the same mistakes over and over again during the one hundred years of their lives.

5. The Qin dynasty ruled China from 221 to 208 B.C.E. During his short reign, the First Emperor of the Qin (r. 221–210 B.C.E.) constructed a magnificent palace, which was destroyed when the population rose in rebellion soon after his death and insurgents entered the capital. The Western Han dynasty ruled China throughout the second and first centuries B.C.E. The stories of the violent warfare following the collapse of the Qin and resulting in the establishment of the (Former or Western) Han dynasty (206 B.C.E.– 8 C.E.) were popular with storytellers, in fiction, and on the stage.

So I conclude that light and shadow are like a dream, a flash:
Why should we slave and suffer to become nobles or dukes?
If you want to escape in this human life from bars and cage,
Closely guard your own cinnabar,[6] don't seek for it outside!

Speak:

Long ago, in the early years of the Warring States period,[7] there lived a recluse by the name of Zhuang Zhou, who was also known as Zixiu. His religious name was the Realized Person of Southern Florescence, and he is best known as Master Zhuang. He was a descendant of King Zhuang of Chu,[8] and his family had adopted that posthumous title as surname. He hailed from Meng district in Suiyang. From his earliest youth, his scholarship had been broad and deep. At one time, he served as the administrator of the Lacquer Grove, but he abandoned his job because of the death of his wife, and when he entered the mountains, he had the good fortune to find an enlightened teacher who instructed him in the secret techniques of longevity. He lived in hiding in a deep valley in the Zhongnan Mountains,[9] where he had built a hermitage. In front a clear brook wound around his door, and in the back green bamboos encircled his dwelling. In these beautiful surroundings, he practiced self-cultivation and found pleasure in embracing the Way. This master practiced the

6. In Chinese alchemy, cinnabar is the basic material used in the production of the elixir of life. In internal alchemy, the language of alchemy is used in a metaphorical fashion, and cinnabar is used to refer to the seed of immortality within the adept's body.

7. The Warring States period refers to the fourth and third centuries B.C.E., when seven states were engaged in almost constant warfare, until the empire was unified by the First Emperor of the Qin in 221 B.C.E.

8. The ancient state of Chu was based in the modern province of Hubei. This area was then the southern margin of Chinese culture. King Zhuang of Chu ruled from 613 to 591 B.C.E. Zhuang (grave, serious, correct) was his posthumous title, under which he was revered as an ancestor by the royal family.

9. Zhongnan Mountains is another name for the Southern Mountains, the hills and mountains to the south of the Han and Tang capital Chang'an (modern Xi'an).

Way with complete devotion and pursued realization with all his heart. Each day he recited some chapters of the *Yellow Court*,[10] while he also composed the *True Book of Southern Florescence*. When he had stead-fastly maintained this practice for a number of years, he finally achieved the way of the immortals.

One day when the spring weather was gorgeous and the scenery at its most colorful, Master Zhuang, confronted with these blooming flowers, simply had to tell his acolyte, "Bring me my drum and my clappers so I can while away the time. Wouldn't that be great?" Having been ordered to do so, his acolyte brought him his drum and clappers. Singing while walking, he arrived and said, "As pine and moon filled half the window, I was fast asleep, / But the apricot precluded pure dreams, so I came to the red dust.[11]

Recite a poem:
At dawn I leave and plow the fields, at nightfall feed the cow;
The wooded spring and breezy moon are both without a worry.
Of all titles the only one I think noble is that of prime minister,
But how can such fame and glory last till our hairs turn white?

To the tune "Qingjiangyin" [Clear River Introduction]:
My brownish hair is a stubborn mess that can't be coiled in knots;
By nature I'm lazy and just go along with the times.
Singing a song, I go where my fancy will take me,
Followed by deer of the fields that frolic and play.
At this very moment
I will not raise the issue of desire for fame and profit!"

10. The *Huangting jing* (*The Yellow Court Classic*), which may have been composed in the second century, is one of the most popular texts in early religious Daoism. The text is written in heptasyllabic verse and describes the human body as a landscape densely populated by gods. It teaches a variety of techniques for "nourishing life." See Isabelle Robinet, "*Huantingling*: Scripture of the Yellow Court," in *Encyclopedia of Taoism*, ed. Pregadio, 511–14.

11. "Red dust" is a conventional expression for the common world.

Speak:

Master Zhuang said to his acolyte, "How I regret that I once passed the examinations![12] But because I came to despise profit and emoluments, I lost my zeal for waiting on princes and lords. I did not seek the glory of carriage and cap[13] but coveted the joys of mists and clouds. I observed the many successes and failures of the Shuns and Jies of past and present throughout the whole world,[14] and this put an end to all my worldly desires. Right now, I have swept away all delusions of the dust and have parted with the world. I have forgotten the number of the current year in order to find my own pleasure;[15] embracing Heaven and Earth, I will live forever. I burn some tattered autumn leaves, and when I have used up all yellow flowers,[16] I drink some remaining bitter tea; when I am done reciting the *Yellow Court*, I stroke the branch of a lonely pine.[17] As soon as I am intoxicated by a mysterious dream, I live at ease in a divine valley, and I do not know which pleasure between heaven and earth could be greater. Just look: Our mists and clouds so bland and thin are visited by none,/ And undisturbed behind my door, I nourish nature and emotion.

Recite a poem:

Throughout the world, men waste their lives in busy pursuits;
All they gain by their efforts is that their temples turn gray.
The immortals see through the affairs of the human realm:
For all eternity, therefore, their heads will never turn white.

12. This is an anachronistic reference to the system of competitive examinations for the selection of officials as it developed over the course of imperial China.

13. "Carriage and cap" refer to the perquisites of high office.

14. Shun is one of the perfect rulers from the mythical past, while Jie was the last evil ruler of the Xia dynasty (ca. 2100–1600 B.C.E.). The two names represent here good and bad kings and emperors.

15. In traditional China, years were counted from the start of the reign of the current ruler. Not knowing the current year means that one is living outside society.

16. The term "yellow flowers" refers to chrysanthemums. Since these flowers bloom in the autumn, they are a symbol of perseverance in adversity.

17. The pine is another symbol of perseverance in adversity, since the tree remains green in the winter.

To the tune "Shuahai'er" [Playing the Child]:
In man's life, I think, light and shadow are like a speeding arrow;
In man's life, alas, light and shadow once gone will never return.
Poems and elegies, songs and tunes I write one after the other.
Next to my couch I have a vat, which I open at will for a drink;
The remaining books inside my bags are all I need for reading.
Today I will chant wildly, drink without restraint;
Empty the jug and finish the cup.

The affairs of a hundred years are only a single dream,
The events of a thousand autumns a few games of go:
In man's life one cannot limit oneself to one's youth.
Don't let your heart be deluded by material desires;
When you encounter wine and song, write a poem!
My advice to you all: don't be shackled by idle cares!
Take all sorrow and sadness, worry and frustration
And entrust them to a single book of new lyrics!"

Speak:
When these lyrics of Master Zhuang's were done, he said to his acolyte,
"The people of this age busy themselves in pursuit of worldly affairs—
how could they understand that this floating life resembles a temporary
lodging? How could they know that I enjoy such pure and simple plea-
sures by living in the mountains? In truth: Rising but late, I do not know
how high the red sun stands; / When idly walking, I rely on white clouds
for companions. Moreover, this immortal realm is separated from the
mortal world. If you live in these mountains for a single day, you have no
idea how many dynasties have replaced one another in the world of dust.

Recite a poem:
Pure and simple, the immortal realm is free from pollution;
The world of red dust is separated from Cinnabar Terrace.[18]

18. "World of red dust" refers to the human world of strife and struggle. Cinnabar
Terrace is one of the names for the dwelling place of the immortals.

When you hear the song of flutes descend from the clouds,
You know that fellow immortals arrive, riding their cranes.

To the tune "Langtaosha" [Waves Washing the Sand]:
I practice the Way, hidden in these mountains,
Living here on this cloudy peak.
I do not care for gown and cap,[19] by nature I am lazy.
When I carefully consider the affairs of the human world,
They all turn out to be empty.

My hermitage is only a few rooms,
Embraced by a brook, surrounded by mountains.
Carefree—the gate remains closed throughout the day.
Three cups of simple wine and a few poems
As I am warmed by the burner's fire.

On my head, I wear a yellow cap,
My feet are shod in boots.
A hemp rope loosely ties together my linen robe.
The gourd at my waist contains a miraculous drug:
Nine times recycled divine cinnabar.[20]

Leaning on my staff, I walk through the hills:
Beyond the wood a rushing stream.
I do not strive for tiny profit or for idle fame:
Those overgrown graves, mound upon mound, amid the shrubs
Are lords and ministers of previous dynasties.

Recite a poem:
Living in hiding by a wooded spring, I do not count the years—
Quite a few times the blue seas have changed to fields of dust.
And ever since I mastered the secrets of this life everlasting,
I've refused to tell those without reason to the common crowd."

19. "Gown and cap" refer to the outfit worn by officials.
20. This refers to the spiritual presence/transcendent being created by the adept through the exercises associated with internal alchemy.

Speak:

Master Zhuang said to his acolyte, "In my opinion, the affairs of this world last no longer than a spring dream and are as insubstantial as autumn clouds. There is no need to plan and scheme and weary your mind: all affairs have been predetermined!

To the tune "Jinshanghua" [Flowers on Brocade]:
　Unlock your forehead's sorrowed frown,
　Loosen up for a while if only temporarily!
　I deeply ponder how years and moons rush by,
　How jade hare and golden crow[21]
　Come and go as quickly as a shuttle:
　How sad that light and shade are irreversible!
　When you have the chance to drink some wine, relax!
　When you can loudly sing, sing at the top of your voice!
　The gray hairs at your temples
　This year will be more than last year,
　So get together with your friends each day,
　Have fun without a worry in the world!
　What's the point of running around
　In a hurry, all busy, occupied, in haste?

Recite a poem:
　Let me dispel these worries by leisurely playing my drum:
　Xianyuan in his wisdom and sagacity was the inventor.[22]
　When I beat it during the day, the divine immortals descend;
　When I beat it at night, all ghosts and spirits are frightened.

---

　　21. "Jade hare" refers to the moon, since the moon is inhabited by a hare that is constantly engaged in the preparation of the elixir of immortality. When jade is mentioned in poetry, it is associated with the color white (not green). The golden crow is the three-legged crow that inhabits the sun.

　　22. Xianyuan is one of the many names of the Yellow Emperor, a ruler from the mythic past who is credited with many inventions. According to legend, the Yellow Emperor achieved immortality and rose to heaven in broad daylight.

When I strike it below a pine tree, the frightened tigers roar;
When I sound it next to a river, the startled dragons chant.[23]
As I sit, I think of the flowing river that will never return
And remember the deceased—how can they come back to life?
Once flowers fade, how can their colors persist for all times?
Once the moon starts to wane, the mirror cannot be repaired.[24]
The later waves on the Yangtze press the earlier waves forward,
And in this world our old friends are replaced by new people.

To the tune "Qingjiangyin":
When our Great Boundary is there,[25] there's no way to escape:
It's much better to enjoy your life a little!
Those who competed for fame and fought over profit
Now all rest in their graves in the overgrown suburbs.
Nothing compares to my study of longevity and its true pleasures!

Recite a poem:
A hidden corner of mists and clouds—that is my dwelling;
As far as one can see green mountains encircle the location.
Oh how I love these mountain birds and mountain flowers!
In my opinion this place far surpasses the palaces of kings.

To the tune "Huangying'er" [Yellow Oriole]:
The affairs of this dusty world seem to drift in the air—
Alas, when will this floating life come to an end?
Nothing compares to my rejection of merit and fame:
I devote myself to Complete Realization Teachings.
I've discarded all private possessions
And now wear a single Daoist robe.
Each day as I watch the world of dust,
I clap my hands and laugh out loud.

23. Each river and lake has its own dragon.
24. The moon is compared to a mirror because mirrors in ancient China, made of polished bronze, were round.
25. "Great Boundary" (*da xian*) is a set expression for the moment of death.

Refrain:
> Without a worry in the world:
> Those pure and simple pleasures
> All day are like a swelling flood!

> I built a straw-thatched cottage as my hermitage,
> Visit woodcutters and fishermen, who are my friends.
> White clouds fill this place all around, swept by none.
> Pines and flowers age by themselves,
> Fragrant dust spontaneously drifts by:
> Who knows the immortal scenery inside this grotto?[26]

Refrain[27]

> Wild apricots and mountain peaches—
> Those I pick as snacks with my wine.
> I sing and drink all by myself, ridiculed by none.
> When deeply drunk, I collapse in a stupor;
> When I wake up, the road home is long.
> In the deep green shade I find the Isle of Penglai![28]

Refrain

> Two topknots, a rope around my waist,
> And in my medicine gourd a superior peach.[29]
> The people of this world don't know the miracles inside the mystery.
> Silence reigns throughout these mountain woods,
> I find my pleasure beyond these mountain wilds.

---

26. The secluded realm of the immortals is often characterized as a grotto. As a world on its own, it may also be called a grotto heaven.

27. The text of the refrain is provided only the first time around.

28. The Isle of Penglai is one of the floating islands in the Eastern Ocean that are home to the immortals.

29. In the garden of the Queen Mother of the West on Mount Kunlun in the mythic west, the peaches ripen only once every three thousand years. Eating one of these peaches ensures immortality.

Nothing compares to my rejection of merit and fame;
I devote myself to Complete Realization Teachings.

Refrain

Recite a poem:

Upon entering these deep mountains, I built a cottage;
Having rejected merit and fame, I don't care for profit.
A clear breeze, a bright moon, without any restrictions,
Accompany me in my undisturbed study of the Way.

To the tune "Zheguiling" [Plucking a Cassia Branch]:

Ever since I arrived here in these mountains,
Few people have come to this hidden location: my mind is at ease.
As halcyon bamboos intermingle,
Green scholar trees sieve the light.
How many times I've witnessed yellow chicks chirping and
    twittering!
As planets move and people change,
I've seen the waning moon and fading flowers innumerable times!
Too lazy to read books and histories,
I am addicted now to poetry and wine.
Leisurely I will recite the *Yellow Court*
And happily observe the mountain peaks.

What are the things I feel like doing during daytime?
One melody on fragrant strings,
A few games of encirclement go.
The tea is brewed in an earthen jug;
Incense is added to the stone tripod;
Wine overflows a chalcedony cup.
Oh how quiet—half a couch is good enough for sleep!
Carefully choosing my words, I have a few new poems.
Closing my eyes, supporting my chin,
I always smile—no frown on my face!
Escaped for all time from cage and coop,
I'll never again be tied up or shackled.

Recite a poem:

    A clear brook amid white rocks and far from the red dust:
    When peach blossoms have fallen, I don't count springs.
    Thatched houses in a hazy village with roosters and dogs;
    The persons I meet are all people who once fled the Qin."[30]

Speak:

When Master Zhuang had finished these lyrics, he said to his acolyte, "Let me tell you in a few lines so you will know how many dynasties I have seen rise and fall, all those changes early and late. Indeed: Sadly observing these thousand autumns, I'm overwhelmed by tears; / Depressed as different dynasties succeed one another.

Recite a poem:

    The Warring States fought one another, then Qin was emperor;
    The Fiery Liu chased the deer but was replaced by the Xin.[31]
    An imperial heir in Sichuan versus stalwart warriors in Wu;[32]
    A crafty hero in times of chaos, a minister in time of peace.[33]

30. The poet Tao Qian (365–417) describes in a long poem with a prose preface how a fisherman going up a river passed through a grove of blooming peach trees and next found himself in a hidden valley. Its inhabitants lived a simple and contented life—even though they could hear the crowing roosters and barking dogs of neighboring villages, they felt no urge to visit them. They told the fisherman that their ancestors had settled there after fleeing the warfare that had engulfed China upon the collapse of the Qin, and that they had had no contact with the outside world since then. When the fisherman eventually returned to his home village, all attempts to go back to this Peach Blossom Fount failed.

31. The Western Han dynasty (206 B.C.E.–8 C.E.) was founded by Liu Bang (256–195 B.C.E.), who adopted the element fire as the emblem of his dynasty. "Chased the deer" refers to the competition for world mastery. The Western Han was supplanted by the short-lived Xin dynasty (9–23), founded by Wang Mang, but his regime is usually condemned as a usurpation.

32. At the end of the second century C.E., the Eastern Han (25–220) was torn by civil war, which eventually resulted in a tripartition of the empire. The southeast was the domain of the state of Wu, which maintained its independence until 280. The southwest (modern Sichuan) was eventually conquered by Liu Bei (161–223), who claimed the imperial title as a descendant of the imperial clan of the Han dynasty.

33. This line characterizes Cao Cao (155–220), the warlord who eventually dominated northern China and whose son became the first emperor of the Wei dynasty (221–265).

The Jin combined East and West: a buffalo replaced the horse;[34]
The empire was split into north and south: Song became Chen.[35]
The Sui, the Tang, and the Five Dynasties all belong to the past,[36]
And next Kaifeng welcomed the Song as the imperial house."[37]

Speak:

When Master Zhuang had said this, he addressed his acolyte as follows: "Living here in these mountains I have seen time and again how all-under-heaven descended into chaos. But now, following the coup d'état at Chen Bridge, the Great Ancestor of the Song has ascended the throne.[38] He is magnanimous, humane, respectful, and frugal; wise

34. The Western Jin, founded in 265, ruled the entire Chinese realm until the early years of the fourth century. Following a devastating civil war, one of the princes of the imperial house moved to modern Nanjing, where the dynasty continued to rule as the Eastern Jin until 419. The ruling house of the Jin was surnamed Sima, and the second syllable of that name is written with the character meaning "horse." Rumor had it that the prince who established the Eastern Jin had actually been fathered by a low-ranking clerk surnamed Niu, a name that is written with the character that means "buffalo." Fanciful as this traditional interpretation may be, one wonders whether the phrase perhaps originally referred to the different landscapes of northern and southern China, with northern China as a landscape fit for horses and southern China as the home of the water buffalo.

35. The founding of the Eastern Jin marked the beginning of a political division between northern and southern China, which would last for almost three hundred years, until the unification of the empire by the Sui (589–617). Both the Song (420–476) and the Chen (557–588) were southern dynasties.

36. The Tang (618–906) was succeeded by five short-lived dynasties that ruled northern China in quick succession from 907 until 959.

37. The Song dynasty was founded in 960. It ruled all of China from its capital Kaifeng until 1126, when northern China was conquered by the Jurchen. From Hangzhou, it continued to rule southern China up to 1278, when the Mongols completed their conquest of the Chinese world.

38. Zhao Kuangyin (927–976) was one of the major commanders of the Later Zhou dynasty (951–959). According to the later official account of events, when ordered to lead the army against the Khitan Liao dynasty in the northeast, his troops, upon arriving at Chen Bridge, forced him to claim the throne for himself by dressing him in imperial yellow. In this way, he became the founder of the Song dynasty (960–1278). His posthumous title was Taizong (Great Ancestor).

and filial, caring and good. Later my immortal friend Chen Tuan wrote a poem containing the lines 'From now on all-under-heaven will be without war, / So I can sleep soundly once back in the mountains.'[39] Among the famous ministers of the successive dynasties, I am afraid, there have been many who did not know when to timely retire, so they suffered execution or banishment—all because they refused to give up their office and live in retirement! How could their life compare to that of us who have abandoned the family—we follow our fancy amid springs and rocks and proudly laugh in mists and clouds! In my opinion the people of this world covet only profit and emoluments without any awareness of impermanence. How could they understand that years and months are like a stream? How do they not realize that light and shade are like a shuttle? Even if you have all the gold of the world, you cannot fashion it into a youthful face. An official of the highest rank doesn't have a single day of ease.

Recite a poem:
>　The prime minister at court does not consider
>　That waiting on kings is like living with tigers.
>　Since ancient times a high position is bound to result in disaster:
>　Once out on the river, it is too late to plug the leak in your boat!

To the tune "Chao Tianzi" [Received in Audience by the Son of Heaven]:
>　I lock the unbridled mind inside my breast,
>　Discard a floating fame beyond the clouds.
>　Green hills, blue rivers, and a little thatched hermitage:
>　I'm fed up with the riches and glories of the red dust!
>　When talking strategy, I'm too lazy to second Liu Kun on the
>　　　border;[40]

---

39. Chen Tuan (d. 987) was a famous Daoist master, closely associated with Mount Hua. It is said that he could sleep for one hundred days on end. In 984 he was received at court by the second emperor of the Song dynasty.

40. Liu Kun (271–318) was one of the most effective generals of the Jin on the northern border in the early decades of the fourth century, but he was eventually defeated and killed.

When dropping my line, it doesn't have to be at Yan Ling's Rapids;[41]
When sleeping soundly, I do not dream of the Yang Terrace of Chu:[42]
I find my pleasure in my untrammeled freedom!

Never loosen the shackles on the monkey of the mind;
Always tightly control the reins of the horse of the will.
He who knows the right moment to make up his mind is the true
    hero.
Otherwise you are a fool deceived by others.
Thousands of bells and hundreds of four-in-hands are only an idle
    show;
The eight kinds of jewels and nine different tripods—what is their
    use?
The five noble ranks and seven high offices are insubstantial and
    empty:
They resemble the single dream of yellow millet.[43]

Recite a poem:
    Ever since I built [a hut] of creepers and vines in the halcyon dust,
    I burn one stick of pure incense each time I recite the *Yellow
        Court.*
    How could any idle person arrive here at the gate of my grotto?
    The only one who is allowed to listen is the crane atop the pine."

Speak:
Master Zhuang called out to his acolyte, "Just look, the patched cassock
with its hemp rope that we who have left the family wear far surpasses

41. Yan Ling was a study companion of Liu Xiu (6 B.C.E.–57 C.E.), the founder of
the Eastern Han dynasty. When Liu Xiu ascended the throne, Yan Ling chose a life of
retirement, and even when called to court and offered a high position, he persisted in his
refusal to serve.

42. When visiting Mount Wu, one of the kings of Chu, while sleeping on the Yang
Terrace (Yangtai), was visited in his dream by the local goddess, who shared his couch.

43. In a well-known tale dating from the Tang dynasty, Li Fuyan's "Lu sheng," a young
man on his way to the capital to sit for the examinations stops at an inn near Handan, and,
dozing off while waiting for the yellow millet porridge to be cooked, he experiences a full
career in his dream. When he awakes, he has understood the emptiness of all earthly glory.

the purple robe with its golden belt of the prime minister at court. In my opinion his gold and sable and purple seal ribbon cannot compare to our Daoist garb and linen scarf. How can their crimson wheel hubs and embroidered saddles compare to our straw sandals and feather fans? Who are the prime ministers here in the mountains, the grandees here in the mountains? We have exchanged the morning audience for pure quietude.[44]

To the tune "Huangying'er":
    My padded cassock surpasses a robe of gauze;
    All gold around your waist doesn't compare to my rope.
    Seated on my rush cushion,
    I clap my hands and laugh out loud,
    Laughing at you high ministers at the morning audience,
    Who don't compare to the joy of us who left the family.
    Our black scarves against the sun
    Surpass by far your hats of raven silk.
    I take my pleasure in carefree quietude and ease
    And all day long am filled with joy!

    How I pity those people in the world out there
    Whose befuddled thinking doesn't distinguish true and false!
    What are they scheming for with such intense effort?
    When I call to mind both past and present,
    When I discuss army and administration,
    Nothing compares to my feigned foolishness, my feigned dullness, my
        feigned stupidity.
    When I rest amid white clouds, there's nothing that burdens my
        mind;
    When I achieve enlightenment, I dream in the shadow of a pine
        tree."

44. The morning audience at court took place at daybreak, which meant that ministers had to get up in the middle of the night.

Speak:

Master Zhuang said to his acolyte, "How many heroes have there been in past and present? Yet they were all unable to avoid the ordeal of Impermanence. You had stalwart warriors like Cao Cao, Liu Bei, and Zhuge Liang;[45] you had heroic fighters like Xiang Yu, Yue Fei, Han Xin, and Peng Yue.[46] Some of them became the ministers of princes and some of them achieved noble rank, but their careers all turned out to be one Southern Branch dream!"[47] The acolyte replied, "Teacher, the ancients have left us this saying: 'Riches and glory are frost or dew on the grass; / Merit and fame are a floating bubble on the river.' Even if you are a prime minister or a prince, you will not escape from the process of birth and death, whether early or late." Master Zhuang said to his acolyte, "That proverb precisely fits my meaning. Continue to listen to me. In past and present success and failure are hard to predict; / Between heaven and earth there is no end to the sorrow of grasses and trees.

Recite a poem:

How I am moved to sighs by people of this world—
They'd better seek the Way and practice immortality.
A linen robe and padded cassock far surpass a gown of gauze,
While fish drum and clappers are my companions.

---

45. Zhuge Liang (181–234) served both Liu Bei and his successor as prime minister. These heroes were (and are) household names in China because of their important role in the sixteenth-century novel *Romance of the Three Kingdoms* (*Sanguo yanyi*).

46. Xiang Yu (232–202 B.C.E.) initially was by far the most successful general in the wars following the collapse of the Qin dynasty, but for all his valor, he eventually lost out to the low-born Liu Bang, who managed to attract crafty advisers and capable generals such as Han Xin and Peng Yue to his cause. Yue Fei (1103–1142) was a general of the Southern Song dynasty (1126–1278) who was positioned to reconquer northern China but was recalled to the capital at the instigation of Prime Minister Qin Gui, who was in the pay of the enemy. Once Yue Fei had returned to the capital, he was soon thrown into prison on trumped-up charges and killed. Both Han Xin (d. 196 B.C.E.) and Peng Yue (d. 196 B.C.E.) were major generals of Liu Bei; following the establishment of the Han dynasty and the final defeat of Xiang Yu, however, both were executed on trumped-up charges.

47. In a well-known tale dating from the Tang dynasty, Li Gongzuo's "Nanke taishou zhuan," a man falls asleep and has a spectacular career, rising to high rank. When he wakes up, he realizes that his career took place in the kingdom of ants under the southern branch of the acacia tree in his garden.

When hungry, I eat some wild fruits from the hills;
When thirsty, I drink from the valley's clear spring.
Since the number of my merits has now reached three thousand,
I freely roam in immortal gardens, riding a crane.[48]

To the tune "Zaoluopao" [Black Gauze Robe]:
How much I like this game and fun of mountain roaming,
So carefree and without a worry!
Who knows the cloudy bridge across the little mountain stream,
The thatched cottage constructed beneath a solitary peak,
The old grotto facing the sun,
The steep cliff and weird rocks?
The black gibbon and white crane,
The golden toad and the Jade Cord—[49]
These accompany me on my leisurely roaming.

Recite a poem:
How quiet is the scene in this immortal realm of mists and clouds:
A hidden place in the deep hills, reached by a long and rocky path.
Seated in silence in my thatched hall, I leisurely read the chronicles,
And deeply moved, I cannot bear to speak of dynasties long gone."

Speak:
Master Zhuang asked his acolyte, "Tomorrow is the third day of the Third
Month. That is the birthday of the Realized Person of Purple Yang.[50]
On the one hand, I want to congratulate him on this great occasion,
and on the other hand, I want to visit some famous mountains and immortal
friends. You should stay here in the hermitage and closely guard the cinna-
bar oven, and I will take your younger fellow disciple along when I descend

48. This is not a poem (*shi*) but a lyric to the tune "Xijiangyue" (West River Moon).
49. The "golden toad" refers to the moon, since the moon is inhabited by a toad. The
Jade Cord is one of the stars of the Big Dipper.
50. Realized Person of Purple Yang (Ziyang Zhenren) is the religious name of the
immortal Zhou Yishan, who appeared to Yang Xi (330–386) in his visions and bestowed
on him the Shangqing (Highest Clarity) revelations. These revelations, written down by
Yang Xi, mark a major phase in the development of religious Daoism.

the mountain." Once Master Zhuang had given these instructions, he changed into a Daoist robe with a ribboned scarf, a feather fan, and straw sandals. He told the acolyte to follow him and carry his zither and luggage. Walking at leisure, he went on ahead and said, "My feather fan will wave away the fog beyond the dust; / One step of my straw sandals scatters clouds upon the hills. Indeed, this is an out-of-the-way place in the deepest mountains with exceptional scenery: I see the rocky road, stony and steep; an inn of fragrant flowers; / A grotto gate so lightly closed and hidden by white clouds. I am overjoyed by the beautiful sights that fill my eyes, by the brilliant scenery that has no end. In truth: Slowly I follow the road traces of the immortals, / And heavy at heart, I leave the mountain woods."

Recite a poem:
> He told his immortal acolyte to pay close attention to his orders
> And quickly prepare his luggage so they might go to Jasper Pool.[51]
> Because he wanted to congratulate a true immortal on his birthday,
> He went on the spur of the moment for a walk through verdant hills.

To the tune "Huangying'er":
> Visiting his friends, he left the mountain woods,
> Moved to laments by the quick changes in the human realm:
> Friends and relatives of earlier years had all passed away.
> "Repeatedly I have witnessed how the Yellow River turned clear;
> Repeatedly I have seen how the peaches of immortality ripened,
> Yet no one believes in the long years and months inside a gourd.[52]

51. Jasper Pool is located on Mount Kunlun.

52. When Fei Changfang (who is said to have lived during the Eastern Han) served as a market clerk in Runan, he noticed how a medicine seller each day after nightfall disappeared into a bottle gourd that he had hung on the wall of his house. Fei treated the man with unwavering deference, and eventually the man accepted him as his disciple. He then told him to follow him and jump into the gourd. Once inside the gourd, Fei found himself in palatial surroundings, and his master disclosed to him that he was a celestial immortal who had been banished to earth for a minor infraction. See Campany, *To Live as Long as Heaven and Earth*, 161–68.

When I consider this body of mine,
I will not seek glory and riches, not go and love the red dust!

Recite a poem:
When I have not visited the Yueyang Tower for a few years,[53]
Several hundreds of autumns have passed in the blink of an eye.
There are only two phenomena that always remain the same:
The green mountains do not change, and rivers flow forever!"

Speak:
When Master Zhuang had finished this short lyric, he walked on, followed by his acolyte. When he had crossed the border of Yancheng district of Huai'an prefecture, he found to his joy that the spring weather was mild and pleasant and the scenery was brilliant and lovely. Indeed: The scenery of mountains and rivers has not changed at all, / But the people in cities and suburbs are not the same anymore. He never tired of watching the scenery, but at the same time heaved many a heavy sigh. "I know that the local magistrate here hails from Huayang district in Chengdu prefecture in Sichuan. His name is Liang Dong, and he is also known as Dacai. As an official, this man is pure and honest, and in his administration he is loyal and capable. He administers the law without partiality and comforts the population with his benevolence. Since he assumed his post, robbers and bandits have disappeared and school buildings have been restored. Pure and incorruptible, he treats others with leniency; creating harmony among the people, he settles lawsuits through generosity. Since his youth this man has loved the Way and for a long time he has sought enlightened teachers. Since I observe that this man has the style of an immortal and the bones of the Way, I will have to go into the district capital and pay him a visit to see how strong his commitment to the Way may be."

53. Yueyang Tower in Yuezhou is located on the eastern bank of Lake Dongting. The place was often visited by Lü Dongbin, one of the famous Eight Immortals. In one well-known legend, he converts the sprite of a willow tree there and leads him to enlightenment.

As he was walking along, he all of a sudden saw an exposed skeleton in the open fields of the overgrown suburbs. The bones were in a mess, and the four limbs had been scattered by the dogs and crows that had fought over it for food. On top of that, the cranium had been cracked by herding boys with their whips. When Master Zhuang saw the skeleton, tears poured from his eyes. Overcome by his emotions, he said, "Skeleton, I don't know what sins you may have committed during your lifetime that you suffer such a bitter retribution upon your death. When I see the degree of your corruption, you look even worse than a pig or a dog! Alas, your bones are all dispersed!"

Ballad of lamentation:
    Once Master Zhuang went out for a walk in spring,
    To a village beyond the fields in the overgrown suburbs.
       As soon as he crossed the border of Yancheng district,
    He spotted a skeleton—its bones as white as silver!
    In the sockets of its eyes spiders wove their webs,
    And its teeth tightly clenched two copper coins.
       For fun the herding boys, having released their cows,
    Had placed the skeleton inside an abandoned grave.
    With one stroke they had beaten a hole in its cranium
    Because they wanted to grab those two copper coins!
       Master Zhuang felt compelled to address those boys;
    He immediately called out to those two herding boys:
    "Be warned! Don't beat that skeleton to pieces, because
    If the relatives see that, they will be angry with you!"
       Those herding boys replied in the following manner:
    "Dear gentleman, you are enjoying the spring scenery.
    We can beat this skeleton to pieces without any worry
    Since he lacks an heir, has no son, is without descendants!"
       When Master Zhuang had heard the words they spoke,
    Tears quickly, spontaneously coursed down his cheeks.
    "How sad that this skeleton has not son or issue at all,
    Now this corpse lies exposed in this overgrown grave.
       In truth, if at thirty you have no son, flowers don't bloom;
    If at forty you have no son, your relatives will shun you.

If at fifty you have no son, people will all despise you;
If at sixty you have no son, the tree is without its roots.
  If a tree has no roots, its branches can no longer grow;
If a man has no son, he will grow poor in his old age.
Even if your gold and silver surpass the Northern Dipper,
It will all be in vain if you have no son in your old age!
  These words are not a statement without any meaning:
I, Master Zhuang, am wounded at heart as I lament you.

To the tune "Xijiangyue" [West River Moon]:
  Today in the fields of overgrown suburbs
  I spotted a pile of white bones, all mixed up.
  Not uttering a single word, it was lying in the yellow sand,
  Bleached by the sun, exposed to wind and rain.

  Skeleton,
  During your life you piled up gold and amassed jade,
  But after death, you can't display that glittering glory.
  Now your short breath has been cut off, you clench your silver teeth
  As you lie on your back below the West River Moon.

Recite a poem:
  The white bones are strewn about the overgrown mounds:
  As soon as one sees them, one cannot but shed some tears.
  During the night a ghost appears, spreading its radiance;
  In spring and autumn there is no heir to offer sacrifice.
    Windblown creeping vines move one to sad emotions;
  Rain-soaked stirring crickets call forth long-lasting pain.
  Because I have failed so far to summon this pitiable soul,
  I stand alone in the setting sun, silently heaving a sigh.

To the tune "Taoyuan yi guren" [Remembering Old Friends of Peach Fount]:
  How pitiable
  These white bones in overgrown suburbs
  Facing misty willows and fiery apricots.
  Who is there who comes to visit them?

Can I bear to take these few tears of a broken heart
And entrust them to the blood wept by the *dujuan*?[54]
When I think back on the past, I am so saddened:
Impossible it is to recall those old-time roamings.
In vain I face the western wind, overcome by emotion.
As I precisely observe you in all detail,
Your status and glory and beauty
Now are all frost and snow on the grass.

Recite a poem:

Carefully pondering past and present, one is filled with sorrow:
Riches and status are all equally buried in a single heap of earth.
Emperor Wu of the Han and his jade halls don't exist anymore;[55]
Shi Chong and his Golden Valley—a river flowing to no avail.[56]

Light and shadow resemble a dawn that soon turns to evening;
Grasses and trees encounter spring, which is followed by autumn.
I have to get rid of all those idle thoughts that occupy my heart—
Let me put those questions that bother my mind to this skeleton!

To the tune "Shuahai'er":

Ever since I grasped the intention of the universe,
    Clear and transparent, my Numinous Terrace has been
        radiant as if cleansed.[57]
Ever since I drummed on the tub, I haven't had a wife,
And following my fancy, I go south or north, east or west.
    Only because the scenery in Luoyang is so famous,

54. The word *dujuan* can refer both to the azalea and its bright-red flowers and to the cuckoo, which is said to bleed from its beak as it calls. The cuckoo is also said to be the transformation of an ancient ruler of Shu (modern Sichuan) who died in shame after he had raped his minister's wife.

55. Emperor Wu of the Western Han (r. 140–89 B.C.E.) pursued an aggressive expansionist policy. In later poetry, he is often mentioned as an exemplar of the ephemerality of glory and power.

56. Shi Chong (249–300) was the richest man of his time. His competitive display of his wealth at his garden estate at Golden Valley has become proverbial. It also caused the envy of a powerful minister who engineered his death.

57. The Numinous Terrace (*lingtai*) is the mind.

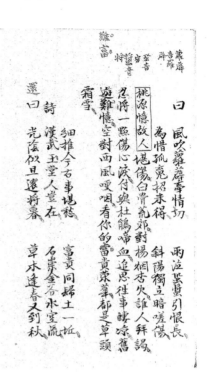

Master Zhuang sighs over the skeleton.

I came here on the spur of the moment to enjoy verdant spring.
When by chance I passed through the overgrown suburbs,
 I saw a skeleton that was lying there exposed,
And involuntarily I was moved to sad sighs.

While traveling I encountered a skeleton amid overgrown graves;
I could not stop myself from crying as tears flowed down my face.

Skeleton,
I step forward and inspect you meticulously,
I step backward to ponder the case in silence:
Alas, your four limbs and five innards are gone without a trace.
 Hungry crows, I see, have pecked through the cap of your skull,
Famished dogs have ripped off the skin below your chin:
The appearance you offer is truly one disorderly mess.

In the setting sun your eye sockets have lost their pupils;
A chilly breeze whistles through the holes for the ears.

Skeleton, in my opinion
If you have people watch you in this kind of manner and way,
It must be because you refused to practice[58] during your lifetime.

Skeleton, let me ask you
Whether your surname was Zhang or Wang,
Whether your surname was Liu or Xu,
Whether your surname was Qian or Zhao or Sun or Li?
    Perhaps you were a Feng or a Chen, a Chu or a Wei?
State it clearly: a Jiang or a Shen, a Han or a Yang?
Let me know: a Zhu or a Qin, a You, a Xu, a Shi, a He, or a Lü?
    Perhaps you are a Jiang, a Tong, a Yan, or a Guo?
A Jia, a Lu, a Lou, or a Wei?

Skeleton, if you are
A Kong, a Cao, a Yan, or a Hua, please tell me so
Since I don't know
Whether Xi, Ji, Ma, or Qiang is your true surname.

Skeleton,
You must have been a macho man or a married woman,
An elderly graybeard or a youthful child—
Where did you live and what was your name?
    You may have been a lustful merchant from another district or
        county,
A common citizen, a government soldier, or an artisan—
Why did you die out here in these abandoned wilds?
    It must be the just desert for your sins—
Who today is now to blame or to praise?

Skeleton,
You may have been a traveling merchant, a man or a woman,
You may have been a soldier or artisan—from which place?

---

58. That is, to practice a lifetime of religious exercises.

Skeleton,
You must have left your hometown with lots of cash
And for the sake of merit and fame come to this place—
It was your bad luck and misfortune to meet with villains.
   You must have cut your own throat with a knife beyond recovery,
Or after a long and incurable illness have lacked the medicine,
And who would be your substitute whence you got here?[59]
   As a result you cohabit in one busy crowd with ants during the
      day
And shivering for cold, sleep with foxes at night.

Skeleton,
On her cushion your wife is still vainly longing for you—
How will she ever receive glad tiding brought by a goose?[60]

Skeleton,
Could it be that you suffered from wind and cold or the summer
      heat?
Could your karmic disease not be treated by any medicine,
Or had consumption poisoned your diaphragm, beyond any cure?
   Was it a magic poison or a demonic possession from which none
      could save you?
Were you a dumb or a mute, silly or deaf, or an advanced case of
      leprosy?
Did you have ulcers in your ears, painful piles, or was it diarrhea and
      cholera?
   It couldn't have been syphilitic sores or burning carbuncles,
Or ulcerous boils that covered your back?

Laid down on your cushion by a chronic disease, a lingering illness,
One day you passed away, beyond the cure of even miraculous drugs.

59. That is, who could take your place in death?
60. When the Chinese ambassador Su Wu (d. 114 B.C.E.) was captured by the
Xiongnu, he managed (according to later legend) to alert his countrymen to his situation
by tying a letter to the leg of a migrating goose.

Skeleton,
Could it be you lost your life out of love for the cup,
Killed yourself out of lust for sex,
Or suffered a stroke over the contested division of money and fields?
   Or did you perhaps die in a fight over a woman following an
      affair,
Or couldn't you live with your losses in gambling den and casino,
Or were you locked up after committing a crime of some kind?
   Or could it be that you teamed up with others, formed a gang,
And faced the enemy on the battlefield?

Wild words and stupid mistakes are all the result of wine;
Broken friendships and family dissent are all because of money.

Skeleton,
Could it be that engaging in trade, you lost your capital,
That hauling money or grain, you didn't bring the check,
Or that you long had owed a debt and were put under pressure?
   Or could it be you were implicated in a crime and died an unjust
      death?
That you got involved in a fight and in the melee suffered an injury?
Did you jump into a river, fall into a well, or did you hang yourself?
   Most likely you ran into your archenemy while on the road,
Or met with a band of robbers while traveling.

Why did you have to discard your body and life in such a hurry?
Without thinking of your parents—it's their body, hair, and skin![61]

Speak:
Skeleton, loquacious as I am, I have used many words to ask you whether
you were male or female, what your name and surname might be, and
from what disease you died, but you haven't given any answer. It must
be because I have not specifically mentioned your case, so I will ask you

---

61. It is the duty of a filial son to take good care of his body and avoid any injuries,
since his body is not his own but a gift from his parents.

for your trade and business during your lifetime. Perhaps you will answer then. Skeleton, indeed,

> Yesterday you were still riding your horse here on the street,
> But today you're already a corpse that sleeps out in the fields.

To the tune "Shuahai'er":

> Skeleton,
> You must have been living in poverty in a back alley,
> Or living in sickness amid grassy marshes,
> Growing melons, selling greens, or cobbling shoes.
>> You must have been studying the Way of ancient kings by your cold window,[62]
> Or were you crushed to death while digging through a wall or scaling a fence?[63]
> Verily, you rested in trust as you roamed in the arts!
>> Even though you had the ambition to nourish a lofty aim,
> You were betrayed by calligraphy, painting, zither, and go.

> Once a hero has departed, all glory is gone:
> All one sees is bones strewn on the ground.

> Skeleton,
> You must have been someone who rows a boat as a ferryman,
> Or a man who pushes a wheelbarrow or leads a mule,
> Or a porter who carries loads and lives by his strength.
>> You must have been a tile maker, a bricklayer, or a kiln operator,
> One who brings in the harvest, pulls the harrow, rents out houses,
> One who winnows the chaff, sows the rice, does all the pounding.
>> You must have been one who digs ditches, bores wells,
> One who cuts and carves and polishes stones.

---

62. As a student preparing for the state examinations.

63. This line appears to be out of place, since it seems to describe the activities of a thief and not of a student. The author may have been thinking, however, of stories of students who studied by the borrowed light from adjoining rooms and of students who scaled walls pursuing an amorous affair.

Skeleton, if you had led
An honest life, you would not have suffered disaster,
But greed for profit and gain will lead to misfortune.

Skeleton,
You must have been one who repairs felt socks, impregnates fishing
    nets,
Washes handkerchiefs, or starches hats,
One who repairs hair ornaments or sells fake chignons.
  You must have been one who repairs pewter, crams porcelain, or
    fixes copper,
One who polishes mirrors, straightens needles, or works in pewter;
A plasterer, a carpenter, or a painter.
  You must have been a basket weaver or a cooper,
A blacksmith or a leather stitcher.

Skeleton, indeed,
Since ancient times, one needs a trade to make money,
But never should one seek for gain beyond one's due.

Skeleton,
You must have been someone who buys up rags, fixes old shoes,
Takes down old houses, sells secondhand clothes,
Or operates an antique shop, dealing in bric-a-brac.
  You must have been a peddler, shaking his bell, a basket on his
    back,
One who gathers a crowd by beating his drum and sounding his
    gong
And entices all little kids to come out and play in the street.
  You most likely sold fragrance and soap,
Beeswax and rouge.

Skeleton, in my opinion
You engaged in many kinds of business during your lifetime,
But today all is finished since you met with Impermanence.

Skeleton,
You must have been a butcher of cows and sheep, a man who kills
    dogs;

One who slaughters pigs, or a man one who gelds horses,
Or one who raises chickens or nets birds in order to make a living.
  You must have been one who hunted animals with hawks and
    with dogs,
One who caught the frightened fish with nets and with weirs,
Or one who amused himself by shooting with bow and arrow.
  Because you committed these karmic sins while alive,
You suffer this kind of desolation upon your death.

Skeleton, if you ever
Took a single life, you have to pay back that life—
You forgot that you'd suffer retribution right now!

Skeleton,
You must have been a shipwright or a house builder,
One whose craft was cutting silk and gauze,
Or one who turned gold and silver into jewelry,
Who climbed mountains or dived into the sea to seek pearls and
    halcyon feathers.
  But even if your possessions amounted to ten thousand strings,[64]
    it's no treasure;
Even if your house numbered thousands of rooms, it is all
    insubstantial,
Because now suddenly everything is all lost and gone.
  All that remains is you, lying here all alone on the yellow earth,
Suffering that your whole body is covered by frost and snow.

Skeleton,
The most sorrowful moment of the late night is the hour
When the full moon, alas, shines on your orphaned soul.

Speak:
Skeleton, I have asked you about all manner of trades and crafts, but you
don't give any answer. So you probably do not belong to those vulgar types.

---

64. Traditional Chinese copper coins were round with a square hole in the middle.
These coins were strung together on strings of nominally a thousand coins. Thus large
amounts of money often were counted in strings.

Perhaps you are a man of intelligence, wisdom, and understanding. So let me question you once again, listing the hundred schools of philosophy and the nine kinds of specialization. Perhaps you will answer me then.

Skeleton,

If you weary your three inches of breath in a thousand pursuits,

One day you'll meet with Impermanence and all will be finished.

To the tune "Shuahai'er":

You must have been one who prays for prognostications, consults the trigrams,

Is used to writing amulets, capable of sanctifying water,

Cracks the carapace,[65] reads faces, and communes with the mysterious.

You must have been one who knows the veins of the earth, its winds and waters,[66]

Who can clearly distinguish the inauspicious and auspicious heavenly signs,

Who observes the plum,[67] computes fates, and splits characters.[68]

You must have been a blind guy who tells ballads,

Or a quack physician who sells delusions.

Skeleton,

With your thousands of miraculous skills, you didn't know death;

With your hundreds of divine drugs, you could not save your life.

---

65. One of the ancient techniques of prognostication in China consisted of heating the carapace of a turtle (or the shoulder blade of a mammal) and predicting the future by reading the pattern of the resulting cracks.

66. This line refers to geomancy, the siting of buildings and graves on the basis of the energy configuration of the landscape.

67. A method of divination by which the applicable trigrams are determined on the basis of the number of strokes of randomly chosen characters.

68. A method of telling the future by deriving meaning from the constituent elements of the characters of names or objects that one has seen in dreams.

Skeleton,
You must have been a great hero who united the court norms,
A wise minister who participated in government,
One of the Three Eminences, the Eight Excellencies, or Seven
    Nobles.
   You must have been a heroic type who handled his lance and
     lifted up tripods,
A chaste and virtuous concubine who stepped into fire or jumped
    from a cliff,[69]
A butcher or wine seller, or a clerk with knife and brush.
   You most likely were a friend more loyal than lacquer and lime,
Or a shaman teacher who impersonated both gods and ghosts.

Skeleton, alas,
Your talents, which covered the world, have become a dream;
The heroism throughout your life has all turned into ashes.

Skeleton,
You must have been an artisan, a merchant, a physician, or a
    soothsayer,
A fisherman, a woodcutter, a plowman, or a herder,
A rake like a drifting weed, a courtesan like a fickle flower;
   A romantic student who cuts the water and carves the snow;
An irascible robber who blocks one's way and bores through walls;
A monk or a priest, a slave or a maid.
   You must have been a Hun and caitiff from north of the Wall
    who submitted;
A dark-skinned barbarian bringing tribute from southern jungles.

Skeleton, you
Once, accompanied by floating clouds, returned under an evening
    sky,
But now you stay all alone in the setting sun amid the autumn
    sounds.

69. Committing suicide in order to maintain her chastity when confronted by bandits.

Skeleton,

You must have been one of those who took his family and fled from
  the Qin,[70]

The one who returned in shackles to save and restore Qi,[71]

Or the one who, flaunting his riches, shattered a coral tree with a
  smile;[72]

   The one who honored gentlemen according to the rites, gathering
     three thousand guests;[73]

The one who repaid his country by sustaining myriad stones by the
  wheelside,[74]

An extraordinary man, excelling above all.

   You must have been the one who at Goose Gate Banquet in his
     rage upset the jade cups;[75]

70. The regime of the First Emperor of the Qin was renowned for its cruelty, and
many were said to have fled to the safety of hideouts deep in the mountains.

71. Guan Zhong (d. 645 B.C.E.) was sent as a prisoner by the state of Lu to the state
of Qi, where he later rose to a high position and made its ruler one of the mightiest lords
of his time.

72. Shi Chong (249–300), while attending a party at the house of the powerful Wang
Kai, beat Wang's coral tree to pieces, and then let the enraged Wang Kai select a replace-
ment from his own collection of much larger coral trees.

73. Tian Wen, the lord of Mengchang (second half of fourth century B.C.E.), attracted
three thousand retainers because of his magnanimity.

74. This line perplexes me. A stone is a weight measure for grain and is equivalent to
somewhat more than a hundred pounds. The line may contain a reference to the story
of Ling Zhe. Ling Zhe was a man with an insatiable appetite. For that reason, nobody
wanted to hire him as a laborer. Because he did not want to steal, he was lying flat on
his back one day below a mulberry tree hoping that some of its fruit would drop into his
mouth. He was observed in this state by Zhao Dun (late seventh century B.C.E.), one of
the highest officials of the ancient state of Jin, who took pity on him and had him fed.
Later, one of Zhao Dun's political rivals tried to have Zhao killed during an audience at
the ducal court. When Zhao Dun fled in his carriage, it turned out that his rival had had
one of its linchpins removed. When one of the wheels of the speeding carriage fell off,
Ling Zhe stepped up and supported the axle, even though it ground away the flesh on
his shoulder to the bone.

75. After Liu Bang captured Xianyang, the capital of the Qin dynasty, in 206 B.C.E.,
he and Xiang Yu met at Goose Gate. When partisans of Xiang Yu's tried to kill Liu Bang,
the latter was saved in the nick of time by the intervention of his general, Fan Kuai (d. 189
B.C.E.), who had started out as a dog butcher.

The one who at Xianyang's market took off his golden tortoise
    while drunk.[76]

Skeleton,
The east wind, close to the graves, blows through the fragrant
    grasses;
The setting sun behind the hills stimulates the *dujuan* to weep
    blood.

Skeleton,
You may have been a fisherman or a woodcutter,
A plowman or a herding boy,
A hermit of the mountain woods, a companion of mists and clouds.
    You must have been a wandering scholar strumming the zither
        and writing characters,
A romantic student composing rhapsodies and chanting poems,
Or a portrait painter who transmits the soul in making pictures.
    But now it's too late for the embroidered brocade of your
        breast,[77]
And buried now are those baroque pearls from your mouth.

Skeleton, in my opinion, you possessed in vain
The brocaded embroidery of your breast—it could not maintain
    your life;
Those baroque pearls from your mouth, unable to save you from
    danger.

Skeleton,
Even if you mastered the texts of the *Six Strategies*, the books of
    the *Three Tactics*,[78]
Had the skills to settle the universe and to support the state,
Were a man who raised his spear and drew his sword to pacify the
    land;

---

76. When the official He Zhizhang (659–744) first met the poet Li Bai (701–762), he pawned his golden tortoises (insignia of his high rank) so they could continue drinking.

77. "Embroidered brocade" is a common image for an educated man's literary talent as perfected by study.

78. *Six Strategies* and *Three Tactics* are the titles of military handbooks.

Even if your writings like those of Confucius and Mencius were
transmitted for all eternity,
And your martial arts surpassed those of Guan Yu and Zhang
Fei,[79] who were united in friendship,
And though you might have as many tricks up your sleeve as Pang
Juan and Sun Bin,[80]
Even if I were a Yuan Tianzheng, I'd be unable to determine
your status,[81]
Even if I were a Li Chunfeng, I'd be incapable of distinguishing
your rank.[82]

Skeleton, just look:
Only the cloudy mountains display an ambition of a thousand
years;
The wind and trees harbor in vain a sorrow that lasts for all eternity.

Skeleton,
Rich and noble people destroy their families,
The smartest people do not outlive their time;
Those who are poor and destitute are succored by none in their
need.
Those who old in years have no sons or daughters are bereft of
support;
Children who lose their parents at a tender age have none to rely on;
When husband and wife fight with each other, misfortune will
follow.
It must be that your children didn't take care of you,
Or that your parents were partial in their love.

---

79. Guan Yu (d. 219) and Zhang Fei (d. 221) were the two sworn brothers of Liu Bei.

80. Pang Juan and Sun Bin lived during the Warring States period. Both studied civil
and military sciences with Guiguzi (Ghost Valley Master) and later served different kings.
Pang Juan was jealous of Sun Bin, but for all his efforts, he was eventually defeated.

81. Yuan Tianzheng was a famous early-seventh-century astronomer and diviner. He
is credited with the authorship of some divinatory works that circulated widely in late
imperial China.

82. Li Chunfeng (602–670) was a famous Tang-dynasty astronomer and diviner.

Skeleton,
When will you repay the labor and care of your father and
     mother?
The love and affection of husband and wife have now come to an
     end.

Skeleton,
You must have been a great hero and a stalwart warrior,
Or someone mild and warm, tender and virtuous by nature,
Who read the sutras, recited the name of the Buddha, filled with
     compassion.
   You must have been some romantic and dashing outrageous
        fellow,
Some noble and loving, caring and generous filial son,
A child adopted from a distant branch, or a son-in-law who moved
     in.
   Did you die because of discord among siblings
Or violent conflicts in the elder generation?

Skeleton,
Even as a hero, you will forever harbor this thousand-year grief:
The windy trees and freezing mist will in vain break your
     heart.

Skeleton,
You too must have watched 'the three cards,'[83] fingered the dominoes,
Played backgammon, and engaged in chess;
You must have mastered all games like throwing darts and shooting
     arrows.
   You were accomplished in all ways of strumming the strings and
        blowing the flute;
You were a rare talent in all games like hitting horses and hiding
     tablets:
An all-around playboy, a romantic groom!

83. "Three cards" is the name of a still widely popular card game.

But even if you mastered the arts of the hundred crafts,
You could not escape from rebirths on the six paths.[84]

Skeleton,
Even before the western wind had arisen, the cricket had noticed;
Secretly it announced Impermanence, which you ignored till death.

Skeleton,
You were filled with pride as you were escorted by men and
> horses,
And when you were fickle, you displayed a tiger-like might:
You too once hoped to acquire that unearned[85] power of empty
> fame.
> You too once despised others because of your many riches and
> > great pride—
Today, now the times have turned against you, you're abused by
> dogs,
So on this day you have experienced both rise and fall.
> Your only use is to serve as the plaything of silly boys,
To be whipped and beaten by country lads.

Skeleton, in my opinion,
Even if heroes would want to mourn you, they wouldn't know
> where;
> Now freezing crows in ancient trees caw in the light of the setting
> > sun."

Speak:
Master Zhuang said, "Skeleton, I have just listed to you the six arts of the
gentleman, the nine areas of specialization, and the hundred schools of
philosophy, but you do not give any answer, so I have no idea what kind

---

84. The six paths of rebirth are usually listed as rebirth as a god, a human being, an
asura (malevolent nature spirits), an animal, a hungry ghost, or a denizen of hell.

85. The word here translated as "unearned" is "dog selling." In a number of expres-
sions, "selling dog meat" is used to mean selling customers not the real item but a cheap
substitute.

of man you may have been. So be it! Skeleton, I will recite to you in brief the sins and crimes you may have committed during your lifetime. Please listen to me. Indeed,

As human beings we should never act against our conscience:
Whoever in past and present got off without any punishment?

To the tune "Shuahai'er":
Skeleton,
You must have been a broker or perhaps a manager
Who harmed his customers so Heaven targeted you—
You acted without honesty, against your conscience.
    You must have employed bucket-like pecks and pint-like sizes
        without fair measures;
Steelyards and balances with heavy and light weights;
Low-grade silver, bronze, and pewter for use in the market.
    But in deepest darkness there cannot be no retribution;
In the blackest of hells you'll be punished by Heaven.

Skeleton, just look:
Dishonest money cannot enrich the fate of a beggar;
Status and riches are all determined by prior karma.

Skeleton,
Because your mouth refused to speak of the Way and of duty,
You had your heart always hope for a sudden stroke of luck:
Riding the mist in the easterly breeze—an utterly foolish act!
    Racing after patronage, you never once rested on the roads;
Lusting after clouds and rains,[86] you refused to go back home;
Running into the Star of Disaster, you planned and schemed.
    You must have harmed your store of virtue by building a sky
        bridge;[87]
Diminished your hidden karma by shooting a treacherous arrow.

---

86. "Cloud and rain" (*yunyu*) is the common euphemism for sex.
87. The First Emperor of the Qin, legend has it, tried, in his hubris, to build a bridge across the sea to reach the floating islands of the immortals in the Eastern Ocean.

Skeleton,
You must have ruined your good fortune by your treachery;
For lack of luck, Heaven had you rest among these graves.

Skeleton,
Could it be that your ancestors as officials brought harm to the
    people,
Or that your father in his personal life could not curb his passions?
Relying on their power and wealth, they boasted of their authority.
  Could it be that they annexed paddies and fields, annexed
    buildings,
And invaded neighboring fences and walls to construct their
    houses,
In their stupidity making plans for a thousand years?
  When retribution is slow, it will come down on sons and
    grandsons;
When it is fast, it will revert to yourself as the foundation.

Skeleton,
Even if you acquire wealth to fatten yourself for a while,
You can't escape an evil reputation, which will last forever.

Skeleton,
You must have convinced someone else to climb a high pole
And then in a sudden reversal have pulled away the ladder,
And as you were watching from the side, you had great fun!
  Most likely, while all smiles toward people, your heart
    resembled a tiger's,
And while not saying a word, your viciousness was that of a
    snake—
Who would ever see through all the tricks you had up your sleeve?
  Because you made use of such devious schemes,
You've landed today in this urgent danger.

Skeleton,
With the mouth of a buddha you spoke words of virtue in public,
But in your heart you nourished a poisonous serpent at all times.

Skeleton,
Most likely no one had any idea of the needle hidden in the silk,
People did not recognize the knife hidden in your smile—
All you wanted was to avail yourself of others' defects to grasp
  their belongings.
 All you wanted was to join those in power at the moment to
  accumulate a hoard;
To tell tales without any foundation in order to create dissension;
To toady to the rich and famous while spreading rumors.
 You were completely devoid of goodness and given to
  deception;
Didn't show any sign of sympathy, or of love and compassion.

Skeleton, your only intention was
To hide a knife in your smile so you might cut off their flesh,
And turn a favor into a feud by robbing people of their cash.

Skeleton,
You must have always harbored treacherous and insolent designs,
Deeply hidden schemes to overturn the order of things,
Made vicious plans to entrap and kill people in secret.
 With a dagger in your sleeve, you welcomed his carriage, then
  stabbed the king;
Drawing your sword, you cut your gown and so turned your back
  on your mother:
You were devoid of all common decency and filled with private
  revenge.
 When collecting the land tax, you turned nothing into
  something;
When pronouncing a verdict, you took falsehoods for true proof.

Skeleton, I see how you
Falsely made a show of fairness while secretly scheming for profit;
Deceptively spoke empty words, so manifesting two different
  faces.

Skeleton,
Did you ever donate a boat of grain to help out the poor and
    needy?
Take off a coat of brocade to come to the aid of an old
    acquaintance?
Build a bridge and repair a road in a display of humanity and
    duty?
  Did you ever rescue a noble prince from hunger with one bite
    of rice?
Show compassion to a starving filial son with a few pecks of grain?
Arrange for a proper marriage of orphaned boys and girls?
  Did you ever, hating its death, bury a snake by the wayside?
Lengthening their lives, release songbirds into the air?

Skeleton, I urge you
To broadly display your gracious virtue by doing good deeds
And out of goodness rescue other people from their troubles."

Speak:
Master Zhuang said, "Skeleton, I have listed at great length whatever you
may have done during your lifetime, your mistakes and crimes, but you
still refuse to answer. So be it. You must have decided that you will not
own up to the many sins I recounted. Skeleton, I'm afraid you are not
the corpse of a man, you must be the body of a woman or girl. So let me
enumerate the things you women do to question you.
  Skeleton, most likely
  You didn't respect you parents-in-law and were jealous,
  Or you deceived your husband, so destroying all norms.

To the tune "Shuahai'er":
  You must have been the main wife in charge of all servants,
  A concubine or a secondary spouse,
  A concubine's maid or a young servant to be bossed about.
    Perhaps you were a girl like a fickle flower, standing in the gate,
      leaning from a window,
  Or a matchmaker arranging marriages, running through alleys,
      following the streets,

Someone like a saleswoman, a wet nurse, or a midwife?
   You must have been an orphaned virgin,
A widow perhaps or a nun.

Skeleton,
Where would I have to go to mourn your fragrant soul?
Your physical remains rest in vain by this cold stream.

Skeleton,
If you were no hero among women in maintaining the norms,
You must have been a long-tongued wife without any morals.[88]
Perhaps you were a woman who had married for a second time.[89]
   Perhaps you had married your husband following an affair;
Were a kidnapped wife who had run away and fled her home,
Or someone without protection who had been seduced.
   Alas, once upon a time you made a mistake,
And now at present your regret comes too late.

Skeleton,
To comfort your soul we've the poem of 'Dew on Leeks,'[90]
But where will we ever be able to find your fine figure?

Skeleton,
You must have visited your eastern neighbor, then talked to your
      western neighbor;
Run off to your neighbor to the south, then run off to your
      neighbor to your north.
You lacked the Three Obediences and Four Virtues, didn't prepare
      the meals.[91]
   When did you ever present fine foods in the room of your
      parents-in-law?

88. A "long-tongued wife" is a woman who loves to speak ill of others.
89. In late imperial China, most widows remarried, but the practice was widely and strongly condemned by moralists.
90. "Dew on Leeks" is an ancient song lamenting the brevity of life.
91. As a daughter, a woman should obey her father; as a wife, her husband; and as a widow, her grown-up son. The Four Virtues refer to proper speech, proper appearance, diligence at work, and careful behavior.

All day long you hung out with your sisters-in-law, voicing your
   complaints.
Leave it to you to spill for no reason at all the family secrets you
   learned while in bed!
   If you were not destined by the Lonely Star to a life as a widow,
You sure would have created a mess by your total failure.

Skeleton,
You may have left some shreds of brocade from your earlier days—
I am moved to great sadness each time because it breaks my heart.

Skeleton,
Most likely when you were a man you were no good provider
As you visited the bordellos to hang out with their beauties,
And pursuing your joys, paid for sex, chanting of breeze and moon.
   'Sunny Spring' and 'White Snow': their singing voices so subtle;[92]
Halcyon jackets and red skirts: their dancing sleeves so low;
Such sophisticated pleasures are beyond human comparison.
   But now you are without your red-tasseled white horse,
In the company of wild ghosts and mountain pheasants.

Skeleton,
Since ancient times none has been master of his length of life,
Because once your luck has run out, you can't stay any longer.

Skeleton,
Now your eyes are dazzled, what do you see?
And clenching your teeth, whom do you hate?
Your breast, I'm afraid, must be filled with frustration.
   Most likely your grown-up sons and daughters have not been
      married;
Your houses and barns have not been repaired:
Repeatedly you've been unable to fulfill your ambition.
   At present, with your head to the south and your feet to the north,
Your hands are pointing to both east and west.

92. "Sunny Spring" and "White Snow" are conventional designations of the most
demanding and most exquisite songs.

Skeleton, I see that
Clenching your teeth and angrily staring, you are still filled with
     hatred;
Your feet to the north, your head to the south—watching the
     setting sun.

Coda:
Skeleton,
The bamboos of the Southern Hills won't suffice to write out your
     follies and wisdom;[93]
The waves of the Eastern Ocean are not enough to wash away your
     rights and wrongs:
Now today I will dig a deep hole and bury you at the Yellow
     Springs.[94]
Skeleton,
In this way I'll let you be a happy ghost beyond destruction and
     birth!

Skeleton,
You will become a soul who dwells forever at the Yellow Springs—
Unable to withstand the doubled sorrows of the windswept trees."

*Newly Composed, Enlarged, and Expanded, with a Forest of Appreciative
Comments: Master Zhuang Sighs over the Skeleton in Northern and South-
ern Lyrics and Songs,* part 1

The End

Newly Composed, Enlarged, and Expanded, with a Forest of Appreciative Comments: Master Zhuang Sighs over the Skeleton in Northern and Southern Lyrics and Songs, Part 2

Composed by the Shunyi Mountain Recluse Du Hui of Kunling;
Printed by Chen Kui (also known as Yangwen) of the same city.

93. Writing brushes are made of bamboo.
94. Yellow Springs is a common designation for the world of the dead.

Speak:

"Skeleton, I have questioned you by listing the doings of women, and you still haven't answered me. So now I will list to you your sufferings, since no one is coming to see you now you have died, to question you once again and see how you will reply to me.

Skeleton,

You're caught up in a butterfly dream and myriad miles from home,

In the third watch of the night, the moon rising above an azalea
    branch.

To the tune "Xinshuiling" [New River Tune]:

A single skeleton among the fragrant grasses of a wild field,

A single skeleton,

And this skeleton has one mouthful of silver teeth.

His eyes observe the vaults of heaven and the seasons

As by the side of the ancient road

He silently rests among overgrown graves.

Skeleton,

Most likely you yourself are the cause

Of your own suffering,

Of your own suffering.

Skeleton, I see that

Your noble breath of a thousand rods stretches across the skies,

But your lonely soul will for all eternity suffer this freezing cold.

To the tune "Zheguiling":

Skeleton,

Who might you be?

Having died, you lie in these overgrown suburbs, in a hole in the
    field,

Your mouth spitting out its white teeth.

While in this world you rode a horse, high in the saddle,

But once dead, you don't display your glory anymore.

You must have been a prime minister or high official,

A Uighur or a Tartar,

新編增補評林莊子嘆骷髏南北詞曲上卷終

骷髏兒南山作書不盡你的冤苦填東海波洗不
盡你的毒恨我今日掘深坑埋你在黃泉內骷髏
我教你做一個無滅無生快活的鬼骷髏我看
你　定做黃泉招滯魄　不堪風木倍傷情

西　骷髏我看你
咬牙怒目常懷恨　腳北頭南望落暉
整齊幾番不逐平生志你如今頭南腳北手指著東

Master Zhuang interrogates the skeleton.

Or perhaps a Chinese.
In their distant village, your father and mother are desperately
    waiting for you;
Your wife, who is as pretty as a flower, is desperately longing for you.

Skeleton, your
White-haired father and mother are filled with sorrow to no avail,
The rouged and powdered beauty is overcome by sadness—in
    vain.

To the tune "Qiaopai'er" [The False Card]:
Skeleton, year upon year the grief of seeing peach blossom and
    startling dew,
The sorrow of suffering frost and snow, exposed to the winds.

Skeleton,
You eagerly anticipate the festival of Clear and Bright;[95]
You anxiously wait for the season of Double Brilliance.[96]
But when the festival of Clear and Bright has arrived,
And when the season of Double Brilliance has come,
Which son or grandson offers his sacrifice to you
On the third of the Third Month, the first of the Tenth?[97]

Skeleton, you
Return together with the floating clouds to the evening colors,
All alone accompany the setting moon amid autumn sounds.

To the tune "Gu meijiu" [Buying Fine Wine]:
Just when I passed by an overgrown grave mound
I came by chance across a skeleton.
The skin of that skeleton had been picked to pieces by crows and
    ravens,
While yellow dogs fought in a ferocious manner over the bones.
Ah! As soon as I saw this, my tears flowed down,
My tears flowed down.
And when I saw that sighing mouth, wide open and never to be
    closed again,
Drop upon drop of hot tears soaked the sleeves of my shirt.

Skeleton, I see how
Your skin has rotted away as the flying birds were picking it to
    pieces;
Tendons and bones are still interconnected as the dogs haul them
    off.

95. Clear and Bright (Qingming) is celebrated on the 105th day following the winter
solstice. Family members visit the graves of their relatives to clean them and make offerings.
96. Double Brilliance is celebrated on the ninth day of the Ninth Month.
97. The third day of the Third Month was, in ancient times, a lustration festival, but
in late imperial China it was identified with Clear and Bright. Ancestors also expected
sacrifices on the first day of each semester—the first day of the Tenth Month is the first
day of winter.

To the tune "Deshengling" [Victory Song]:
    All alone and forlorn one single skeleton:
    Freezingly cold amid the grave mounds.
    The desire for fame and profit
    Today has been wiped out,
    And by this time
    You're free from all worries and cares.
    Skeleton,
    At present your breath has finished,
    Your heart doesn't guard it anymore.
    The only result is that blue rivers and green mountains remain
        unchanged.

    Skeleton,
    While in this world, alas, you may have been a hero,
    At present all you can do is to sleep here in the earth.

To the tune "Yan'er luo" [A Goose Falls Down]:
    Once upon a time, you roamed these suburban fields with other
        gentlemen;
    During that springtime outing, peach trees were red, willows
        green.
    Clapping, you sang at the top of your voice; drinking, you chanted
        to music,
    And in your heart knew no sorrow or worry.
    Skeleton,
    But at present you are so stupid;
    You don't care anymore for the fight over profit and fame.
    I'm moved to sadness, my tears gush down:
    You have completely shed the heroic aura
    Of the days you were alive.

    Skeleton,
    You only thought that as a hero your life would last forever—
    You had no idea that today you would lie amid these graves.

Speak:

Skeleton, in my opinion it is the rarest occurrence in ten thousand kalpas to acquire a human shape, but you allowed your body to be lightheartedly wounded. Because you created so much evil karma during your lifetime, today you are a plaything of dogs in these overgrown suburbs.

To the tune "Qingjiangyin":

> Your white bones cover the ground but are gathered by none;
> Time and again, they are drenched by the rain.
> As the hare runs and the raven flies,
> Dogs and crows fight most viciously,
> While the herding boys beat you just for fun.

> Skeleton,
> The saddest song of ten thousand miles may sound miserable,
> But the desolation of a lonely soul is even more to be pitied.
> Skeleton, in my opinion, you're truly in dire straits:
> You have no son or daughter, you have no way out.
> During your lifetime you refused to practice religion,
> Following your death, there was no one who cared.
> When the evening arrives, you are all alone
> And spend the night all by yourself.

> Skeleton,
> No drug can cure the horror of unending night;
> No amount of money can buy you a second life.

Speak:

Skeleton, I've been thinking that you may have harmed your life through wine, sex, money, or rage. You may have had a capital of ten thousand strings, a lovely wife and a young son, but none can substitute for you. Now keep on listening to me. Indeed: Wine can confound your nature and generate fights; / Sex is the root of ruining families and destroying states. / If you search for riches beyond measure, you'll end up in trouble; / If you suppress your rage, no misfortune can strike. Just look,

Husband and wife originally are birds that share a grove,
But when the Great Boundary comes, each goes its way.

To the tune "Dongwujin" [East Five Close]:
Skeleton,
It must be that wine or sex, money or rage wrecked your life.
Let me analyze these four words for you
As I slowly, so very slowly, lament your fate.
Skeleton,
Du Kang's invention of wine was transmitted throughout the
       world:[98]
The finest blessing from heaven, the sweetest drink on earth!
He invented this pungent fragrance and gave it so much taste.
Liu Ling was completely drunk each day,[99]
Li Bai chanted his poems and drowned while reaching for the
       moon.[100]

Skeleton,
That Liu Ling addicted to drink—
Where is that Liu Ling at present?

Skeleton, I
Urge you not to take pleasure at all in your addiction to drink;
Rather, preserve your true nature, grasp emptiness's mystery!

---

98. One legend tells that people who drank the wine brewed by Du Kang would become so drunk that it would take a thousand days for them to wake up from their stupor.

99. Liu Ling lived during the middle decades of the third century. He is one of the famous Seven Sages of the Bamboo Grove. In later legend, he is famous for his addiction to alcohol, perhaps because his only surviving piece of writing is a *Hymn to the Virtue of Wine* (*Jiude song*).

100. The famous poet Li Bai was well known for his addiction to wine. According to legend, he died while trying to embrace the reflection of the moon in the river.

Skeleton,

Once long ago the Brilliant Emperor of the Tang favored Lady
    Yang[101]

Because Lady Yang was exceedingly charming:

She excelled in singing and dancing atop a halcyon plate.

But Lady Yang lost her life when trampled to death by horses.

Skeleton,

That exceedingly charming Lady Yang—

Where is that Lady Yang at present?

Skeleton,

I urge you never to desire a flower with such intensity:

Rouged and powdered beauties are the root of disaster.

Once long ago, one Deng Tong was extremely wealthy:[102]

The piles of cash looked like mountains, his dwelling resembled
    the sea.

The court outlawed the use of his coins and his notes:

Eventually he died of starvation beneath a pile of cash.

Skeleton,

That mighty and wealthy Deng Tong—

Where is that Deng Tong at present?

---

101. Lady Yang was the favorite concubine of the Tang emperor Xuanzong (r. 712–756) during the final years of his reign; she dominated the inner court and lavished favors on her relatives. When An Lushan rebelled in 755 and approached the capital, Chang'an, in the spring of the following year, the emperor fled the city. He had traveled only a short while, however, when the imperial guard demanded that Lady Yang and her distant cousin, Prime Minister Yang Guozhong, be killed since they were held responsible for the rebellion of An Lushan. After the emperor allowed Lady Yang to commit suicide, her body was trampled to dust by the horses of the guard.

102. Deng Tong was the favorite of Emperor Wen (r. 179–164 B.C.E.) of the Western Han, who had granted him copper mines and allowed him to mint money, making him the richest man of his time. Following the death of Emperor Wen, his son and successor, Emperor Jing (r. 163–141 B.C.E.), rescinded Deng Tong's privileges, and Deng Tong eventually died as a beggar.

Skeleton, just look:
Riches and status in our lives are predetermined,
Don't desire any money that's outside your fate.

Skeleton,
Just think of Zhang Liang and of Fan Li:[103]
The hegemon-king, so fierce and violent, fought over profit and
    fame.[104]
He cut his throat at Raven River, so his head fell to the ground.
Skeleton,
Han Xin and all his merits,[105]
All his merits—where is he now?

Skeleton, I
See that you heroes have been buried in the earth—
As soon as you are overcome by rage, it's the end.

Skeleton,
In the morning you fawn and in the evening you fawn;
By fawning and toadying you try to establish your family.
But then today on this day Impermanence arrived!
Skeleton,
You clench your fists to no avail,
You clench your fists and clench your teeth.

---

103. Zhang Liang (d. 185 B.C.E.) was one of the advisers of Liu Bang, the founder of
the Han dynasty. When Zhang Liang observed the fate of Han Xin and other generals,
he insisted on leaving the court. Fan Li (fifth century B.C.E.) was one of the advisers of
Gou Jian, the king of Yue. After he assisted Gou Jian in destroying the kingdom of Wu,
he left the court and became a rich traveling merchant. Both Zhang Liang and Fan Li are
often cited as examples of men who knew to retire from political strife in a timely fashion.

104. The hegemon-king of Western Chu (Xi Chu Bawang) was Xiang Yu. Despite
his personal valor and his initial success, he was eventually defeated by the troops of Liu
Bang. When a boatman offered to ferry him across Raven River so he could raise new
troops in his hometown, he refused the offer since he could not bear the shame of having
to face the relatives of the men he had led into battle and who were now dead.

105. Han Xin was one of the most effective generals assisting Liu Bang. Following the
founding of the dynasty, Liu Bang grew suspicious and had him killed.

What's the use now of a capital of ten thousand strings?
A mansion of a thousand rooms turns out to be useless!

Skeleton,
Alas, those fine garments on their racks you'll not be able to
        wear,
Those hundred kinds of rare delicacies you'll be unable to eat.
You'll be unable to ride that spirited lean horse,
You can't take along the gold and silver you amassed,
And your young son and lovely wife can't substitute for you.
Skeleton,
Forget about your heroism,
Your heroism when alive.

Skeleton,
When all of a sudden King Yama arrives and invites you,[106]
You will depart for his dark realm with two empty hands.

Skeleton,
At seventeen or eighteen you became husband and wife—
Considered carefully, you were bewitched by a ghost.
If you don't believe me, just look at the birds in the woods.
Skeleton,
When the Great Boundary arrives—
When that arrives, each flies off on its own.

For all the love between husband and wife, they must part;
The deep affection of father and mother one day will cease.

Skeleton,
Our human life is like a bubble on water;
Light and shadow never rest in a hundred years.
And when all goes wrong,
And you have lost your human shape,
Where can that human shape be found again?

---

106. King Yama is the lord of the underworld and the highest judge in the ten courts
of hell.

Skeleton, just watch,
In the shadows of the evening sun the cricket chirps its song,
Secretly it invites Impermanence and dies without knowing.

Skeleton,
Your mother bore you after carrying you for ten months in her
    belly,[107]
And who were you when you barely had been born?
Only when you grew up into an adult you became you.
You wore some fine clothes and ate some fine foods,
But today all of a sudden Impermanence has arrived.
Skeleton,
Let me ask you: what you wore and what you ate—
Where are they now, those things you enjoyed?

Don't say that this body was easily acquired:
Your parents worried about you without end.

Skeleton,
I will now bring you gladness:
Assisting all mortal souls, I will ensure your rebirth,
And I will so enable you to escape from the cycle of rebirth.
Skeleton,
If you succeed in becoming a man,
You should as a man never forget righteousness.
Out of compassion I will save you, assuring your rebirth;
If you successfully become a man, don't forget my favor.

Skeleton,
Now moving out of compassion for you,
I've selected a high spot on this slope.
Tearing this square cloth, I wrap you in a short coat,
And digging a hole, I bury you here.
I will recite some chapters of the *Yellow Court*
So you will quickly be reborn in heaven.
It's not the case that I now covet you.

107. In China, a pregnancy is said to last ten months, counting from the month of
conception to the month of birth.

Skeleton,
You have ruined my process of self-cultivation;
My self-cultivation says good-bye to the Way.[108]

Skeleton,
I now will ferry you across so you will be reborn in heaven—
You won't go to the realm of shade to be judged for your sins.

Recite a poem:
In the shadows of the setting sun a single skeleton
Is lying upside down in the field, amid the graves.
As soon as your throat regains three inches of breath,
You'll covet wealth, love sex, and flaunt your style."

Speak:
Master Zhuang said to his acolyte, "Once long ago when King Wen of Zhou traveled through the suburbs, he came across white bones and had people bury them.[109] Because of this act of hidden virtue, he created a dynasty that ruled the world for eight hundred years. You and I are people who have left the family and by rights we should come to the rescue of all living souls and at all times be filled with sympathetic compassion. If I see this skeleton here exposed like this, I am truly deeply moved. We should display compassion and bring him back to life as a human being. Then we will not have come down from the mountain in vain." The

108. In order to achieve immortality, one has to free oneself completely of all emotions and attachments.

109. King Wen was the father of King Wu, the founder of the Zhou dynasty (traditional dates, 1122–249 B.C.E.). The *Huainanzi*, a text compiled in the second century B.C.E., contains the line "When King Wen buried the bones of the dead, the nine kinds of barbarians submitted to him." The commentary specifies that "when King Wen was building the Spirit Tower, bones of dead people were found. At night, he dreamt that these people called out to him, asking for a burial, and at dawn King Wen had them reburied according to the rites for the Five Grandees." Throughout Chinese history, the burial of abandoned bones (that is, of people who do not belong to your own family) has been considered a very virtuous deed, bound to bring blessing to the person who performs the action.

acolyte replied, "Master, you are absolutely right." Master Zhuang then said, "Skeleton, I spoke to you again and again, but you did not wake up. I lamented you again and again, but you still did not wake up. Now I want to save you so you can be a human being once again. But alas, your skin is gone and your flesh has rotted away, while your bones are dispersed in all directions! So be it. In truth, saving the life of a single human being surpasses the building of a pagoda of seven stories. I'll have to call my acolyte here so he can put the bones of the skeleton one by one in their proper place." Only the three bones of the arm below the left shoulder were missing. Master Zhuang thereupon broke a willow branch in three pieces to make up for the missing parts. Master Zhuang took off his Daoist gown to cover the skeleton completely. From his gourd he quickly took a divine cinnabar pill for saving the world that had the power to bring the dead back to life and put it in the skeleton's mouth. He then told his acolyte, "Take the divine ladle from my medicine bag and fetch some running water." When Master Zhuang had received this water, he spat it out all over the skeleton and addressed the following prayer to Heaven: "For us who have left the family, compassion is the root and good deeds are the gate. While traveling I have found this exposed skeleton and I cannot bear to abandon it to its fate, so I want to bring this person back to life." Thereupon he recited some magical words and called out to the skeleton: "Now you have eaten this drug, I order you to come back to the world of light."

After a little while, one saw that the skeleton started to move, however slightly. When Master Zhuang took away the Daoist robe, he saw that the skeleton had grown flesh and skin: his appearance was the same as before, and he had regained his human shape. By the looks of it, he might not have the strength to mount a horse, but he definitely had the mind of his mature years. When he opened his eyes and saw Master Zhuang, he said, "Master, thank you very much for saving me so I could become a human being once again, but I'm completely naked, so I cannot thank you properly." Master Zhuang hastily took off his underwear and gave it to the skeleton to wear. The latter then got up and thanked Master Zhuang with a proper bow, saying, "Master, now today you have been so kind as to bring me back to life as a human being, I am like [a parched field] that after a long drought receives some rain, or [a straggler] who far from home runs into an old friend." Master Zhuang then asked, "Tell me truthfully your hometown and your name." The skeleton replied, "Master, I am deeply grateful to you for saving my life. In my case it can be said that in earlier days I followed the example of the cicada escaping from it chrysalis, but that today I have returned in the shape of a crane.[110] Please listen to my precise report.

To the tune "Huangying'er":
    My home is in Fuzhou city;
    Being a merchant, I went to the capital,
    But halfway I unfortunately attracted a fatal disease—
    When I soon lost my life, my body was left unburied.
    I am deeply grateful to you for saving my life,
    The favor you've done me
    Is as high as a mountain, as wide as the sea.

Recite as ballad verse:
    Master, I'm deeply grateful to you for saving my life;
    The favor you've shown me is like a mountain, a sea!
    You ask me for my name and where my hometown is,
    Listen, since I'll provide you with detailed information.
        Dear sir, the name of this humble person is Wu Gui,
    And my family is registered as inhabitants of Fuzhou.
    I wished to seek profit to establish myself back home,
    How could I know I was destined to die on the road?
        Crow and hare, dog and raven were my companions,
    Wind and frost, snow and moon became my neighbors.
    My white-haired parents heaved their sighs all in vain,
    My wife, still so young, soaked her gown with her tears.
        Master, I'm grateful to you for your benevolent action,
    You were so kind as to save me, bring me back to life!
    Now there's the pack I was carrying and my umbrella—
    Now nicely return those to me so I can go back home."

110. Immortals may manifest themselves in the shape of a crane.

To the tune "Xijiangyue ci" [West River Moon Lyric]:
　　When Master Zhuang heard him say these words,
　　He ever so softly, sarcastically laughed three times:
　　"You devious scoundrel, as soon as you have regained human shape,
　　Your mind comes up with a criminal scheme.

　　All that was left of you were some bleached bones,
　　East and west, north and south—dispersed all over.
　　By the side of your corpse no umbrella or silver was to be seen.
　　The words you speak really fill me with anger!"

Speak:
That skeleton said, "Master, if you return my pack and umbrella to me, then I will go back and that's it. But if you refuse to return them to me, you and I will go into the city of Yancheng and argue it out [before the magistrate]." Master Zhuang laughed sarcastically and said, "You devious scoundrel, you don't even understand life and death! A moment ago, I brought you back to life as a human being, and now you are threatening me." The skeleton replied, "Daoist, don't blabber on. You and I will go and see the magistrate." Master Zhuang said, "Fine, I will go along with you."

That skeleton grabbed Master Zhuang and his acolyte by the hand, and there they went. Repeatedly they ran into other travelers, who urged him to desist, but he would not listen and dragged them right to the district offices of Yancheng. The district magistrate had just taken his seat in the hall. Outside the gate the skeleton cried at the top of his voice, "Your Lordship, allow me to lodge an accusation!" Magistrate Liang promptly asked his underlings who was screaming like that outside the gate, and they replied, "Your Lordship, there's a fellow there who is screaming and shouting while holding on to a Daoist." The magistrate told them to bring them all inside. They immediately fetched Master Zhuang and the two others and had them kneel down in the hall. The skeleton shouted, "Your Lordship, I am a merchant who trades in gold. When I passed through this place, I was robbed of my gold and silver, pack and umbrella by these two Daoists. They have been arrested by me and I have hauled them here so I can lodge an accusation against them." The district magistrate told him to present his written accusation, but the skeleton said, "I am a single merchant from a different township, so I don't know anyone here who could write out my accusation for me. I can only give you an oral statement." The district magistrate said, "Since you have no written accusation with you, you have to tell me the whole story according to the facts, without any lie!" The skeleton said, "Your Lordship, please listen to my detailed accusation.

Statement of accusation:
The person submitting this accusation, Wu Gui, is thirty-one years of age and a registered inhabitant of Fuqing district of Fuzhou prefecture in Fujian. For business reasons, I passed through this district, where I ran into this Daoist, whose heart was set on robbery but who pretended to practice self-cultivation. He robbed me of my umbrella and my pack with all my gold and silver. Prostrating myself, I hope for your commiseration so you will retrieve the stolen goods and apply the law."

Speak:
Magistrate Liang thereupon questioned the Daoist, saying, "How did you rob his gold and silver, his pack and his umbrella? Make a truthful confession so no torture needs to be applied." Master Zhuang replied, "Your Excellency, please still your towering rage and manifest an intention of loving life. Please consider that I, this poor monk, am free of any duplicity and cohabit with the thunder.[111] I have devoted my whole life to self-cultivation and would never harm others against my conscience. Because I wanted to visit a friend, I descended from my mountain, and when passing through, I happened to see this skeleton as it lay exposed in the overgrown suburbs beyond the fields. This poor monk made a vow to save him and bring him back to life as a human being. Who could have known that I would bring about this disaster today? Indeed, even if my whole body would be mouths, they could not tell all; / Even if I had tongues all over my limbs, I could not explain it fully. Your Excellency, please listen to my detailed statement. Throughout my life I never

---

111. Thunder was believed to strike evil people dead.

committed a deed that should cause one to frown, / So in this world there should not be anyone who has to gnash his teeth.

To the tune "Langtaosha":
    I live on the Isle of Penglai,
    And my name is Master Zhuang.
    Since my youth I have studied the Way and practiced self-
        cultivation.
    Because today I was free and had nothing to do,
    I came here to enjoy the spring."

Speak:
The district magistrate exclaimed, "Daoist, as far as I know, Penglai is the dwelling place of the divine immortals. On top of that, Master Zhuang lived during the time of the Warring States and achieved the Way a long time ago, at least more than a thousand years ago. How could Master Zhuang still roam in this world? Don't talk such nonsense! Hurry up and make a truthful confession so you won't have to be beaten." Master Zhuang replied, "Your Excellency, please listen once again to my statement. How I hate that dissension originates from speech, / But because of this vexation I must force myself to talk.

To the tune "Langtaosha":
    I saw him buried in a lonely grave,
    His flesh rotted away, his skin all gone.
    As a result his bones were devoured by dogs and crows.
    Filled by feelings of compassion,
    I saved him and restored his soul."

Speak:
The skeleton said, "Your Lordship also knows that the dead cannot be brought back to life, so how can bleached bones be revived? These are all brazen lies! You can't believe him." The magistrate said, "These two Daoists stole his gold and silver. Now they have been arrested by him, they have no way to escape their punishment but to come up with a devious scheme in order to befuddle me. Hand over his gold and silver, his

pack and his umbrella!" And he ordered his underlings, "These thieves will refuse to confess unless we use torture and give them a beating." He urgently told them to take action: "Apply the instruments of torture to that Daoist!" Master Zhuang said, "Your Excellency, there is no need to apply torture. Allow this poor monk to submit a detailed statement. In truth, Fodder at night is not to blame for a sick horse losing weight; / Wrongfully acquired money will not enrich a man destined to poverty. Moreover, all travelers coming and going have seen this skeleton as it lay exposed in the overgrown suburbs beyond the fields. Your Excellency, in truth: It is impossible to cover the eyes of the whole world with the hands of single man. I beseech Your Excellency to conduct a detailed investigation. As long as one does not create wind and waves in this world, / One does not have to fear any vexations in one's breast.

To the tune "Langtaosha":
>   I brought him back to life in a human shape,
>   But he immediately conceived an evil plan,
>   Since he wanted to obtain my pack and umbrella, gold and silver.
>   If Your Excellency doesn't believe me,
>   I will take the divine cinnabar pill from his mouth
>   So he will stop breathing and leave for the land of darkness."

Speak:
The district magistrate said, "Daoist, what is your proof if you brought him back to life?" Master Zhuang replied, "Your Excellency, the clothes that skeleton is wearing were all given to him by me. Below his left shoulder the three bones of the arm were missing, and I have supplanted those with a willow branch. Your Excellency, if you don't believe, just fetch one bowl of water and all will become clear." The district magistrate then ordered his servants to fetch the water and give it to the Daoist, to see what he would do. The skeleton protested, "Your Lordship, he is a magician, so you cannot believe him and send for water." When Master Zhuang had received the water, he spat it out all over the skeleton. The skeleton cried out, "Master, please spare my life!" but he spat out the cinnabar pill, which turned into fire and disappeared into the earth. Two gods pounded on his head and threw him down in front of the steps. Unable to speak anymore, his face turned the color of ash. Little by little, his shape dissolved and his features became too horrible to watch.

When the district magistrate had him lifted up so he could have a look, he found inside the clothes apart from a bunch of bleached bones three pieces of a willow branch. Master Zhuang remarked, "Your Excellency, just look at this skeleton. He had barely left the eastern prison[112] and returned to life,/ When he went off to King Yama and entered the cycle of transmigration."

To the tune "Langtaosha":
>Seeing this pile of bleached bones before the steps,
>The district magistrate was frightened out of his wits:
>The three souls and seven spirits had gone to the Yellow Springs,[113]
>And the bones of his arm were replaced by a willow branch
>As the skeleton lay on his back and looked up to the skies.

Speak:
Master Zhuang said, "Your Excellency, in my opinion this skeleton resembled in outer appearance a human being, but his beast-like heart could not be fathomed. I had saved his life, and yet he schemed for my gold and silver. Indeed: The human heart is never satisfied—a snake devouring an elephant;/When the affairs of this world come to a climax, the mantis seizes the cicada./Skeleton, your devious heart has destroyed your store of good fortune;/For lack of luck, Heaven had you rest amid the grave mounds. Your Excellency, one becomes a human being because of the accumulation of goodness, and one annihilates one's body through the accumulation of evil. Show gratitude for favors received and accumulate goodness,/And for myriad and thousands of years you won't turn to dust." Master Zhuang continued, "Your Excellency,

Recite a poem:
>My bold ambition, rising highly, pierces the blue vaults of heaven,
>For now I live in this world of dust and suffer its winds and waves.
>That stupid fool did not recognize this guest of mist and clouds,
>And had me, a divine immortal, come here and bend my waist."

112. The "eastern prison" is the earth prison (hell) below the Marchmount of the East, Taishan.

113. In traditional Chinese thought, every human being has three souls and seven spirits that disperse when he or she dies.

Speak:
When Magistrate Liang had seen this, he hurriedly descended the steps and welcomed him, saying, "Master, please rise! I am but a mortal man with limited vision, so I did not recognize the shape of a divine immortal. Moreover, you and I had no preexisting appointment for a meal of chicken and millet,[114] but fortunately you were so kind as to come and visit me. It must be because of a karmic bond from a former existence, Master, that I now am allowed to meet you! Indeed: You may wear out your iron shoes and never find your man; / But when you do, it happens without any effort." Master Zhuang replied, "Your Excellency, I had to go to great effort to save him and bring him back to life as a human being. How could I know that his devious heart would try to harm me? Skeleton, in my opinion your innards were too vicious! The heart of a beast, the face of a man, the shape of a snake! You always had the evil intention of harming ordinary people, but the eye of Heaven is as clear as a mirror. Skeleton, you could hide your crimes in the world of light, but in the realm of darkness you cannot escape from your evil karma. Indeed: Other creatures are easily saved, but man is hard to save, / So I would rather save other creatures than save human beings." The district magistrate said, "Master, you have to be on your guard against the knife in a smile, and you have to stay away from tigers among men. In my opinion, that skeleton killed his fellow men without a trace of blood because he carried his sword on his tongue. Skeleton, now today you should not carry a grudge since you initiated an affair that turned against you, and you should not be angry because you harmed others who then harmed you. Skeleton, in the world of light you have Heaven and Earth, in the world of darkness there are gods and ghosts. Even if you may employ a thousand kinds of schemes, / If Heaven does not allow them, they will all be useless."

To the tune "Shanpoyang" [Mountain Slope Sheep]:
    Alas, that skeleton
    Busied himself all his life to amass a fortune—
    However much he achieved, it was of no use.

---

114. Chicken and millet are the simple fare to which true friends treat one another. The allusion goes back the tale of Fan Juqing and Zhang Yuanbo of the Eastern Han.

When by and by you grow older,
Your features are slowly bound to fade.
Even if you pile your gold as high as the Northern Dipper,
You cannot buy an escape from the cycle of birth and death.
Your relatives may be as close as sons and daughters,
But when Impermanence arrives,
None can substitute for you on the wheel of transmigration.
Oh how sad:
Your breath becomes a clear breeze,
But your flesh turns into mud.
Oh how sad:
As before you will in the suburbs
Accompany the mounds of earth.

Speak:
Magistrate Liang promptly ordered his underlings to gather the bones of
the skeleton and take them outside. They were not allowed to bury them
but had to throw them away in the overgrown suburbs, outside the fields,
so he would once again suffer the retribution of dogs and crows. A local
stele would be erected in front of the bones with an inscription narrating
the story of the skeleton so when people would later read this, they would
reform their evil ways and convert to goodness. If this account would be
transmitted in this way, people as vicious as wolves definitely would not
deviously harm people. The legend would live on for a thousand years
and myriad people would spit on the skeleton and curse him. But Mas-
ter Zhuang said, "Your Excellency, that may well be so, but I, this poor
monk, long ago made a vow that I would everywhere commit good deeds
and throughout my life never once harm a living being. Your Excellency
may perhaps turn your back on him, but I will never turn my back on
him, since I am afraid that that might damage the virtuous behavior of
a man who, like me, has left the family." The district magistrate replied,
"Master, you didn't harm him, he deviously harmed you!"

Magistrate Liang hastily told his servants to leave them alone and
invited the master to the Pavilion of Quiet Joy behind the hall for a
discussion. Master Zhuang and Magistrate Liang walked to the small
pavilion, where they sat down as host and guest. When no one else was

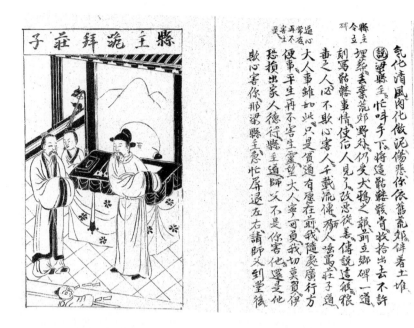

The district magistrate kneels before Master Zhuang.

around, the magistrate hurried to kneel down and said, "Master, please consider that I, Liang Dong, have loved the Way since my earliest youth but so far have not yet found a gate for entrance. Now you have fortunately honored me by your visit, and I hope that you will instruct me. Master, you have acquired the right breath of Heaven and Earth and completed the perfect truth of Heaven and Earth. If you will show me the way out of my delusions, I will resemble a dried-out fish that is revived by a bucket of water, an exhausted bird that is allowed to rest on a branch." Master Zhuang replied, "Observing that your energy and appearance are clear and exceptional and not of the common kind, I came here on purpose to wash your dusty gown. But I was worried that you might not have the right mind and would be unable to understand the Way." The magistrate declared, "I, Liang Dong, have harbored a mind that is set on the Way for quite a long time. My only fear is that my karma of dust might not yet be finished. Master, if you refuse to instruct me, I will lack, I'm afraid, a Yangzhou crane, and I will not be able to fly off to Penglai."[115] Master Zhuang said, "Your Excellency, please rise and listen to another word of mine. Just look: How sad it is to see these many heroes: / They're not aware they're trapped in cages of desire! Just think of that skeleton: he refused to spread a fragrant reputation for a hundred generations, but insisted on leaving behind his stench for ten thousand years." Master Zhuang continued, "Your Excellency, just look: The swimming fish desires the bait, swallows the hook, and dies; / Birds of all kinds covet the food and then are captured by a net.

Recite a poem:
    Since ancient times but very few have lived to see a hundred—
    Who understands the trick of life eternal without ever dying?
    Each day again they hotly covet only fame and profit,
    Each morning they desire and love their children and their wives.
      They scheme to be the greatest hero in this present moment,
    But unaware that in their body breath and blood both dwindle.
    Make efforts early on to find a strategy for life,
    Make sure your bones will not end up in muddy fields.

To the tune "Yan'er luo," followed by "Deshengling":
    Glory and decay are based in nature;
    Riches and glory cannot be trusted.
    People in their multitude are all different,
    But all too often their hearts are not good.
    With empty hands they want to scale heaven,
    Out of the blue they aspire to immortality.
    Profit and fame: fish swallowing the bait;
    Light and shadow: an arrow leaving the string.

115. In an early anecdote, three friends each tell of their ambitions. The first wants to become prefect of Yangzhou, and the second wants to become very rich. The third then wishes to fly to Yangzhou on the back of a crane with a hundred thousand strings of cash. Here, the meaning of the Yangzhou crane seems to have been reduced to that of an immortal crane.

Alas, the crow and the hare just circle each other!
The proverb:
Sea and land continually change and shift."

Speak:
Master Zhuang said, "Your Excellency, when I look up, I do not fear
Heaven, and when I look down, I do not fear man. Because I want so
little, people all ridicule me for being stupid, but I laugh at the foolish-
ness of those people because they are so greedy. Just look at this skeleton:
because his evil deeds during his lifetime were too many and because he
refused to practice self-cultivation, he suffered the retribution of today.
So I urge you, Your Excellency, to bravely retire from the rushing stream,
and to turn around in your moment of success. You should avail your-
self of the greening spring, which is the right season for self-cultivation.
Don't wait until pleasure has reached its climax and sadness follows. How
many men haven't I seen who raised empires, supported the state, fought
to be the first, and competed for fame and profit—even they could not
avoid Impermanence! Your Excellency, let me tell you the secret teaching
of the cultivation of the truth, the causes and condition from beginning
to end. In my opinion the official career is a sea of suffering, but if you
are willing to turn around, you're on the other shore.

Recite a poem:
    Abandoned graves, mound upon mound, are overgrown by weeds,
    Those who are left unburied once wore gold around their waists.
    Without desires, you are far better off than with desires,
    And to advance is not as lofty as retiring quickly.
        The golden fish that takes the bait will end up in the steamer;
    The wiser bird that flees the cage will soar into the skies.
    Immortals are not bothered by the business of red dust:
    They grow their own green hemp to weave a linen robe.

To the tune "Langtaosha":
    In this human life
    At ten, you've reached the proper age for practice,
    Since you are not bothered yet by idle worries.

The great boat has not sprung a leak and can be kept intact;
The golden cinnabar, that relic,[116] has not yet been damaged:
A pure and perfect Yingzhou![117]

At twenty, you will take a wife:
A living demon like a flower!
The love between husband and wife may be praised in this world,
But it topples the exquisitely beautiful pagoda of the seven jewels:
The cinnabar flees from the tripod!

At thirty, you're your mansion's slave.
Like a silkworm sleeping in its cocoon
Your body is tied up from head to toe in threads.[118]
If man would only know the miracle of mystery,
He would grow wings and soar to the immortals.

At forty, you have many sons and daughters
And you are occupied by family affairs.
Don't wait until your primal yang has been dispersed, your harmony
    been damaged.
You cannot cross the ocean in a boat that's made of paper:
It can't withstand the many windswept waves!

At fifty, you are slowly turning older,
But you refuse to turn around
And claim a dashing style that puts the younger men to shame.
But if you wait until your primal yang has been completely wasted,
Your cinnabar is lost and cannot be retrieved.

At sixty, you are old and shriveled.
Your sons and daughters and their kids are flowers before your eyes.[119]

---

116. The word *śarīra* originally referred to the bead-like relics that were left on the cremation of the Buddha.

117. Yingzhou is the name of the one of the three floating islands in the Eastern Ocean that are home to the immortals.

118. The words *si* (thread) and *si* (thought, longing, desire) have the same pronunciation.

119. Also, stars in your eyes because of poor eyesight.

Avail yourself of this moment to practice cultivation and seek
    pleasure,
Don't ever idly pass your precious time!"

Speak:

The district magistrate said, "Master, if I carefully consider the principle
of things, one should take one's pleasure. Why should I shackle my body
with an idle fame? Before my eyes I see all those heroic and stalwart
fellows, these men fighting over fame and profit, but none of them has
any thought of Impermanence, so they are stubbornly stupid people. If
they would understand the cycle of birth and death, they would devote
themselves to practice and love the Way!" Master Zhuang replied, "Your
Excellency, not so quickly! Let me give you a detailed exposition. Let me
ask you about glory and decay, rise and fall—they are like floating clouds
in the sky: one moment there, gone the next.

Recite a poem:

Mercury and lead: how many years do these last in the world of
    men?[120]
How few those who understand, how few those who engage in
    practice!
But if we would allow all those who are foolish to achieve the Way,
The divine immortals in this world would resemble a massive
    stream.

To the tune "Qingjiangyin":

As a human being in this world, we don't live forever,
But how many of us have this insight?
In vain you carry the sorrows for sons and daughters:
Who of them is able to save you?
When the Great Boundary arrives, you can't be protected.

Light and shadow and affairs of this world are without end,
So it is best to turn around very quickly!

---

120. In the discourse of internal alchemy, lead and mercury correspond to the original
spirit (and innate nature) and to original breath energy (and life destiny).

As long as you've something to eat, don't get into trouble.
A human life may last a hundred years,
But in the end you will be buried below the green grasses."

Speak:
Master Zhuang said, "Your Excellency, let me tell you about some prime ministers who buried their title and practiced the Way. Just watch: Riches and status are like dew on flowers; / Profit and fame are like frost on the grass. Your Excellency, please listen carefully, avoid being in the situation [to which applies:] It's too late to rein in a runaway horse at the edge of a cliff; / It's too late to plug a leak when the boat is out on the river. Your Excellency, observing the patterns of heaven up above and scrutinizing the arteries of the earth here below, I have come to know that you have a mind that will grasp the wonders of the Way, so you should follow me and refine your cinnabar.

Recite a poem:
  Since ancient times generals and ministers have met with danger;
  Coveting and loving their high positions, they fooled themselves.
  The only ones to grasp this idea were Zhang Liang and Fan Li;
  One left for the hills, one sailed away: those were smart choices.

To the tune "Shanpoyang":
  Man's life, alas, resembles a shooting star, the sinking moon;
  It's better to bury your title and grasp the miraculous mystery.
  In ancient times Zhang Liang, Yan Ling, Fan Li, and Xu You[121]
  Abandoned merit and fame to study the practice of the Way.
  Their bodies were wrapped in a coat of rough linen,
  And behind a bamboo fence they collapsed in a stupor.
  Snoring away, snoring away, they slept till the sky brightened at
      dawn.
  If you guard your pure quietude like them,
  You too will escape the vexations of right and wrong.

121. Xu You was a hermit in the days of the mythic emperor Yao. When Yao offered him the empire, he refused. In one version of the legend, he washed out his ears afterward because they had been soiled by Yao's offer.

Your Excellency, now listen well:
Study eternal life and never grow old, roaming freely.
Abandoning merit and fame is by far the best option.

Recite a poem:

My thatched cottage is quite low; it's just a few rooms;
It is surrounded all around on four sides by green hills.
I don't allow any cloud of depression to rest on my bed;
Before the sun is about to sink, the door is already closed."

Speak:

The district magistrate said, "Master, my meeting with you here today is like observing the blue sky after sweeping away all clouds and mists, and like finding the Great Way after clearing away all shrubs and brush. You led this mind that lived in a stupor and died in a dream to a realm that is lofty and brilliant, perfect and great. Verily, If there is karma, people meet one another despite a distance of a thousand miles; / If there is no karma, they will not meet even when face-to-face. I am determined to practice the Way, but my only fear is still that you, Master, will refuse to instruct me, Liang Dong. But when clouds accompany the green pine, they reach the blue heavens; / When a crane follows a phoenix couple, it enters the azure skies." Master Zhuang replied, "Your Excellency, just look: After a thousand years, who can distinguish wise from foolish? / Weeds and tares wherever one looks—they all share a common grave. Your Excellency, if you are willing to leave the family and practice the Way, I will instruct you so you will transcend the mortal world and enter the sacred realm. I am only afraid, Your Excellency, that you will covet your office and love your position and will not be able to abandon your home and garden. Don't say: The perch may taste great, but I will not return; / Carrying in vain a southern cap, I'll follow the prisoner from Chu."[122] The

---

122. This couplet is quoted from a poem by Zhao Gu (806–852). While serving in the capital, Zhang Han (fl. 300), who hailed from Suzhou, remembered the taste of his hometown perch and decided on the spot to return home. But the poet decides to stay in the capital, and so, shackled by his desire for fame and profit, he can be compared to the homesick prisoners of war from Chu who had been taken north in 582 B.C.E.

district magistrate said, "Master, please listen to my statement. Right now I want to jump out of the cage of desire; I'll never again dispute right and wrong with the men of this world." Master Zhuang then said, "Your Excellency, Don't go forward when you are at your most success- ful; / Realize that the affairs of this world are constantly changing. / The best for you is to follow me and retire to the mountain woods; / You will be blessed if you say good-bye to this world of men." The district magistrate said, "Master,

To the tune "Shanpoyang":
I have made up my mind
To leave the family and study the Way.
Never again will I love fickle flowers and wild grasses.
Here and now I abandon all merit and fame,
Abandon them to study the cultivation of the Way.
My body will be wrapped in a coarse linen coat
As I watch the hustle and bustle of the red dust—when will it end?
I am only too happy to wear a cassock and head scarf,
And watch for a while the crying gibbons.
Master, please listen to me:
I will study eternal life and never grow old.
Master, please listen to me:
Abandoning merit and fame is by far the best option."

Speak:
Master Zhuang said, "Your Excellency, just look: The Long River of ten thousand miles flows on without end, / So moor your boat as soon as you can moor your boat. / People of this world don't know the dangers of wind and waves: / Don't wait for wind and waves and stop when dan- ger arises!" The district magistrate replied: "Master, my foolish mind is blocked, so I hope to receive your instruction." Master Zhuang then said: "Your Excellency, in order to rectify the heart one practices the Way. Its name can be heard, but its body cannot be seen; its virtue can be revered, but its shape cannot be observed. If you are willing to practice the Way, I will give you a detailed exposition of the essential teaching of the cultivation of the truth. You should make every effort

to remember it well. Alas, it is hard to acquire a human body, but the scenery so easily shifts. So how can one escape from retribution for one's sins if one does not even practice a little? The best option is to achieve enlightenment as early as possible, accept one's lot, and wait for the end. If at the crossroads you make one single mistake, your regret will be too late. Just look: When refining the medicine, you have to fully understand all subtle details; / When cultivating the cinnabar, you have to fully grasp its mysterious wonders. When you understand axis and trigger of Heaven and Earth,[123] they are not distant; when you grasp motion and stillness of yin and yang, they are not difficult. If you are not brave and fierce, devout and sincere, it will be impossible to achieve the outer medicine; you have to be diligent and attentive in all your activities if you want to complete the inner medicine. When the inner and outer medicines are both perfected, you can join the divine immortals. If you solidly settle the business of the medicine, adjust and change the firing periods, it will resemble the refining of the energies of the Five Sprouts[124] and ingesting the brilliance of the Seven Dazzlers.[125] If you fix your thought and practice massage, ingest the pure and spit out the turbid, it will not be difficult to reverse aging and return to the infant,[126] to change and transform and ascend as if flying. You have to fully understand yin and yang and deeply penetrate the process of creation, because only then will you be able to pursue the two energies[127] on the Yellow Road and to gather the three parties[128] in the mysterious palace. If you collect the five phases together and unite the four images[129] in harmony, the dragon will chant and the tiger will roar. If

123. "Trigger" refers to the mysterious mechanism that engenders the movement of Heaven and Earth and their creative powers.

124. The Five Sprouts are the energies of the five organs of the body and the energies and life force of the Five Phases that fill the universe.

125. The Seven Dazzlers are the sun, the moon, and the five visible planets. The term is also used to refer to the seven stars of the Big Dipper.

126. "Infant" refers to the immortal embryo.

127. The two energies are yin and yang.

128. The three parties are spirit, essence (seed), and breath (energy).

129. The four images are the emblems of the four directions: green dragon (east), red bird (south), white tiger (west), and dark warrior (north).

the water boils in the jade tripod and the fire burns in the golden stove, just a little bit of effort will protect you eternally, without end, and you will find unlimited pleasure in that which is so of itself. Restore the energy of generating yang and shed the shape of killing yin, and as soon as controlled rhythmic energy is complete, you will emerge from the embryo and achieve divinity. Your name will be listed in the registers of the immortals and your position will be that of a realized person. That is the moment when a real hero makes his name and achieves his ambition. Our Way is not transmitted without good reason, but because you have the karma, I have fully exposed it to you. I have, further, secret oral instructions in the form of two regulated poems and one lyric. If you memorize them well and embody them in your practice, you will not be far from entering the Way. Your Excellency, The road to Penglai is verily not all that far: / It's right here in your heart, it's only an inch or a foot.

Recite a poem:

You should widely seek for true lead with concentrated mind.[130]
You should make every effort; make good use of each moment.
Strictly hold on to the spirit of earth: the mercury inside cinnabar;
Firmly subdue the soul of heaven: the gold that is in the water.

If your Way is lofty, dragons and tigers will submit themselves;
If your virtue is great, demons and gods will show their respect.
You'll live as long as heaven and earth, none knowing your age,
And your heart will no longer accommodate any vexations.

You must clearly research the dark trigger of heaven and earth;
You'd better be devout and sincere in maintaining the secrets.
Never slacken in your sincere intention of protecting the secrets;
If you slacken and lightly divulge them, you'll see no success.

If you achieve the outer cinnabar, you can become an immortal;
If you complete the inner medicine, your Way will have power.
The divine power of transformation equal to heaven and earth—
You must clearly research the dark trigger of Heaven and Earth.

130. Lead is one of the substances used in outer alchemy; the term acquires a metaphorical meaning in inner alchemy.

Recite a lyric to the tune "Zhegutian":
> It completely depends on the person to invert the effects of
>   practice;
> Following man or reverting to the sacred depends on the same
>   body.
> When by inversion you reach the sacred, the truth is not false at
>   all;   .
> When you follow along and grow into a man, the false is not true.

> There is no intention of going,
>   but there is cause for coming:
> You must grab another man's treasure and join it with your silver.
> If you forget your shape for nine years, follow the adjusted cycle,
> Your work will be done: your mortal body will change into a god."

Speak:
When Master Zhuang had chanted these, he said, "Your Excellency, this
is the outline. The benefits are without end. Work hard on it! I have
clearly shown you a broad and level road, / Don't take my good advice
for evil counsel." Then he pointed with his hand toward the south, and
suddenly two immortal cranes descended from the sky. Master Zhuang
said, "Your Excellency, if you are willing to devote yourself to the Way
with all your heart, you should follow your teacher and go to the Zhong-
nan Mountains and cultivate the Way." While the flabbergasted Magis-
trate Liang twisted his beard and looked around, Master Zhuang and his
acolyte each mounted a crane and rose into the sky. [Master Zhuang]
said, "Your Excellency Liang, you must memorize those essential words
of a moment ago with all your heart. You cannot slacken in your efforts!
If you are willing to abandon your family and cultivate the Way, I can
assure you that your name will be registered in the Purple Office,[131] and
that you will have a position in the ranks of the immortals. Returning to
the immortals I arrived, flying across the nine peaks: / These miraculous
words and numinous sounds sweep away all vulgar dust. / To the sound
of an iron flute I disappear on my crane; / Where the five-colored clouds

---

131. The Purple Office refers to the palaces of the immortals.

gather together, you'll find Penglai." Having finished this lyric, he said, "Your Excellency, verily so: These sagely times right now are rich in rain and dew; / We part for only a short moment, so don't hesitate!" When he had said this, he was completely gone.

District Magistrate Liang bowed down, facing the sky, and said, "I, your disciple, will execute your orders. I will never revert on my decision or slacken in my efforts. Master, I, Liang Dong, in my eager devotion cannot bear to be so lightly parted from you, / And standing upright on the steps below the eaves gaze after you till my eyes give out." After Magistrate Liang that day had been enlightened by Master Zhuang, he immediately returned to his living quarters, where he told his wife, "You and I as husband and wife are birds sharing a branch: / But when the sky brightens, each flies off on its own. When the Great Boundary arrives, who can substitute for whom? I am moved to sighs by light and shadow that resemble a shuttle, and the years and months that are like a stream. I am occupied by the thought that Impermanence doesn't spare old or young: I wish to escape from the cycle of transmigration, and I have to flee from this burning house![132] Today I had the good karma to meet a teacher who enlightened me—lost on the road, I returned to the right. A single sentence from him opened the shackles of miraculous mystery; half a word from him revealed the secrets of death and life. I want to abandon my office and cultivate the truth to protect and maintain my body and life. You should take good care of our house and garden and raise our children and grandchildren." His wife said, "My husband, you are mistaken. Right now you are destined for carpets on top of carpets and tripods arranged in rows, you will wear a purple gown and a golden belt—isn't that great? Why would you want to suffer the privations of wild mountains and desolate fields? What's your reason? How many people have you seen who achieved the Way? How many lived forever? It is far better to serve the state with utmost loyalty and to raise your children and grandchildren. In that way you will enjoy pleasure during all your predestined years. Wouldn't that be wonderful?"

132. The burning house has been a common image for the world of desire since it was first used in that meaning in chapter 3 of the Lotus Sutra. For an English translation, see, for example, Hurvitz, *Scripture of the Lotus Blossom*, 58–61.

The district magistrate replied, "My dear wife, I don't covet profit and riches, and I don't seek glory and status. I will find my pleasure in stillness."

Recite a poem:
>Even if you travel to the ends of the earth, the shores of the sea,
>The human heart will not resemble a river that flows on forever.
>Once you have received great favors, you should hurry to retire;
>When you are extremely satisfied, it is the right moment to rest.

>When fights over right and wrong have not yet entered your ears,
>The love and affection of earlier days are already turning to hatred.
>If I do not leave for the hills right here and now, I strongly fear
>That my service to my lord and king will end in disaster for me!"

Speak:
The wife tried every means at her disposal to make her husband change his mind, but he refused to change his mind, so she went to her room for a good night's rest—she would come up with some other plan the next morning.

That night, the district magistrate put on another set of clothes and secretly left his official quarters, heading straight for the Zhongnan Mountains, and he said, "With my two hands I have opened the way out of the cycle of life and death; / This one body of mine has jumped through the gate of right and wrong." When his wife found out the next morning, she dispatched servants in all directions to find him, but none knew where he had gone. She wept and collapsed on the floor; she fainted and then came to after a while. That very day, she collected her luggage and went back home. But let's not talk about the magistrate's family.

Let's talk about District Magistrate Liang. He abandoned his wife and children, discarded his seal, and stepped down from his office to enter the mountains and cultivate the Way. He avoided right and wrong and so preserved body and life. "Today I shed my purple gown and put on Daoist garb; / Having discarded my silver belt, I tie a rope of hemp around my waist." Living in retirement in the Zhongnan Mountains, he built a thatched cottage and constructed a fence around his yard. "At ease, I pick wild greens and cook them with their roots; / And next I chop some firewood that I burn with all the leaves." During the four seasons there were never-fading flowers, and at each of the eight nodes there were scenes of perpetual spring. On the ridges one heard the pines sough like roaring tigers; in the valleys you heard the springs resound like chanting dragons. The peaks were so steep that they blocked the route of the migrating geese; the mountains so lofty they separated the cover of drifting clouds. Even though the mountains were so lofty and the ridges so steep, he suddenly saw cinnabar cliffs of a hundred yards and green walls of ten thousand rods. "I wonder whether these could be places where divine immortals gaze into the distance:/One can only paint them in pictures but one cannot go there. It is impossible to take in all the scenery here in the mountains. Just look at this purity! I'm afraid only a few people understand this. But I enjoy here now this pure ease and pleasure. My limitless right and wrong have now come to a stop,/And those many worries and cares from today are all finished.

Recite a poem:

My purple gown I've taken off, exchanged for coat of hemp;
I've entered the deepest mountains to flee right and wrong.
But all those many fools and simpletons who serve at court
Won't understand till the sword comes down on their neck.

To the tune "Guizhixiang" [Cassia Branch Fragrance]:

A yellow cap, a linen mantle,
Hempen shoes and a black staff:
I've cast off the lifestyle of sons and younger brothers[133]
And am dressed in the manner of the mountain woods.
I order my immortal boy,
I order my immortal boy
To close the simple gate:
None will come to visit.
Carefully consider the gurgling murmur of the valley brook,
The fragrance everywhere of the chrysanthemums.

---

133. The locution "sons and younger brothers" (of high officials) refers to the moneyed and fashionable young men-about-town.

Merit and fame I do not want;
My possessions I abandoned.
The best option for me is to build a thatched cottage
And each day devote myself to the study of the Way.
From which I gain this freedom,
From which I gain this freedom
From worry and from vexations,
This pure serenity and pleasure.
Quickly turning around is best:
Your merit completed, you'll ascend to the highest heaven!

I entered the hills to study the Way,
Left the family to cultivate the Way.
I did not crave for the golden seal and its purple cord,
And jumped out of the many pleasures of the red dust.
Like the green pine that withstands the cold,
Like the green pine that withstands the cold,
I'll live forever without growing old,
Having abandoned the burning house.
Quickly turning around is the best:
Your merit completed, you'll ascend to the highest heaven!

A thatched cottage newly built;
The simple gate securely closed.
There are steep ridges and lofty mountains
Embracing this spot, surrounding this spot.
You have pine and cypress, dense and dark,
You have pine and cypress, dense and dark,
Encircling the place on all sides all around,
It's fit for free and easy roaming,
And no idler is allowed to loudly clamor.
Quickly turning around is the best:
Your merit completed, you'll ascend to the highest heaven!

Recite a poem:
   The thatched cottage with its simple gate, far from the wind and
      dust:

Plowing my fields at the valley's entrance, I follow Zizhen's
    example.[134]
The gurgling spring requires no labor to manage the sloping fields;
In the deepest mountains I unexpectedly discover people of the Qin.
    The pines I planted with my own hands age with a dark-green
        color;
The clouded peaks on which I rest my body are so very silent in
    spring.
I've only sesame seeds to serve instead of a chicken and millet
    meal—
The white clouds that come and go never despise me for my
    poverty.

To the tune "Zui taiping" [Drunk on Great Peace]:
Don't harm your heart with worry and vexation,
Make sure to spend your time in joy and laughter.
In the arena of fame and on the road of profit I slaved for many
    years,
But now I have abandoned that dream of yellow millet
As I was awakened on the road to Handan.
This heart like a white cloud loves only the Isle of Penglai;
Desire for the red dust was terminated at Luoyang Bridge.[135]
Untrammeled, I am filled with pleasure.

---

134. According to Yang Xiong (53 B.C.E.–18 C.E.), "Zheng Zizhen from Gukou refused
to bend his will [to the ways of the world (that is, refused to serve as an official)] and
plowed his fields at the foot of the mountains, and in this way his fame shook the capi-
tal." According to a later source, the virtuous Zheng Zizhen would not wear what he was
not entitled to wear and would not eat what he was not entitled to eat and consistently
refused invitations to join the administration.

135. In order to ensure funding for the completion of the Luoyang Bridge in Quan-
zhou, a legend tells, the bodhisattva Guanyin manifested herself as a beautiful girl in a
boat who promised to marry the man who could hit her with his silver—her beauty was
such that the boat was soon filled with cash. But the man who brought her home in a
bridal sedan chair found, upon arriving at his house, that the chair was empty and in this
way achieved enlightenment.

To the tune "Shenzui dongfeng" [Very Drunk in the Easterly Breeze]:
The sun flies to the west
And cannot be tied down with even the longest rope;
The river flows to the east,
And no rock or pillar can stop it and halt the stream.
In busy crowds people cover the roads:
All their efforts are for fame and profit.
But how can we know who is right and who is wrong?
Just read a chapter about eternal life,
Don't long for riches and glory that are but floating clouds.

Recite a poem:
To my joy I entered the deepest mountains, hiding even my
    shadow;
I was fed up with frequenting court and market, where long I
    toiled.
In my earlier years I had only little ambition for mists and
    clouds,
But later in life I fully understand the feeling to flee from the
    world.
    Now I lay myself down to rest amid the clouds in this empty
        valley
And do not compete over first place on the steps of Dragon Tail.[136]
From now on the realm of my ears will be pure and undisturbed:
Never again will I hear the chatter and buzz of praise and blame.

To the tune "Shanpoyang":
I have discarded merit and fame
To study the Way and its practice:
My wish is not to receive any five-colored appointment to office!
I've said adieu to dragon lofts and phoenix pavilions
And never again will hear the imperial summons.

136. Dragon Tail refers to the high steps leading up to the Tang-dynasty audience hall
of the main palace.

I've taken off my purple gown
And put on a padded cassock,
A hemp rope and straw sandals.
I don't care whether others laugh
At my dirty face and unkempt hair.
Watching the clouds and hills, I'm satisfied all day;
Roaming at ease beyond the red dust,
I've abandoned riches and status.

To the tune "Qingjiangyin":

My court boots I've taken off—I now wear straw sandals;
My ivory tablets I've all thrown away.
I've put aside the fish of purple-gold[137]
And exchanged it for a hemp rope as belt.
Raven gauze cap and black silk gown,[138]
You, too, I don't love anymore!

Recite a poem:

I don't care for merit and fame and have fled the world of dust
And now find joy by the side of a brook, at the edge of a wood.
When the wild flowers set fruit, I'm informed spring has passed;
When the water plants grow sprouts, they announce a new year.
    The gulls are my friends when, passing, I wade through the creek;
Returning from gathering mushrooms, I'm welcomed by cranes.
Sipping from a brook, I still my thirst, when hungry, I eat berries;
I built my hermitage high in a pine to sleep amid white clouds.

To the tune "Huangying'er":

I'm living on a mountain slope,
Bamboos are my neighbors, pines my companions:
No one travels on this side of the mountain or that.

---

137. Officials of the fifth rank and higher of the Tang and Song dynasties wore a fish-shaped tally at their belt.
138. Such a cap and gown were worn by officials.

I do not pay the emperor any tax on field or stream;
The local official has no way to bother me at all.
My loose shift and wide sleeves bury the disaster of fame.
Other people may laugh at me,
But what does it matter if I don't reply?

I'm only too happy to play the simpleton—
Even for the highest appointment I won't come back.
There is no harm in stepping back from the rushing current.
I've broken open the cage of desire,
I've wrenched apart the lock of gold:
At present I've discarded that cap and that belt.[139]
Without any guile,
I practice self-cultivation, discussing the Way;
My merit completed, I will ascend Mount Tiantai.[140]

Recite a poem:
The winding path with its twists and turns goes around in coils;[141]
For ten miles the waves of the pines refreshingly enter my ears.
When you practice the truth at this spot, never say you are tired;
Once merits and practice are finished, you'll soar, riding a crane.

To the tune "Chao Tianzi":
I'm resting at ease on a bamboo couch,
On the window sills I've pasted paper.
I've hung up a bed curtain with plum flowers,
My pouch is made of green silk brocade,
The shelves are filled with the classics.
A breast filled with moonlight and breeze,
An outer appearance of mountain woods:
Enjoying this transparency, I have no outside longings.

139. The cap and belt that came with official rank.
140. In many legends, Mount Tiantai is the home of immortals and gods.
141. Sheep's intestines.

I scrutinize the *Yellow Court* in great detail,
Compare and evaluate the *Southern Classic*:
To aim for the Way is most lofty and noble.

The people of this world, I see, are all sharp,
And I, alas, am only an idiot and simpleton.
But when I objectively watch those shrimps,
Their rise and fall is all determined by fate,
So don't try to scheme for success or failure.
Body and world are an empty boat,[142]
Light and shadow a passing guest:
How many years can you playact the hero?
I made my hundred worries turn to ashes,
So freeing myself from my double frown:
A square inch[143] now is wider than the sea."

Speak:
Living in the Zhongnan Mountains, District Magistrate Liang ate pine seeds when hungry and drank from creek and spring when thirsty as he devoted himself to strict discipline and pure practice. Dark gibbons presented him with fruits, clinging to the vines as they descended, and white deer brought him flowers, coming by crossing the creeks. Hiding his surname and burying his name, he practiced the truth and nourished his name. "My heart resembles the white clouds in always being at ease; / My will is flowing water that can choose either east or west."

One day when his practice was perfected and his merits were completed, he disappeared by flying off to the skies.

Recite a poem:
Once you've grasped the Heaven of nonaging that precedes
heaven,

---

142. The empty boat drifting along on a stream is a conventional image for an untrammeled existence.
143. The heart.

You'll refine the Absolute Yang at the open hole of the Caudal
Gate.[144]
Reining in the white tiger, you will nourish it on the western
hillocks;
Shackling the green dragon, you'll hide it away in the northern
ocean.[145]
Guard with greatest attention against the free roaming of the
maiden,
Don't allow the lord of metal to display his madness and
extravagance.
When under the crescent moon, lead and mercury unite in the
oven,
The elixir spontaneously is formed, your body exuding a
fragrance.

Recite a poem:
Once your merits are completed, you'll lightly roam the clouds on
a crane;
All you'll leave behind will be your medicine oven and the *Southern
Classic.*
The mist-covered cage and the stone tripods—secrets for a
thousand years:
The golden elixir, eternally united, takes nine transformations to
complete.
There is a recipe for changing your bones so you will be able
never to die;
When you obtain the formula for practicing the truth, you will
live forever.
If the people of this world manage to understand the precelestial
principle,
They all will be able to join the Banquet of the Peaches of
Immortality.

144. The Caudal Gate is the place where the waters of the sea drain away.
145. The tiger is associated with west and yin; the dragon, with east and yang.

Recite a poem:
> When the nine-transformed elixir is achieved, the Way is truly
>   perfected;
> Once your three thousand merits are completed, you will be an
>   immortal.
> Golden characters on jade tablets will proclaim the imperial
>   summons;
> Walking on colorful clouds, you will pay your respects to highest
>   heaven.

Recite a poem:
> Who knows that in this mystery all things are topsy-turvy reversed?
> How can they understand you can grow a lotus even in a raging
>   fire?
> When all elements of yin have been excised and the elixir is formed,
> You'll ride a crane to Jasper Pond and meet with the other
>   immortals.

On the Revision of the Skeleton Collection
> The lyrics and songs of the skeleton have long been riddled with
>   errors,
> So I collated and corrected them during these leisure days of
>   summer.
> I've added and extended poems and lyrics to complete the
>   collection—
> Later readers may greatly benefit from these as an aid to their
>   singing.

When I visited Yishan, I saw the tale of the skeleton that he had compiled.
It was to the point and concise. Impressed, I presented him with the follow-
ing poem:
> Miraculous lyrics and songs—a standard for a hundred generations
> As they demonstrate pure tones, elegant tunes, and limitless
>   thought.

The seven-word poems, winding and sinuous, are full of deep wit;
The springtime beauty of the six concepts[146] restores the ancient
style.
   The subtle lyrics, filled with meaning, contribute to moral
teaching;
The right breath, whirling with energy, supports the original
merit.
A brightly shining classical mirror, more important year after year;
Inherited texts, expanded and continued, for singing and
chanting.

Reprinted by this bookshop

146. The "six concepts" refer to six terms used in early criticism to analyze the *Book of Odes*, China's oldest collection of poetry. Here the term refers more generally to classical beauty.

Ding Yaokang (1599–1671) was born into a leading family of Zhucheng in Shandong. As a young man, he spent some time in the Jiangnan region, but he soon returned home. His quiet life as a country gentleman, however, was disrupted by the Manchu invasion of Shandong in 1642 and the subsequent Manchu conquest of China of 1644 and following years. He eventually moved to Beijing, where he served for a while as a teacher of Manchu students. Still later, he was appointed by the new regime as magistrate of Hui'an in Fujian, but he never took up that position.

Throughout his life, Ding was a prolific writer. He wrote a great amount of poetry, which he had printed in a number of collections. He was fascinated by the issue of retribution and in 1630 compiled the *History of Heaven* (*Tianshi*) to show the universality of the process of retribution using hundreds of examples culled from a wide range of sources. He also left a collection of prose essays, some of which provide a vivid account of how he and some other members of his family survived the violence of the 1640s. After his move to Beijing, he also took up playwriting, producing three *chuanqi* plays and one long *zaju*. And during the last years of his life, he concluded a long vernacular novel in sixty chapters.

This novel, *A Sequel to Plum in the Golden Vase* (*Xu Jinpingmei*), is a continuation of the late-sixteenth-century novel *Plum in the Golden Vase* (*Jinpingmei*), set in Shandong and often said to have been written in Shandong dialect. Ding's novel describes the fate of the surviving protagonists of that novel and of the reincarnations of some of the deceased characters during the years of conquest of northern China by the Jurchen Jin dynasty in 1126 and later. In its description of foreign conquest, Ding's novel is a thinly disguised account of the violence and social disruption accompanying the Manchu conquest. Once the novel had been published, Ding was denounced to the authorities for having slandered the Manchus, and for most of the Qing dynasty (1644–1911) the novel could circulate only in a heavily shortened version of forty-eight chapters known as *Flowers Behind the Curtain* (*Gelian huaying*).

Like *Plum in the Golden Vase, A Sequel to Plum in the Golden Vase* contains a fair number of descriptions of performances of prosimetric storytelling, often including (a shortened version of) the text that is performed. This reflects the relative openness of Shandong authors of the seventeenth century toward these genres of vernacular literature (Ding Yaokang himself is credited with having authored three short prosimetric compositions). As for the prosimetric texts he included in his novel, it is impossible to determine the degree to which he may have revised them. One of the texts Ding included in his novel (in chapter 48) is *Master Zhuang Lamenting the Skeleton* (*Zhuangzi tan kulou*).

Ding's version of *Master Zhuang Lamenting the Skeleton* is obviously much shorter than the version provided by Du Hui. It is also formally much simpler, because all the songs (with the exception of the first two) are now sung to the melody "Shuahai'er." While the basic outline of the plot remains the same as in Du Hui's account, Ding's version allows the revived skeleton a number of songs when making his case before the judge. In these songs, he not only accuses Master Zhuang of being a dangerous charlatan and a crook but also makes the outrageous claim that he had been sent back to life by King Yama, the highest ruler of the underworld, because of his moral behavior while alive!

DING YAOKANG

Master Zhuang Lamenting the Skeleton

Sing:
> The changing scenery startles the mind: time passes in a flash!
> A hundred years of shifts in fortune since all warnings are
>   ignored!
> The clouds and hills that fill the eyes are the truly lasting joy—
> Wealth and power in the end all together turn out to be empty.
>
> Buying some wine to have a drink,
>   I ask woodcutters and fishermen,
> What ever compares to our carefree leisure in mountain and valley?
> In idle moments I've taken some lines from the life of Master Zhuang
> And written them up into this tale of his lament over the skeleton.

Speak:
Long ago, in the early years of the Warring States period, there lived a
recluse with the name of Zhuang Zhou, while his religious name was
the Perfected Person of the Southern Florescence. He hailed from Sui-
yang. From his earliest youth, he had studied the classics and histories,
and at one time he served as administrator of the Lacquer Grove of the
Zhou dynasty. Because he lost his wife, he sang a song while beating
out the rhythm on a tub, and then abandoned his position and retired
to a mountain valley in the Zhongnan Mountains, where he wrote the
True Classic of the Southern Florescence, which has been transmitted as
the *Master Zhuang*. After he had practiced cultivation and refining for
many years on the mountain, he achieved the way of immortality. One
day he said to his acolyte, "Hidden deep in the mountains, you and I
have devoted ourselves to cultivation, and we may have achieved the
way of the elixir, but as long as we do not go into the world of men

to assist and ferry across the living beings, we will be unable to complete the work of three thousand eight hundred hidden acts of virtue, and we can become immortals only of this earth—we will not be able to be received in audience by the Jade Emperor in highest heaven. So today you and I will leave for Luoyang to see which person we can ferry across." There is a song to the tune "West River Moon" that serves as a description:

Sing:
The people of this world cause me to heave a heavy sigh:
They'd much better seek the Way and practice immortality.
A linen gown and patched jacket are far better than garments of
    gauze.
The fish drum and bamboo clappers are my companions!

When hungry, I eat the wild greens to be found in the hills,
When thirsty, I drink from the pure well down the valley.
My works and deeds have reached the full number three thousand,
So now we will for a while roam through the world of men.

Speak:
While walking they had reached the environs of Luoyang. In those abandoned fields they suddenly saw a pile of bones exposed to the elements. This involuntarily moved Master Zhuang to a sad sigh. A poem reads,

When, traveling, he discovered a pile of bones in the wilds,
Master Zhuang was deeply moved and he burst into tears.
"Whose relative may you happen to be, or whose friend?
All because you refused to practice cultivation when alive!

["Shuahai'er"] Sing:
I step forward and inspect you meticulously,
I step backward and ponder the case in silence:
Alas, your three souls and five innards are gone without a trace.
    Hungry crows, I see, have pecked through the cap of your skull,
Famished dogs have ripped off the skin below your chin:

The appearance you offer is truly one disorderly mess.
　　In the setting sun your eye sockets have lost their pupils,
And a chilly breeze whistles through the holes for the ears.

You must have been a macho man or a married woman,
An elderly graybeard or a youthful child—
Where did you live and what was your name?
　　You must have been a lustful merchant from another district or
　　　　county,
A common citizen, a government soldier, or an artisan—
Why did you die out here in these abandoned wilds?
　　It must be the just desert for your sins,
Today no one weeps and no one knows.

You must have left your hometown with lots of cash,
And for the sake of fame and glory come to this place—
It was your bad luck and misfortune to meet with villains.
　　You must have cut your throat with a knife because of a fight,
Or after a long and incurable illness have lacked the medicine,
And who would be your substitute once you got here?
　　As a result you assemble with ants during daytime,
Sleep with foxes at night.

You must have lost your life out of love for the cup,
Have killed yourself out of lust for sex,
Or worked yourself into a fit over the division of fields.
　　Or were you killed by the husband you had foully abused?
Or were you ruined completely by gambling and suing?
Or were you executed after committing a major crime?
　　None came to your rescue when you were hungry and cold,
Or when you met with danger on the battlefield.

Speak:
Skeleton, I've asked you, whether male or female, for your name and surname, but you haven't given any answer. It must be because I have not specifically mentioned your case, so I will ask you for your trade and business.

[*Sing:*]
    You must have been living in poverty in a back alley,
    Or hiding yourself in a village in the country,
    Growing melons, selling greens, or cobbling boots and shoes.
        You must have been studying the books, resigned to poverty
            and hunger,
    You must have been robbed by bandits while engaged in buying
        and selling,
    You must have been a roaming stranger, a friend of lofty
        characters
        Who, despite all oracles and prognostications,
    Packed up his books and his zither.

    You must have been someone who replaces woolens, repairs
        shoes,
    Builds new houses, sells secondhand clothes,
    Or operates an antique shop, dealing in bric-a-brac.
        Someone who fixes kettles, crams porcelain, or repairs
            copperware,
    Polishes mirrors, straightens needles, or works in pewter,
    A bricklayer, a carpenter, or a house painter?
        You must be a basket weaver or a cooper,
    An iron smith or a leather sewer.

Speak:
Skeleton, I have asked you about all manner of trades and crafts, but you
don't give any answer. So you probably do not belong to those vulgar
types. Perhaps you are a man of intelligence and wisdom, a member of
one of the hundred schools, a high official or noble traveler who lost the
road far from home. So let me ask you again!

[*Sing:*]
    You must have been a great hero who rectified the court norms,
    A wise minister who participates in government,
    One of the Three Eminences, the Eight Excellencies, or Seven
        Nobles.

You must have been a heroic type who rips out mountains and
    lifts up tripods,
A virtuous teacher who composes rhapsodies and writes poems,
An administrative talent deeply versed in the details of documents,
    A dashingly romantic poet,
An erudite and famous scholar.

You must have been taking your family and fleeing from the Qin,
Or returning in shackles to save and restore Qi,
Or flaunting your riches by shattering a coral tree with a smile?
    Or did you hasten at dawn to the Golden Hall, wearing red
      shoes,[147]
To drink yourself into a stupor at night, surrounded by flashy
    girls
—But even then disaster may strike or fortune rise—
    Unaware that your time had declined, your life would end,
Your luck would recede and misfortune would follow?

Speak:

Skeleton, I have listed to you the six arts of the gentleman, the nine
schools of philosophy, and the hundred specialists, but you do not give
any answer. So most likely during your life you acted without conscience,
against better knowledge, by coveting sex and scheming for wealth. Let
me provide a brief catalogue of your crimes.

[Sing:]

    The words from your mouth must have been as sweet as honey,
    But your heart lacked all goodness and was black like lacquer:
    Twisting your words and devising lies, you concocted evil schemes.
      Trapping people by providing loans, you then would make sure
        to sue them,
    Harming the community to benefit yourself, you relied on the
      power of others,

147. The Golden Hall refers to the emperor's throne hall, where he received his min-
isters in audience at dawn.

By acting the local bully, you made your millions.
  Fabricating false expectations, you fooled and duped the simple
    guy,
Playing your dirty tricks, you watched with folded arms, filled with
    joy.

You must have come from a long line of corrupt officials,
And you in your turn were unable to reform yourself,
Bereft of all loyalty, all filial piety, and all brotherly love!
  You gobbled up the property of others, invaded the fields of your
    neighbors,
You claimed the road, fought over walls, and changed the site of
    buildings,
Foolishly drawing up plans for the next thousand years.
  And the final result: your head points north, your feet point
    south,
And your arms are pointing east and west."

Speak:

When Master Zhuang had lamented the skeleton, he said, "In ancient
times the munificence of King Wen of the Zhou dynasty extended even
to dried bones, and so he laid the foundations for eight hundred years
of rule by his sons and grandsons.[148] We people who have left the family
should also rescue and aid the living beings. I will now greatly display my
compassion and bring him back to life by recalling his soul, as a manifesta-
tion of the powers of us immortals!" From his gourd he took one magic
cinnabar pill, which he inserted into the mouth of the skeleton, and blew
his immortal breath on it. He took off his gown to cover the corpse, but
when he counted his left-side ribs, he came up three ribs short, so he hast-
ily ordered his acolyte to pluck three willow twigs in the southeast. When
he had fitted these three pieces, recited a spell, and spat out a mouth-

---

148. The decision of King Wen (eleventh century B.C.E.) to see to the burial of bones
that had come to light during the construction of his Spirit Tower greatly enhanced his
reputation for virtue and ensured the loyalty of even the barbarians to his cause.

ful of water, that skeleton developed a spirit from his breath and grew flesh on his bones. Having received the primal breath of Prior Heaven, he quickly returned to life. Rolling over, he got up and said, "Many thanks, Reverend, for bringing me back to life, but I'm as naked as the day I was born, so I cannot appear before people." Master Zhuang immediately took some underwear from his luggage for him to wear, but then that guy stretched his body, and with eyes bulging with rage said to Master Zhuang, "I hail from Fuzhou prefecture and my name is Wu Gui. I was traveling with three hundred ounces of silver to do some business in Luoyang. But the two of you murdered me with your sweat-covering drug.[149] First you took my life, and then you cursed me without end. Now I have come back to life, I will let you go if you return to me my money and my clothes. But if you don't give them back, I will accuse you of murder by use of poison at the Luoyang county office, the Henan prefectural office, and every other imaginable office. I'll write out a list of all one hundred twenty missing items and lay my plaint before the emperor. I will beat the drum of announcing injustice to ensure that the two of you are hacked to ten thousand pieces! Your gourd for using medicine and your ladle for dispensing black magic are present as proof!" Stepping forward, he grabbed Master Zhuang without ever loosening his grip, and loudly shouting his accusations, he took him into the city, to the magistrate's office.

When the county magistrate had taken his seat, he saw a sick person pulling along a man of the Way, who entered his gate and cried out he had been wronged, so he ordered him to come forward for interrogation. With tears streaming from his eyes, that man cried out his wrongs, and weeping, he recounted the story of what had happened, saying that Master Zhuang had murdered him with some drug to steal all his belongings, and that the gourd with its drugs and the evil water were available as evidence. The magistrate asked Master Zhuang, "You are someone who has left the family, how could he without reason falsely accuse you if

149. The "sweat-covering drug" (*menghanyao*) is often mentioned in traditional Chinese fiction as a powerful drug that makes people lose consciousness, but it is not clear what substance was meant. In modern times, it has come to be used as one of the terms for chloroform.

you had not murdered him?" And he immediately shouted, "Ready the instruments of torture! If you do not confess the truth, we will have to apply torture." Master Zhuang stepped forward and told the whole story of how he had found the skeleton exposed to the elements, how he had revived it with a magic pill, and how the skeleton had repaid a favor with a feud. That guy said, "Sir, decide the case according to reason—how can a skeleton be brought back to life? This is clearly nonsense! Let me explain to you in detail the crimes of this man of the Way in committing evil by using his magic in killing common people!

Sing:
    Feigning to roam the world and being a man of the Way,
    He treks through counties and districts, crossing passes and fords,
    But in truth he's a scoundrel who begs for food and doesn't pay taxes!
        Secretly in cahoots with highwaymen, he robs traveling
            merchants,
    Conspiring with violent robbers, he hides them inside his
            monasteries,
    And making his rounds to collect his alms, he acts as their scout.
        His instrument is that 'sweat-covering' poisonous drug,
    Come across him and your soul is set to leave for the shades.

    He has magic to hide his body so his body can't be seen,
    Magic to fix your body so you cannot follow his ways;
    He can also step on the stars of the Dipper to trap your soul.
        By nabbing their soul and possessing them, he rapes virtuous
            women,
    By making a fire and burning lead, he produces counterfeit silver.
    And then there is one thing that is really the worst of them all:
        He hoodwinks little children and then kidnaps them
    To gouge out gallbladder and heart to make his drugs!"

Speak:
That guy said, "When he and I were passing the night sometime ago at an inn, he saw how heavy my luggage was and decided to murder me to get at my goods. He put only one little pill in my wine, and I immediately passed out and fell to the ground. He robbed me clean of all my clothes and goods

and, making a show of his compassion, took the trouble of disposing of my remains in the wilds. But because of my many good deeds throughout my life, my case moved the gods and spirits, and I was returned to life!

Sing:

His gourd is filled with a hundred kinds of poison,
And using a trick, he drugged the wine he offered.
Dizzy and wobbly, I was lost in a dark, foggy haze.
    At my death he feigned compassion by shedding tears,
Fearing I might revive, he spat his magic water over me
And then made an exhaustive search for my belongings.
    He dumped my corpse somewhere in the wilds,
Not knowing at all that I might come back to life!"

Speak:

The county magistrate then asked him, "Hey mister, your story is without any proof. How could you come back to life if you had already died? As a magistrate, I cannot judge a weird case like this! What kind of supporting evidence do you have?" That guy said, "I keep to a vegetarian diet, recite the name of the Buddha, and never act against Heaven's principle. All my life I have never spoken a lie, and I am not one of those who betray their duty and forget a favor! So when I was poisoned,

Sing:

King Yama came out in person to welcome me,
And Judge Cui greeted me as a close relative,[150]
Praising me for my pious lifestyle and great virtue.
    Since the golden bridge is meant to receive people of pure
        goodness,
And the hells down below cannot keep a good person like me,
I was hastily sent off and escorted out of the underworld.
    But they broke three of my left-side ribs,
And the scar is still visible at present."

150. Judge Cui is one of the associate judges in the underworld. He was widely venerated throughout China and is best known for his role in the early chapters of the sixteenth-century novel *Journey to the West*.

Speak:

When Master Zhuang heard these words, he said, "'All living beings can be ferried across, but only man is hard to ferry across!' Only now do I realize that love and care may lead to trouble and vexation. Dear Mr. Magistrate, please give me a cup of water and I will make him manifest his original form. He was a most evil and inveterate sinner, whose fate it was to die by the roadside. Disobeying Heaven, I wanted to do a good deed, so it was fitting that I suffered this retribution." The magistrate immediately gave some water to Master Zhuang. Once the latter spat the water out over this guy, he fell to the ground and collapsed in the dust. When they lifted up his clothes, they discovered a pile of bones, and three of the left-side ribs turned out to be willow twigs. Only then did the startled magistrate realize that Master Zhuang was a true immortal who could bring the dead back to life, but that he had run into a sinful soul who betrayed his duty and forgot a favor. Master Zhuang improvised a four-line poem:

> From ancient times to the present—we all end up as a single
> skeleton,
> Exposed to the elements as a corpse, we still refuse to practice
> cultivation.
> It always has been the case that a good heart finds no good
> retribution,
> And all the love and favors one may show will result only in a
> feud!

[Ding Yaokang, *Xu Jinpingmei*, 1302–15; Liu Guangming, *Gudai shuochang bianti xipian*, 136–41 (includes annotations)]

2

One Late Ming Play

Dramatic literature flourished during the last century of the Ming dynasty (1368–1644). The most popular theatrical genre was the *chuanqi* play. *Chuanqi* were long plays that often counted more than forty scenes. While the genre could handle any subject, the basic plot frame was usually provided by a melodramatic love story. Like all other genres of Chinese drama, *chuanqi* was a form of ballad opera, since the arias were written to existing tunes. In contrast to *zaju*, the dramatic genre that had been dominant for the two centuries from 1250 to 1450, which employed so-called northern music and, in its standard form, allowed only one actor or actress to sing throughout the play, *chuanqi* plays employed southern tunes and required all performers (each in turn) to sing. Over the centuries, southern music had developed a number of (local in origin) distinctive performance styles. For most of the sixteenth century, the Yiyang style was predominant, but from the late sixteenth century onward, Kunqu, which had originated as the local style of performance in Suzhou, gained more and more prestige.

While *chuanqi* dominated the stage in the sixteenth and seventeenth centuries, the same period also witnessed the emergence of a new kind of *zaju*. Late Ming *zaju* might vary from one to ten acts in length and use either northern or southern tunes (or even a combination of them) for their arias. These plays, written as closet drama or intended for private performance, could freely experiment with their musical organization and dramatize all kinds of materials that would have been taboo on the public stage of those days. The range of freedom provided by late Ming *zaju* is suggested by the first major work in the genre, Xu Wei's (1521–1593) *Four Cries of the Gibbon* (*Sishengyuan*). This collection consists of one one-act play, two two-act plays, and one five-act play and deals with subjects as diverse as a monk who is seduced by his foster daughter, a frustrated intellectual who takes off his clothes to shame his master, and young women who cross-dress (one to replace her father in the army and the other just to make a living). Playwrights of the next generation would deal with even more outrageous subjects. Other playwrights of the late Ming, such as Wang Yinglin, opted for the genre because of the leeway it allowed them to voice their social criticism.

Wang Yinglin's (d. 1644) play *Free and East Roaming* (*Xiaoyao you*) follows the basic plot of the legend, but he dispenses with the long questioning of the skeleton by Master Zhuang. The skeleton in fact becomes a quite secondary character in the play as the two main objects of satire become Master Zhuang's acolyte and Magistrate Liang. The first is so obsessed with money that he tries by every means to get his hands on the coin in the skeleton's mouth. The second is delighted to be able to judge the case of a resurrected skeleton, since such a case will provide him with the fame that he needs in order to receive a promotion in his bureaucratic career. In the first section of the play, devoted to the acolyte's obsession with money, all the arias are sung to the tune "Langtaosha" (Waves Washing the Sand). In the second part of the play, devoted to the court case, all the songs are sung to the tune "Huangying'er" (Yellow Oriole). We reencounter the tune "Shuahai'er" (Playing the Child) in the final section of the play, where the acolyte and Master Zhuang's new disciple, Magistrate Liang, question their teacher and force him to admit that the Buddhist teaching of emptiness might be superior to the Daoist pursuit of eternal life.

Wang was a polymath who never passed the higher examinations. He served in the metropolitan administration for many years in the final decades of the Ming but always in subaltern positions. He committed suicide out of loyalty to the Ming when Beijing was captured in 1644 by the peasant rebels of Li Zicheng. *Free and Easy Roaming* is his only pre-served dramatic composition. The play's original title was *Master Zhuang on Stage: A New Tune* (*Yan Zhuang xindiao*); it acquired its current title when it was included by Shen Tai in the anthology *A Second Collection of Short Plays of the Glorious Ming* (*Sheng Ming zaju erji*). The translation presented here is based on this latter version. In his edition, Shen Tai made a careful typographical distinction between the *zhengzi* (proper words), which are sung to the melody, and the *chenzi* (filler words), which are spoken quickly. Since the *chenzi* are printed in smaller-size characters in the original, they are set in smaller-size type in this translation.

WANG YINGLIN

Free and Easy Roaming

(The MO[1] *enters and opens the scene.)*

> *A lyric to the tune "Xijiangyue" (West River Moon):*
> What may it be that generates being in nonbeing?
> Just for fun we will discuss emptiness from facts.
> Lively oh so lively—a butterfly entering into a cluster of
>   flowers
> Will wake one up from that single Handan dream.
>
> Chasing and chasing for the juncture of life and death;
> Yearning and yearning in the burrow of profit and fame:
> Who like a flake of snow can tumble down into the burning
>   stove?
> Watch the trick performed of free and easy roaming.

A young acolyte courts disaster by pulling a coin from clenched jaws;
An evil skeleton turns to emptiness by stealing his pack and umbrella.
District Magistrate Liang discards the desire for profit and fame;
Master Zhuang Zhou pierces the juncture of life and death.

[*(The* MO *exits.)*]

---

1. In traditional Chinese plays, the roles are not indicated by the names of the characters but by the role types (stock characters) constituting a theater company. The names of the role types used in this play are the commonly used designations of the seventeenth century. The role of Master Zhuang is played by the *sheng*, or male lead; the role of Magistrate Liang is played by the *xiaosheng*, or secondary male lead; the role of Master Zhuang's boy servant is played by the *chou*, who specializes in the roles of clowns and fools; and the skeleton is performed by the *jing*, who specializes in the performance of heavies and villains. The opening scene is entrusted to the *mo*, who performs more senior male roles.

(*The* CHOU *enters, dressed as an acolyte.*)

I go by the name of Aco Lyte;
My face is pockmarked and my hair is a mess.
But even though my appearance may be ugly,
The inside of my belly is truly quite exquisite.
To my regret my father and mother were poor
And had to sell me, so I have now become a servant.

But no more about this. When other people are servants, they can be the advance party, collect the farewell gifts, and with borrowed authority apply some pressure. Or they can collect rents and debts and conduct commercial transactions, so their food is plenty and their families grow rich. But my fortune had to be poor. I had to become the valet of Master Zhuang Zhou. Not only doesn't he have any authority or power, wealth or status, he also is no gentleman, farmer, merchant, or artisan. Let's forget how dismal his prospects are, it's only that his lifestyle is truly lacking in comfort. For food it is only yellowed leeks and bland rice. We never have a good drink or a hearty roast. His clothes are a worn gown and a padded cassock. I've never seen a bolt of cloth sent to the tailor's. But no more about this. That man has no ability at all, but he knows how to tell a lie! Now words are only a puff of wind, but the brush leaves clear traces. Now who has ever seen fish bait made of fifty pairs of oxen?[2] Who has ever seen a rooster with three legs?[3] Who has ever seen a tree that can shade a thousand miles?[4] Who has seen that roc with wings like Mount Tai?[5] Who has ever seen a Confucius who at fifty still had not

2. *Zhuangzi*, chapter 26. "Prince Ren made an enormous fishhook with a huge line, baited it with fifty bullocks, settled himself on top of Mount Kuaiji, and cast with his pole into the eastern sea" (adapted from Zhuangzi, *Complete Works of Chuang Tzu*, 296).

3. *Zhuangzi*, chapter 33. "A chicken has three legs" (ibid., 375). This is quoted as one of the statements proposed by logicians such as Hui Shi.

4. *Zhuangzi*, chapter 4, describes a tree so large that a "thousand teams of horses could have taken shelter under it and its shade would have covered them all" (adapted from ibid., 65).

5. *Zhuangzi*, chapter 1. "There is also a bird there, named the roc [*peng*], with a back like Mount Tai and wings like clouds filling the sky" (adapted from ibid., 31).

heard of the Way?[6] Who has ever seen an infant that can talk at five months?[7] Who has ever seen a black turtle that is longer than a snake[8] or a black dog that is whiter than snow?[9] And who has ever seen a fire than can burn without heat[10] or a storm that can strike up a conversation with a snake?[11] How can you prove that by the classics and support it with commentary? It's truly all fantasy without any facts. But later those literati and poets, students and gentlemen would all steal some of his remnant words or leftover phrases and, one by one, insert them in their own writings so they would be praised for the strength of their brush and hailed as skilled writers and literary leaders. Bah, I don't know how many people in this world he has taught to aim for the absurd, and I also don't know how many people in this whole wide world he has made adopt mad nonsense as their style. But no more about this. People always speak about "lazy Daoists." Only lazy people can become Daoists. The only thing I know as an acolyte is to go to bed early and sleep till late. Why should I run to north of the Wei and east of the River? Yesterday he ordered me to ready his

6. *Zhuangzi*, chapter 14. "Confucius had gone along until he was fifty-one and had still not heard of the Way. Finally he went south to Pei and called on Lao Dan" (adapted from ibid., 161).

7. *Zhuangzi*, chapter 14. "Shun ruled the world by making the hearts of the people rivalrous. Therefore the wives of the people became pregnant and gave birth in the tenth month as in the past, but their children were not five months old before they were able to talk" (ibid., 164).

8. *Zhuangzi*, chapter 33. "The tortoise is longer than the snake" (ibid., 375). This is quoted as one of the statements proposed by logicians such as Hui Shi.

9. *Zhuangzi*, chapter 33. "White dogs are black" (ibid., 376). This, too, is quoted as one of the statements proposed by logicians such as Hui Shi.

10. *Zhuangzi*, chapter 33. "Fire is not hot" (ibid., 375). This is yet another statement credited to logicians such as Hui Shi.

11. *Zhuangzi*, chapter 17. "The snake said to the wind, 'I move my backbone and ribs and manage to get along, but I still have some kind of body. But now you come whirling up from the North Sea and go whirling off to the South Sea, and you don't seem to have any body. How is that?' The wind said, 'It's true that I whirl up from the North Sea and whirl off to the South Sea. But if you hold up a finger against me, you've defeated me, and if you trample on me you've likewise defeated me. On the other hand, I can break down big trees and blow over great houses'" (ibid., 184).

pack and umbrella and also this fisherman's drum and these clappers. I have no clue where he wants to go. Just listen, the man who—*cha-cha-cha* and *dong-dong-dong*—is coming out onto the stage is not dredging for the moon with a punting pole but more likely piercing the wind with a bamboo splint.

(*The* SHENG *enters, dressed as Master Zhuang in Daoist garb.*)

The invitation gifts from King Wei arrived at my door in vain;
On awakening from the butterfly dream, I drummed on the tub.

Fame and profit, I discovered, are like an illusion and a bubble;
Southern Florescence, once written, contains a million words.

I am Zhuang Zhou. I am also known as Zixiu. My name in religion is the Perfected Man of Southern Florescence. I hail from the city of Meng in Suiyang. I am a descendant of King Zhuang of Chu—our family used the posthumous title as surname. I served as a clerk in Chu, and my office placed me in charge of the Lacquer Grove. Deeply affected by the situation of the times, I roam at liberty beyond the world. At present, following the period of Springs and Autumns,[12] the empire has descended into disorder. The seven states expand their territory and revere effectiveness and profit. Because they venerate possession, they commit grand theft, and while displaying ritual, they teach treachery. They adhere to the law of the lord but turn it into depravity and employ their intelligence to hasten chaos. Alas, pure innocence is not embodied anymore! Alas, the dark pearl[13] has suddenly disappeared. The result has been that the virtues of Yao and Shun are practiced nowhere[14] and even the teachings of Confucius and Mencius are not employed. Filled with frustration and anger and without a way to effect a transformation, I therefore composed

---

12. The "period of Springs and Autumns" refers to the centuries covered by the *Annals of Spring and Autumn* (*Chunqiu*), a chronicle of the ancient state of Lu for the years from 721 B.C.E. to the early fifth century B.C.E.

13. The "dark pearl" refers to wisdom. See *Zhuangzi*, chapter 12. "The Yellow Emperor went wandering. . . . When he got home, he discovered he had lost his Dark Pearl. He sent Knowledge to look for it, but Knowledge couldn't find it. . . . At last he tried employing Shapeless, and Shapeless found it" (Zhuangzi, *Complete Works of Chuang Tzu*, 128–29).

14. Yao and Shun are proverbial sage-rulers from China's mythic past. Yao ceded the throne to Shun, and Shun ceded the throne to Yu, but the last was succeeded by his son and so became the founder of the Xia dynasty (ca. 2100–1600 B.C.E.).

my *Southern Florescence* and lodged my intention in its fables. It's too bad that all people reject me as a heretic, but I do not view these people as my equals. They do not realize that my words may go against the classics but actually protect the orthodox. Because I hate the muddied nature of the stream, I want to purify the source. It may be compared to ascending a mountain or crossing a river—it equally comes down to wading and climbing. It's just as with birds' heads and stalactites—what counts in the final analysis is whether the disease is cured. Ah, the people of this world are plagued by a hundred diseases, but the ones that are most difficult to cure are fame and profit. For me as a monk, compassion is the root, and my intention is to deliver the world, but where in the world is a man who can be delivered? I should try it out once or twice so he might serve as an example. With my eye of wisdom I have found out that District Magistrate Liang Dong of Yancheng in Huai'an prefecture may be tightly caught up in the net of the world and deeply committed to the pursuit of fame but by nature does not belong to the common kind of mortals and has a karmic destiny to become an immortal. I would like to pierce the gate on his cranium and deliver him from the sea of suffering, but I don't yet know the means to do it. I've given it quite some thought, and the only way I have will be to perform some trick. Acolyte, you take the pack and the umbrella and follow me on a cloud-like visit to the Zhongnan Mountains. Give the drum and the clappers and the medicine gourd to me.

CHOU: What is the origin of this fisherman's drum and these clappers? And what is their use?

SHENG: Acolyte, you may not know this, but this set of drum and clappers was invented by His Imperial Majesty Xuanyuan[15] and played by the Immortal Master Guangcheng.[16] When you beat them, you can wake up the most stupid delusions; when you beat them, you can put to rest the most devious rage. When you beat them, you can shake the most conceited prejudices, and when you beat them, you can destroy the most despondent sorrows. The thirty-three heavens up above, the eighteen hells here below, and the four great continents in between—

15. Xuanyuan is one of the names of the Yellow Emperor, a sage-ruler from the mythic past who in later times was credited with many inventions.

16. Guangcheng taught the way of immortality to the Yellow Emperor.

all people, whatever their number, have only to hear this drum and these clappers played and in all cases each and every one seems to have a clear lamp in a dark night and to the very last person they seem to be awakened from their yellow millet dream.

CHOU (*acts out smiling*): Master, it's difficult to imagine that this drum and these clappers would be so powerful. Why don't you play them to me?

SHENG (*acts out beating the fisherman's drum and the clappers*):

(*"Langtaosha" [Waves Washing the Sand]*)

> The fisherman's drum booms and booms loudly;
>> These bamboo
> Clappers are made of dried *qiong*,[17]
> But beat them once and they destroy the Jingyang bell.[18]
>> I'm afraid
> The stick will beat your head to pieces and you'll be in pain,
> And the hidden deer will turn out to be illusionary.[19]

Just look: The sinking moon is still combing the willows on the dike, / and the idle clouds have already swept the pines on the ridge.

(*To the same tune as before*)

> Practicing the Way, I live in hiding in the hills,
> For all the red of the dust of the world,
> White clouds slowly so slowly close my gate.
> But in this puppet booth I'll perform a trick,
> So let's not stop in our tracks.

Acolyte, now our road passes through Yancheng district in Huai'an prefecture, I want to pay a visit to District Magistrate Liang Dong.

---

17. *Qiong* is a type of bamboo.

18. The Jingyang Tower was one of the buildings in the inner quarters of the imperial palace of the fifth-century Qi dynasty. The sounding of the bell alerted the palace ladies to the imminent arrival of the emperor.

19. *Liezi*, chapter 3. "There was a man of Zheng who went to gather firewood in the moors and came on a frightened deer. He stood in its way, struck it, and killed it. Fearing that someone would see the deer, he quickly hid it in a ditch and covered it with brushwood. His joy overwhelmed him. But soon afterward, he could not find the place where he had hidden it and decided that he must have been dreaming" (adapted from Liezi, *Book of Lieh-tzu*, 69).

CHOU: Master, you and Magistrate Liang must be old friends. You must be going there to extract some wealth. But that means you will rile up his rage.

SHENG: Why would we who have left the family need any money and want to extract some wealth? I want to deliver him!

CHOU: Master, today is a perfect day, auspicious for setting out on a journey. I wouldn't spoil your first idea. If you would want to visit famous mountains or meet with friends in the Way, all would be fine and dandy, but if you want to deliver those officials . . . Those officials never talk about these matters. They only talk about how to worm their way up and how to manipulate men, how to obtain a recommendation to speed up their promotion or how to fill their bags and increase their property. And if it is not that, they talk about their townsman Zhang, discussing his pros and cons, or they talk about their fellow student Li, evaluating his rights and wrongs. And if it is not that, they talk about a cure for blackening their beards so they don't have to hide and cover them, or they talk about a fragrance for lifting the blanket so they can engage in sex throughout the night. That kind of talk is what they like to hear. But I'm afraid, my master, that these matters are not your expertise. If you want to go and deliver him, I fear all you will gain from him is a bellyful of foul and stinking rage. That may be easy, but at that time even I, your acolyte, will lose face!

SHENG (*acts out walking*): Don't talk nonsense! Acolyte, what kind of man do you think this Magistrate Liang might be?

(*To the same tune as before*)
> He is
> Predestined to become an immortal,
> > But at present he is
> Imprisoned and encaged by fame and profit.
> > I will
> With a golden needle pierce the central-trigger peak
> And awaken him from the dreams of his midnight stupor,
> Not betraying a good friend.

Just look: The clouds and hills that fill your eyes are effective drugs; / A hundred years of toil and effort are useless and empty.

(*To the same tune as before*)

> Walking on, we arrive at the suburban fields.
> At leisure I stroke a lonely pine—
> How frequent those green willows and red flowers!
>> I only feared that
> In delivering the world I would be hindered by those people,
>> But it is you
> Who has to play the pedant!
> Walking on slowly, we have arrived in Yancheng district.

(*The* CHOU *acts out secretly wrapping a skull in the sleeve of his gown.*)

SHENG (*acts out turning around, seeing this, being taken by surprise, and questioning him*): What's that?

(*The* CHOU *acts out refusing to show it.*)

SHENG: It must be melon you stole from that garden!

(*The* CHOU *acts out shaking his head.*)

SHENG: You little beast! It must be a pig's head you stole from a shop.

(*The* CHOU *again acts out shaking his head.*)

SHENG (*acts out grabbing it, seeing the skull, and being surprised*): Bah, so it was a skull! You little beast, why would you pick up such a filthy thing?

CHOU (*acts out wiping the mouth of the skull and showing it*): Master, don't you see that it clenches a copper coin between its jaws?[20] I want to dig it out. (*Acts out picking up a piece of rock in order to smash the skull.*)

SHENG (*orders him not to do so*): You little beast, why would you want this one coin?

CHOU: Master, do you want me to tell you the use of copper cash? What kind of thing between heaven and earth could be better than this? From past to present and from Son of Heaven to commoner, they all use cash as their capital, and once they have capital, they will make profit, so who doesn't want it? And it is not only living people. Even the ghosts who have died still want it even when they have become gods.

SHENG: How can you say that?

---

20. Ancient Chinese funerary ritual demanded that body openings of the deceased be blocked by objects of value in order to safeguard the integrity of the body. In its simplest form, a coin was placed in the mouth of the deceased before burial.

CHOU: How can I say that? According to all your talk, those shops that make sacrificial paper money can all close their doors!

SHENG (*to the same tune as before*):

> The affairs of this world are one murky mess;
> They are in love with stupid cash!
> From the common people in village and hamlet to princes
>> and dukes,
> They all burn with desire
>> And want
>>>> Their bags to be heavy.
> This really pisses a hero off!

You coin, I have no clue who produced those four characters, / but throughout our lives we are pestered by you.[21]

(*To the same tune as before*)

> Your numinous power is truly divine:
>> You can make
> Rivers run dry and mountains fall down,
>> But you can also
> Support filial sons and loyal officials.
>> Those
> Wives will share cushion and coverlet with them,
>> But without you,
> Their passion will have diminished!

Acolyte, please spare him! This skeleton too must have sons and grandsons. Of course they would blame you if they learned of this.

CHOU: Master, my master, from these words of yours it would appear that you do not understand the affairs of this world at all! In this world it is only the old who pity the young, but you never find any young people who pity the elderly. So if you would say that his father and grandfather would blame me if I broke this skull, that still would make some sense. But if you say that his sons and grandsons would blame me, that would

---

21. Traditional Chinese copper coins are round with a square hole in the center, and they usually carry a four-character inscription along the lines of *Kaiyuan tongbao* (common currency of the reign period Kaiyuan).

never, never happen. In this world all sons and grandsons hate their grandfathers and fathers for leaving them not enough cash. Even this one coin he clenches between his jaws he should have left to his sons and grandsons to buy some tofu. If I now would dig out his coin and give it to his sons and grandsons, they would be greatly pleased with me!

SHENG (*to the same tune as before*):

When you say so I can only beat my breast:

Because of this

Brother Kong Squarehole,[22]

They don't care about

Father and mother or father-in-law.

If you would dig out this coin and give it to them,

Truly

A smile would cover their faces!

When one day Impermanence arrives, you can't take it with you, / And the sons and daughters before your eyes turn out to be of no avail. When people die, I see,

(*To the same tune as before*)

It is because

No thread of breath can pass through anymore.

But the weeping and wailing of sons and grandsons

Are gusts of wind beside your ears

As they lament that their inheritance falls short in wealth.

Just watch how

Water drops before the eaves all fall in the same spot:

Their sons and grandsons

Will closely follow their tracks.

(*The* CHOU *acts out hitting the skull.*)

SHENG: You little beast! If you want that coin so badly, I will give you one coin. Now please spare that skull.

---

22. Kong is a common surname (it is the surname of Confucius), but as a common word it means "hole." Kong Squarehole (Kong Fangxiong) is a common designation for the traditional copper coin with its square hole.

(*The* CHOU *acts out taking the coin but still secretly digging out the other coin.*)

SHENG: Skeleton, O skeleton, you really have to suffer because of this coin! The case of Shi Chong long ago informs us that riches bring trouble,[23] so it is best to distribute them as early as possible. In my opinion it does not matter how much money you have, even a single coin spells trouble. Skeleton, O skeleton, why do you so tightly hold on to this coin and refuse to let go? In my opinion the desire for profit by this acolyte is too deeply ingrained, like an illness that has entered the diaphragm.[24] I will have to perform a trick to call him to his senses. (*Acts out facing the acolyte.*) My acolyte, would you believe that I can bring this skeleton back to life?

CHOU: Master, that's really weird! That's like buying a dried fish and setting it free![25] (*Speaks in an aside.*) Just look, I told you that my master likes to perform tricks!

SHENG: Acolyte, lay out the bones of that skeleton to look just like a living person.

(*The* CHOU *acts out being afraid.*)

SHENG: How come you were not afraid when you were digging out that coin a moment ago?

CHOU: Master, the old saying is, Others guard their silver as they do their lives, / But when I see their silver, I happily risk my life. So of course my gall was as big as heaven when I was digging out that coin.[26] (*Acts out arranging the bones.*) Master, I am missing three ribs. I'm afraid this skeleton must have had the bad luck to run into someone who wanted his coin and dug through his ribs. That man has taken out three ribs.

23. Shi Chong (249–300) was the richest man of his time, but his competitive display of conspicuous consumption created jealousy among the members of the imperial family and soon resulted in his downfall.

24. An illness that has entered the diaphragm is said to be incurable.

25. One of the good works in Buddhism is buying captured animals that are destined for consumption and setting them free.

26. The gallbladder is considered to be the seat of courage.

SHENG: What to do? (*Acts out looking up to heaven.*) I have a solution! I will substitute three dried willow twigs. (*Acts out plucking the twigs and inserting them.*) Acolyte, take off your gown and cover this skeleton.

CHOU: Master, that is impossible. I will need this gown when I am the groom.

SHENG: No problem! I will have a new one made for you.

CHOU: Master, there is still one more matter we have to discuss. When this skeleton is revived, he is bound to open his mouth, and when he opens his mouth, this coin he clenches between his jaws is bound to fall down. This coin will still be mine.

SHENG (*acts out smiling*): This little beast is so calculating!

CHOU: Master, in this world money is no easy matter. It is all acquired by calculation.

SHENG: Don't talk nonsense. Let me take a divine cinnabar pill from my gourd and insert it into his mouth through the crack between his teeth.

CHOU: Master, isn't that the recipe for returning all diseases to spring, the Three-Primes Cinnabar?[27] Such a pill should not be used lightly. You may have to waste quite a lot of words later.

SHENG: That's no problem. You go and get me a ladleful of water from the brook.

(*The* CHOU *acts out fetching water.*)

SHENG (*acts out taking the cup of water in his hands*):

(*To the same tune as before*)

> I contrive a way to display my magical powers;
> In order to convert the ignorant,
> I show a trick and steal the work of heaven.
> When in a moment he revives, it won't be a lie:
>> We'll see
> What he looked like in earlier days!

27. Cinnabar is the prime ingredient of the elixir of life in Chinese alchemy. Ingesting such an elixir heals all diseases and returns one to the prime (the springtime) of one's life.

Who claims there is no *samadhi*[28] that revives the dead? / You must
believe that there are eight lords who bring back youth.[29]

(*To the same tune as before*)

These

Four Elements all turn out to be empty:

Their congregation and dispersal resemble a gust of wind.[30]

After some acrobatics for a while, you turn to scattered
weeds.

Acolyte,

If you want to catch a turtle, just stay close to this vat:

Go and listen at his throat.

(*The* JING, *dressed as the* SKELETON, *acts out lying down on the ground.*)

(*The* SHENG *acts out spitting water.*)

(*The* CHOU *acts out bending down to listen—he jumps up in fright when
the* SKELETON *starts to breathe.*)

(*The* SKELETON *acts out rising to his feet, opening his mouth, and drop-
ping the coin.*)

(*The* CHOU *acts out grabbing the coin.*)

(*The* JING *acts out trying to grab it back, shouting, "Agent, a thief!" and
grabbing the* CHOU's *pack and umbrella.*)

(*The* CHOU *acts out grabbing him by the hair and getting into a fight.*)

(*Extras, dressed as runners, follow the* XIAOSHENG, *who is dressed as Dis-
trict Magistrate Liang and acts out coming upon this scene.*)

XIAOSHENG: Underlings, arrest this group of fighting criminals and take
them to my office. (*Acts out taking his seat in the hall.*)

Day and night the swift current of the Huai River flows on;

Purple clouds drift above the iron pillars of majestic hills.

To my shame I spent three years like a corpse, to no use;

I am worried my final report will list no exceptional case.

I, this lowly official, am Liang Dong. I am also known as Guozhen,
and I hail from Huayang. By an act of grace by His Majesty, I have
been appointed as district magistrate for Yancheng. Even though I

---

28. The Sanskrit word *samadhi* refers to superior wisdom.

29. The "eight lords" are the teachers of Liu An (179?–122 B.C.E.), the compiler of the
Huainanzi, which, despite the diversity of its contents, is often classified as a Daoist book.

30. The Four Elements are earth, water, fire, and wind.

"Underlings, arrest this group of fighting criminals and take them to my office."

have been at my post for three years, I don't have a single forte in administration. When a moment ago I paid a visit to the inspecting censor, he said that I have to be reviewed at the end of my term, but for three years not a single case of exceptional administration could be recorded. If I would produce but one or two cases of exceptional administration, he could then report me to the emperor for promotion to circuit level. In my opinion the great secret in being an official is getting your superiors on your side. There is no need to care for the people. You only have to establish a spectacular name. There is no need to devote yourself to routine administration. Alas, all the slopes throughout this district are covered with locusts, but despite all exorcisms, they refuse to leave, and all hills are populated by tigers, but despite all our efforts to chase them, they refuse to cross the river. The people have created a popular ditty, which states that I do not exorcise the man-eating locusts, but that I only exorcise the rice stalk–eating locusts; that I don't chase away the tigers in the guesthouses, but that I only chase away the tigers in the hills.[31] Bah, I busy myself for the

31. The "man-eating locusts" and the "tigers in the guesthouses" refer to rapacious clerks and runners.

sake of a fleeting name. How can I bear this lack of success in exceptional administration! And right when I was in that bad mood on my way home, I come across this bunch of fighting criminals. Underlings, bring those criminals in for questioning.

(*The extras reply and act out bringing in the three persons.*)

(*The* SHENG *remains standing; the* CHOU *and* JING *act out kneeling.*)

XIAOSHENG: You fellow over there, what do you have to say?

JING: My name is Wu Zhen and I hail from Fujian. I passed through this place because of my business in gold and pearls. Here I ran into these two bandits, who robbed me of my pack and my umbrella. These stolen goods are here as proof.

(*"Huangying'er" [Yellow Oriole]*)

> Me, I hail from Fuzhou;
> Trading in gold and pearls, I was traveling along,
> Shouldering this umbrella
>> And
>>> This heavy pack, this bundle.
> But I ran into these archenemies,
> Who out of the blue used violence.
>> They blocked my way with their cudgel, so I
> Knelt down on both my knees, offering them gold and pearls,
> But fortunately I encountered My Lordship.
>> Your Lordship, this is a clear case of robbery in broad daylight.
> Order them to return the stolen goods
> So I won't end up with empty hands.

XIAOSHENG: You little beast, what do you have to say?

CHOU: My name is Aco Lyte, and I do not know from where I hail.

(*To the same tune as before*)

> My father and mother, beset by poverty,
>> Had me
> Sold off to the hills to become an acolyte.
> When my master goes on a trip, I have to follow along.
>> Your Lordship, what do you think you will find in this pack? It's
> A linen gown with some old repairs.
>> This umbrella is broken,
> But it serves as our protection against wind and rain.

Out of the blue he stole these from us and instigated this case.

> Your Lordship, these two things are not mine either.

(*Acts out kowtowing.*)

> I hope Your Lordship
> Will order him to return these stolen goods
> To my dear master, their rightful owner.

XIAOSHENG: You Daoist, how come you are not kneeling?

SHENG: I, this poor monk, have not committed any crime.

XIAOSHENG: I'll forgive you for the moment. What do you have to say?

SHENG: That fellow over there is actually a skeleton.

XIAOSHENG (*acts out standing up in surprise*): How is such a weird thing possible? He is clearly a man. How could he be a skeleton? Please explain!

SHENG: Your Excellency, in my cloud-like wanderings I am accompanied by this little guy. When on the road he tried to dig out the coin in the mouth of a skull, I gave him a coin, but he still refused to give up, and so I performed this little trick to instruct him. The bones of this skeleton came back to life after I had inserted a divine pill into his mouth.

(*To the same tune as before*)

> In search of the Way I left the woods
> And saw a skeleton on the burrow of foxes and rabbits.
> Because I want to deliver others, I was suddenly moved to
>> compassion
> And inserted a pill into his mouth,
> So his soul returned and his energy developed.
>> I had promised the coin he clenched between his teeth to this little
>> guy, but because
> This coin fell to the ground, they started a fight.
>> Who could have known that once this skeleton had lost his coin,
>> he would steal the pack and umbrella of this little guy?
> I appeal to Your Excellency
> To repay this injustice with a favor:
> This crime cannot be pardoned by Heaven!

JING: I am clearly a man. How can he say that I am a skeleton? Obviously he is a priest who practices black magic!

SHENG (*points to the* JING): How can you still talk back like this? A moment ago it was me who gave you that medicine to eat so you could come back to life. How can you now suddenly deny it?

JING: Your Lordship, don't listen to him. In this world the drugs of physicians can only kill people. They can never revive people.

SHENG: Your Excellency, if you are not convinced, just give me a drink of water. I will spit the water out on him, and he will become a skeleton as before. Then you will know the truth.

SKELETON (*acts out panicking*): Your Lordship, this evil monk knows a magical method to disappear. On no account can you allow him to even see water.

XIAOSHENG (*acts out striking his desk to frighten him*): Underlings, this is clearly a priest who practices black magic. Tie him up tightly and fasten him to a tree, because otherwise he might disappear. Tell the secretaries to quickly prepare the documents to inform the provincial governor in all detail and also all the other relevant authorities. This judicial case will not only be a case of exceptional administration such as has not occurred for three years, but it is also something that has never been seen or never been heard of since the beginning of time and throughout the whole wide world! This is great! Really great! If my review is concluded with this case, I can count on an appointment at circuit level!

(*The extras act out tying up the* SHENG *and fastening him to a tree. They act out placing the fisherman's drum and the clappers on the desk.*)

CHOU (*facing the* SHENG): Back home I told you that if you wanted to visit officials, you would rile up their rage. So what to do now?

SHENG (*to the same tune as before*):
  There is no need for any roaring rage,
  These empty words are truly without trace.
(*Acts out facing the* SKELETON.)
    You truly forget favors and betray righteousness. I'm just afraid
     that when
  Your true shape is exposed, you'll have no hole for hiding!
  Your Excellency, if you are still not convinced, then there is still another weird fact. When this little fellow arranged his bones in good

order, we missed three ribs, which I replaced with three willow twigs. If you now allow this poor monk to spit a mouthful of water on him, he will resume his original shape, and you will see the ribs that are willow twigs, so you will have additional proof.

XIAOSHENG: On no account loosen his ropes, but fetch some water and let him try.

SHENG:

> The ropes must be loosened for a moment
> As I hold the water in my mouth:
> This miracle is bound to astound you all.
> May I ask Your Excellency
>> To inspect
> These dispersed white bones:
>> There will be three willow twigs
> Pressing close to his heart!

(*The* SHENG *acts out spitting water.*)

(*Others have beforehand placed the bones, wrapped in a Daoist gown, at the foot of the desk.*)

(*The* JING *acts out being spat upon, falling to the ground, and going backstage.*)

XIAOSHENG (*in an aside*): How is such a weird thing possible? Now I suddenly see this, my hairs stand on end. Come to think of it, the man became a skeleton, the skeleton became a man, and the man became a skeleton again. The turning wheel of transmigration revolved here in an instant. The tale of man and sheep in the Lankavatara Sutra verily does not deceive us.[32] In my opinion human life in this world is not different from a spark from a rock or a flash of lightning; all our

---

32. "Again, Mahāmati, what is meant by the emptiness of mutual [nonexistence]? It is this: when a thing is missing here, one speaks of its being empty there. For instance, Mahāmati, in the lecture-hall of the Mŗigarama there are no elephants, no bulls, no sheep, but as to the Bhikshus [monks] I can say that the hall is not devoid of them; it is empty only as far as they [that is, the animals] are concerned" (Suzuki, *Lankavatara Sutra*, 67).

efforts for a floating name truly resemble the [wars between the states on the] horns of a snail,[33] and our love and attachment for this burning house[34] cannot be distinguished from a dream. The hot guts that fill my belly will turn to freezing ice. Why should I have to wait for someone else to release this trigger? What do I wait for if I do not turn around right away? Moreover, this Daoist has the style of an immortal and the bones of the Way, he is not one of us common mortals. If I find out that this set of bones indeed includes three willow twigs, he is bound to be a true immortal and I had better follow him and leave the family. (*Turns around.*) Underlings, inspect those bones! Are there indeed three willow twigs?

(*The extras report.*) There are indeed three willow twigs.

XIAOSHENG (*stamps his feet*): That's it! I know. Take these bones to the public graveyard for burial. (*Acts out untying the* SHENG *with his own hands, pushing him to the seat of honor, and kneeling down in front of him.*) Your disciple is a common fellow with limited eyesight, so I did not recognize you as a perfected person. Just now I behaved most rudely in every imaginable way, so I beg you to be so kind as to forgive and pardon me. From now on I want of my own free will to abandon my office and leave the family. I am determined to convert to your teachings and to call myself your disciple. Great Master, I pray that you will accept me as such.

CHOU (*acts out pulling the* XIAOSHENG *aside*): My master is someone who loves to play tricks. You are an official, so you have to consider this

---

33. *Zhuangzi*, chapter 25. "Dan Jinren said, 'There is a creature called the snail—does Your Majesty know it?' 'Yes.' 'On top of its left horn is a kingdom called Buffet, and on top of its right horn is a kingdom called Maul. At times they quarrel over territory and go to war, strewing the field with corpses by the ten thousands, the victor pursuing the vanquished for half a month before returning home'" (adapted from Zhuangzi, *Complete Works of Chuang Tzu*, 284).

34. The burning house as an image for our life in this world with all its attachments derives from a fable in chapter 3 of the Lotus Sutra, in which the teachings of the Buddha are compared to the promises a father makes to his children in order to entice them to leave their burning house.

carefully. You cannot allow him to deceive you and so easily bow down in front of him!

XIAOSHENG: If you talk about us officials, we play quite a lot of tricks each day, and we play quite a lot of tricks in each case. It is the main craft of us officials to deceive others. So how could I be deceived by him? In delivering people, the master employs cunning expedients. His words are nothing but absurd, but his true desire to save the world is sincere and correct in its main intention. You cannot misunderstand him because of this.

CHOU: At present you'd still better go back home to talk it over.

XIAOSHENG: Whenever there is discussion, there is delay. With a single stroke I cut myself free, and the ten thousand dharmas[35] now are all empty. (*Acts out taking off his cap and gown and putting on Daoist garb.*) *A lyric to the tune "Xijiangyue":*

> For ten years I toiled and toiled by the glare of a lamp;
> For three years I hurried and worried with ink and seal.[36]
> Leaving by starlight, returning by starlight—it was all in vain:
> An appointment as official is just the same as a dream.
>
> To my great fortune my teacher enlightened me
> And opened the prison cage of that dusty world.
> Discarding my office, I'll practice the Way in calm serenity,
> Together with the full moon and the clear breeze.

(*Turns around and acts out making a light bow to the* CHOU.)

CHOU: Your Lordship, a moment ago you exuded such authority, and now you are my co-disciple. And I also started out earlier than you. From now on I will call you Brother Liang.

XIAOSHENG: To be an official was only theater—that goes without saying.

CHOU: If you know that being an official is theater, then why did you have to make such a display of your authority and power a moment

---

35. The "ten thousand dharmas" refer to the innumerable elements that, in their temporary combinations, make up the visible world in which we live.

36. The "ten years" refer to the long years of study in preparation for the state examinations; the "three years" refer to the common term of office as a magistrate.

ago? Brother Liang, when my teacher set out on this trip, he said that your desire for fame was too strong, so when he wanted to deliver you, I initially did not support him at all. I had not imagined that you would now truly allow yourself to be delivered by him. Even so, you have to realize that it was not the teacher who delivered you but the skeleton.

XIAOSHENG (*in an aside*): I hadn't thought that this acolyte would show such insight. Now let me use the same trigger to set him going. (*Facing the acolyte.*) Acolyte, let me ask you. When I was an official, my foremost concern was to avail myself of cash. But now I have suddenly freed myself of that. But why were you having that argument with the skeleton a moment ago about that one coin?

CHOU (*acts out stamping his feet*): That's it. I understand! Could it be that that skeleton delivered me? Let me tell this to the teacher. (*Facing the* SHENG.) Master, I will now accept Brother Liang as my councilor.

SHENG: If you are willing to turn around, I will be greatly pleased.

CHOU: Brother Liang's lyric to the tune "Xijiangyue" of a moment ago was written quite well. I will now also write such a lyric using the same rhymes. (*Acts out bowing.*)

A lyric to the tune "Xijiangyue":

> Half my life I toiled and toiled, running here and there;
> All my existence I hurried and worried, all calculating.
> Hot water was replaced by snow—it was all equally in vain:
> To live as the richest man is just the same as a dream.
>
> Fortunately my immortal teacher showed me the way:
> A buffalo skin cannot serve as the covering of a lamp.
> Because when a moment ago I wanted to dig out that coin
>   and put on a mask with such a big mouth, I will now
>   throw this coin to the eastern end of the big river,[37]
> And happy together the three of us will have great fun.

---

37. A lyric to the tune "Xijiangyue" consists of two stanzas of four lines each; in each stanza, the first, second, and fourth lines consist of six syllables each, whereas the third line has seven syllables. In this case, the acolyte has expanded the number of characters in the third line of the second stanza way beyond that number.

Master Liang, the two of us may have been delivered by that skeleton, but a skeleton cannot speak. He can be compared to a firecracker: even though it is filled with saltpeter, without the man who lights the fuse, it is no different from a clod of earth or a piece of rock. How could that skeleton without our master have delivered you or me? Of the two of us, you were led by fame and I was led by profit—this goes without saying. Our teacher originally said that he wanted to go to the Zhongnan Mountains. But as we now have some leisure time on the road, you and I should ask our teacher once again to expound on the two concepts of fame and profit.

XIAOSHENG: You are right. (*Takes the fisherman's drum and the clappers.*) (*The* CHOU *takes the pack and the umbrella. They act out asking the* SHENG *to get under way.*)

XIAOSHENG: The two of us were saved by you from the beaten track of fame and profit, just like a glowing oven melts the snow, like a lamp appearing in the dark night. But please instruct us more about the meaning of these two words.

SHENG: Listen to me.

(*"Shuahai'er"[Playing the Child]*)

> How many people in this world are not fickle liars?
> Scheming for fame and profit, they're drifting weeds.
> But what is the use of their urgent yearning and desire?
> In freely roaming, there's the clear moon and bright wind.[38]
> The dew on grass can be compared to the riches of Tao Zhu;[39]
> A bubble on the water equals all merits of Tang and Wu,[40]
> Because when Impermanence arrives, all becomes a dream.
> > Who is willing
> To bravely retreat from the rushing current?
> > Who is capable
> To rein in the horse that is chasing the storm?

---

38. This line is not found in the *Yan Zhuang xindiao* edition of the play and would seem to be out of place here.

39. After Fan Li had assisted King Goujian of Yue in annihilating the state of Wu, he abandoned the court and became a traveling merchant, amassing incredible riches. In his new life, he was known by the name Tao Zhu.

40. Tang is Cheng Tang, the founder of the Shang dynasty (ca. 1600–1050 B.C.E.). Wu is King Wu, the founder of the Zhou dynasty (traditional dates, 1122–249 B.C.E.).

XIAOSHENG: Master, according to you, fame is empty. But in your *Classic of Southern Florescence* you also say that you have to hold on to your fame, and you also speak about receiving name and fame So isn't it impossible to say that fame is completely rejected by you?

SHENG: The fame that I do not want is that of those who love fame, who buy fame, who angle after fame, who pay for fame, who steal fame, who crave fame, and those with a false fame. You certainly understand that a name is the guest of a deed, so if you make a name by your deeds, your fame will last for all eternity. So how can you not do any substantial deeds because you want to avoid an empty fame? (Seventh Coda)[41]

> Who has accomplishments in learning and scholarship?
> Who is truly outstanding because of his merit and deeds?
> For a thousand years your example cannot be repeated.
>
> Only if your fame fits the facts will your fame endure;
> If the facts do not fit your fame, your fame will be empty.
> Who is willing to support evaluations that always change?
>> Don't think that
> An empty name can be inherited;
>> You must know that
> Common opinion can't be deceived.

CHOU: Master, according to you, profit is empty, but you must know the case of Confucius. Confucius once upon a time told the man who refused grain to give it to his neighbors and townsmen.[42] But I'm afraid that when he ran out of grain in Chen, he must have felt the pangs of hunger and have been quite uncomfortable.[43] So it is difficult to imagine that profit is always rejected by you.

SHENG: The profit I reject is that of those who are addicted to profit, those who fight over profit, those who chase after profit, those who lend for profit, those who angle after profit, those who monopolize

41. Codas are conventionally counted in reverse order.

42. *Lunyu*, VI.5. "On becoming [Confucius's] steward, Yuan Si was given nine hundred measures of grain, which he declined. The Master said, 'Can you not find a use for it in helping the people in your neighborhood?'" (adapted from Confucius, *Analects*, 81).

43. Confucius's distress in Chen is noted in *Lunyu*, XI.2, and XV.2 (ibid., appendix 1, "Events in the Life of Confucius," 173–75). It is a well-known theme in ancient literature and is often referred to in the *Zhuangzi*—for instance, chapters 14, 20, and 28.

此劇集
阿賓白
一韻押
成從史
記攢元
傳宋元
王一段
將末

盛明雜劇

古越雲來王應遴編

新安長吉黃嘉惠評

西湖　道常陳　節閱
泰征王光　閱

逍遙遊

末上開場〔西江月〕何事無中生有無端實裏談空。

栩栩蝴蝶入花叢撼醒邯鄲一夢生死關頭逐逐。

利名窠內憧憧誰能片雪墮鑪紅試看逍遙撮弄。

小道童挖令錢惹禍、刁骷髏奪包傘成空。

梁縣尹摑利名楔子、莊周子透生死關中。

逍遙遊

一

"But as we now have some leisure time on the road, you and I should ask our teacher once again to expound on the two concepts of fame and profit."

profit, and those who die for profit. If it is a profit you should receive, there is no harm in taking it. If you would want to say that we can do without profit, it is difficult to imagine that you have no use of the daily necessities of human life such as clothing and food.
(Sixth Coda)
>   Linen and fur for use in winter and summer;
>   Drink and food, whether simple or sumptuous:
>   Instituted by the Sage, of use to the people.
>   Only when you take profit fairly, it will bring luck,
>   But when your profit is not fair, it will bring disaster:
>   Money is that thing that manipulates all people.
>   But in Yama's palace
>   They don't accept cash or notes,
>   And in the Lotus World[44]
>   They don't despise the destitute.

44. The Lotus World is the Pure Land of the Amitabha Buddha.

XIAOSHENG: The people of this time will refuse to act unless it is for fame, and will refuse to act unless it is for profit. And if they do not secretly receive the benefits of profit and fame while publicly enjoying the reputation of avoiding profit and fame, they will also refuse to act. What is the reason for this?

SHENG: Why should the people of this world consider profit and fame a taboo? But the fame they recognize is not a true fame, and the profit they recognize is not a true profit. If we talk about true fame, then fame would follow you even if you would flee it, then fame would pursue you even if you would avoid it. If we talk about true profit, then it all depends on not taking making profit as profit, but on viewing losing profit as profit.

(Fifth Coda)

> Who is not deeply concerned about fame and profit?
> But they cannot clearly distinguish true from false,
> And rarely know how the steelyard weighs light and heavy.
> A fame as lofty as the Nine Gifts is snow on an oven;[45]
> Profit amassed in a thousand vats is wind on the river.
> In vain you fritter away your mercury and lead.[46]
>> Alas,
> The baroque pearls in your mouth
>>> All result in
> Ice and coal in your breast!

CHOU: Master, in your *Classic of Southern Florescence* you say that Bo Yi died for the sake of fame at the foot of Mount Shouyang, and that Robber Zhi died for the sake of profit at the foot of Mount Dongling.[47] In my opinion, people all have to die eventually, so

---

45. The Nine Gifts are the nine exceptional gifts bestowed by an emperor on a minister to whom he intends to cede his throne.

46. In inner alchemy, mercury and lead are the basic components of the immortal embryo and eternal life.

47. *Zhuangzi*, chapter 8. "Boyi died for reputation at the foot of Shouyang Mountain; Robber Zhi died for gain on top of Mount Dongling. The two of them died different deaths, but in destroying their lives and blighting their inborn nature, they were equal" (adapted from Zhuangzi, *Complete Works of Chuang Tzu*, 102).

instead of dying of hunger and starvation, would it not be much better to be a bandit and become a ghost with a stuffed belly? That would seem to have the advantage.

SHENG: You don't understand. Do you want to leave a fragrant name to the next generations, or do you want to be despised for your foul name for all eternity? That's why it is said that to die from hunger is an extremely insignificant matter, but to lose your honor is an extremely important matter. The people of this world all consider getting an advantage as acquiring profit. I'm afraid that you still cannot make the distinctions when it comes to dying for fame and dying for profit regarding who has the advantage.

(Fourth Coda)

> When it comes to life and death, they both are empty;
> When it comes to advantages, they are quite different:
> No birth and no nirvana is the Diamond's message.[48]
>
> The dispersal of souls and spirits is a common event;
> Beheading the devil of evil makes a man a great hero.
> How could a macho guy be manipulated by monkeys?
>
> How many people are able
> To reverse the beaten track?
> Who is capable of
> Jumping from the barred cage?

XIAOSHENG: Master, you have expounded on the meanings of fame and profit without anything left unsaid. But this discussion today was all

---

48. The Diamond Sutra was one of the most popular sutras in Chinese Buddhism. As a "Perfection of Wisdom" sutra it teaches that both being and nonbeing are equally illusionary, or "empty," and that therefore the pursuit of nirvana is equally illusionary. It is a relatively short text that was often recited at funerals. This may not be unrelated to the gatha that concludes the teaching of the Buddha in this sutra:

All existing phenomena
Are like a dream, an illusion, a bubble, a show;
Are like the dew and like a flash of lightning:
This is the way they should be viewed.

For translations of the Diamond Sutra, see Mu, *Diamond Sutra*, and Red Pine, *Diamond Sutra*. See also Yong, *Diamond Sutra*, and Wood and Barnard, *Diamond Sutra*.

occasioned by that skeleton. Was this skeleton a man or a woman? What kind of occupation did he have? Master, I hope you will instruct me about all of this.

SHENG: The skeleton's occupation and sex have been exhaustively dealt with by those texts in the world that lament the skeleton. But when it comes to his essential nature, I must say that his theft a moment ago of the pack and the umbrella was a trick that I performed in order to enlighten the two of you. If this skeleton were someone who during his lifetime did good, he would now surely have been reborn in heaven. But if he is someone who committed evil, he is now surely suffering in hell. How would I know?

(Third Coda)

Those who do good ascend to Brahman's Palace;
Those who commit evil go down to the hells.
Each is punished for his own sins,
And you cannot bother
Other people to come along.
No need to brag about
Your manly strength of years ago—we all turn white,
Your female charms of days bygone—no rosy cheeks.
When the abacus is finished, we will know the total.
Your single mind
Will receive its due reward;
Your hundred bones
Will be abandoned in the wilds.

CHOU: Master, those who do good and those who commit evil each will receive their own retribution, like a shadow that follows the shape, like water reflecting the moon—that goes without saying. But this wheel of transmigration spins around like a capstan or a windlass without any end. Master, even you, who are a true immortal according to the teachings of the Way, will encounter the end of this kalpa and your life eternal will end in no-life. How could you transcend the wheel of transmigration? What to do in the end?

SHENG: This question of yours resembles a mosquito on an iron statue: it has nowhere where it can bite. The ancients said, "In teaching and learning people take one another as elders." For this question I should bow to you as my teacher. (*Acts out sinking in thought, then stamping his feet.*) That's it! I understand. Eternal life is not as good as no-birth. In this respect, the teachings of the Buddha transcend those of the Way. If you want to escape from the wheel of transmigration, you have to finish birth and death. If you cultivate and uphold the substantial dharma, you will be able to escape from the gate of being. And if you want to know a short-cut, the best option is to strictly uphold name and title and to devotedly convert in order to seek rebirth in the Pure Land.[49] Then you will have found a raft to carry you across the sea of life and death, and with fame and profit you will have thrown weir and trap away for good.

(Second Coda)

> To finish life and death, your vow must be extensive;
> To escape from the wheel of transmigration,
> > You must rely on
> > > The power of deliverance,
> So uphold and recite the six characters *namo Amituofo*.
> > If you devoutly recite them constantly, without mistake,
> The hundred illusions will be removed, so never slacken!
> The six *paramitas*[50]
> > Require
> > > A heart that is sincere.
> > Once you have achieved
> The dharma realm of the blue lotus,
> > You don't have to fear
> Black waves or violent storms.

CHOU (*in an aside to the* XIAOSHENG): That is weird! Our master is a man of the Way. So how come his words of a moment ago resembled a Buddhist person?

SHENG: Only because I wanted to enlighten the two of you did I perform this trick of the skeleton. Only because I wanted to take you to the end

---

49. The Amitabha Buddha had made the vow that he would receive all those who sincerely call on him in his Pure Land in the West. Devotees recite his name as *Namo Amituo fo* (Hail Amitabha Buddha).

50. The six *paramitas* are charity, purity, patience, zealous progress, meditation, and wisdom.

did I point out the road to the Pure Land. Buddhism and Daoism may be two paths, but they and Confucianism all come down to a single principle. As long as you are willing to work on your mind and nature, what kind of difference can there be between the three teachings?
(First Coda)
> Don't harbor doubts because the teachings are different;
> You have to know that the three teachings all converge.
> With decomposed reins
> > You must
> > > Firmly restrain the colt of the spirit.
> Without a numinous drug, your illness cannot be cured;
> Without a golden needle, you can't turn the pupil around.[51]
> How often has the setting sun sent people to their graves?
> > You must realize that
> An enlightened teacher is hard to find,
> > So don't ignore
> This rare meeting with wonderful truth!

(Final Coda)
> The dusty net of profit and fame is only so light;
> The strict conjuncture of life and death so heavy.
> > This fisherman's drum and these clappers
> Can by their beating awaken
> > You from your
> > > Muddled dreams.
> > Please understand that
> Free and easy outrageous jokes
> Don't deceive the people of this world.

> By chance I reined in my running horse at the city of Meng;
> When I awoke from a butterfly dream, the window was red at dawn.
> > Leisurely I adapted the old script to new tunes:
> Don't despise its substantial principle as a performance trick.

---

51. This image is derived from cataract operations.

3
One Youth Book

Following the Manchus' conquest of China, a large number of Manchus settled in Beijing. As their number quickly increased over the following generations, the city became home to a large leisure class of unemployed Manchus, all of whom received a government stipend of some kind or another. Some of them became avid patrons of drama, especially Peking opera as it developed over the course of the eighteenth and nineteenth centuries; others became authors and/or performers of long narrative ballads known as *zidishu* ("youth books" or "bannermen tales"). The genre acquired its name because of its close association with the *baqi zidi* (sons and younger brothers of the Eight Banners)—that is, the fashionable young men-about-town who belonged to the Eight Manchu Banners. Right up to the last decades of the Manchu Qing dynasty (1644–1911), the performers of *zidishu* insisted on their status as amateurs and stressed the wide gulf that separated them from low-class professional entertainers.

Zidishu were sung to very slow music; although they were written basically in lines of seven-syllable ballad verse, the musical tempo allowed for the extension of each line to many more syllables and often resulted in very long lines. *Zidishu* might consist of one or more chapters, each chapter containing between one hundred and two hundred lines. As a rule, each chapter begins with an eight-line poem that was not sung but recited. *Zidishu* enjoyed a relatively high status, and many of them are by known authors who often relied on literary sources. The individual texts were not only performed but also circulated in written form, both in manuscript and in print. The genre was popular not only in Beijing but also in other northern cities with a large Manchu population, such as the secondary capital of the Qing dynasty, Shengjing (Shenyang), and Tianjin. Many *zidishu* were, with only minimal adaptations, later performed as *guci* (drum ballads).

The tale of Master Zhuang's encounter with a young widow who is fanning a grave (and the subsequent developments), as first published by Feng Menglong (1574–1646) in 1624 and later included in the widely popular anthology of vernacular tales *Extraordinary Sights from Present and Past* (*Jingu qiguan*), was rewritten as a *zidishu* at least four times. Such adaptations might be based either directly on the text in *Extraordinary Sights from Present and Past* or on one of the stage versions that opened with the scene of Master Zhuang's encounter with a skeleton. The *zidishu* translated here, *The Butterfly Dream* (*Hudie meng*) by Chunshuzhai, refers in its final comments to such stage adaptations. Chunshuzhai's adaptation includes four chapters, the first of which is devoted to a retelling of Master Zhuang's encounter with a skeleton. But for all the obvious influence of the legend of Master Zhuang's encounter with the skeleton, Chunshuzhai limits himself to an account of a dream dialogue between Master Zhuang and the skeleton, in the manner of the dialogue of Master Zhuang and the skull in the *Master Zhuang*. Little information is available on the author of this version beyond his name, which is not his personal name but the name of his study.

CHUNSHUZHAI

The Butterfly Dream

CHAPTER ONE: THE ILLUSIONARY TRANSFORMATION

Both high and low will end up lying in a single mound of earth:
So let me ask you, what's the use of your insistent seeking?
A lifetime's wealth and status will be gone in just one moment,
And in a single second worldwide fame and merit vanish.
Eternal love of boy and girl is truly an illusion;
Affection in a marriage is a counterfeit emotion.
After a good night's sleep, I suddenly saw through the
dreamscape of the butterfly
And wrote this piece about a skeleton's manifestation,
and lament the skeleton.

Zhuang Zixiu had seen through the red dust and understood the
Great Way;
Rejecting the king of Zhao's invitation,[1] he displayed his true
motives in the book of *Southern Florescence*.
Saddened by the fact that people opened their eyes when they
shouldn't open their eyes,
He lamented that the deluded masses did not turn around when
they could turn around.
Instead of getting to "the spring silkworm will complete its
thread only in death,"
Why necessarily wait for "the bow is put away only when there's
no trace of a bird."

---

1. He rejected the king's offer to join his government as prime minister.

Because of this the master had retired from the world and lived
in the hills;
Grasping the original truth, he wanted to study in detail his own
original features.
This one day he went by chance for a walk on a whim, for no
reason at all,
And in the wild suburbs saw orioles hiding in trees, heard birds
chirping on branches.
Here and there dogs were barking in mountain villages while
bells resounded in ancient temples;
On and off woodcutters sang on steep ridges while fishermen
chimed in from their slender boats.
Underneath a small bridge the brook's water murmured, so
clear it pierced the bones;
In the sparse wood the wildflowers blazed forth, their splendor
filling one's eyes.
This was truly a picture of nature—the wise love its streams, the
humane its hills—
And with increased enthusiasm, the master happily walked on,
roaming at random.
Turning around a hillside, he saw a limitless level plain, wide
and expansive,
And from afar he noticed a pile of white bones lying exposed in
the fields.
When he arrived there, the master observed it with both his eyes
and his mind:
It turned out to be a skeleton that no one had cared to cover or
bury.
The master covered it with earth because his heart was filled
with sympathy,
And facing the skeleton, he heaved many a heavy sigh as he
silently bowed his head
And thought, "This skeleton in former years was just like me
today,
So why does he have to suffer so extremely once he has escaped
from that sack of skin?"

Heaving a heavy sigh, he sat down on a black rock and fell
    asleep with lowered head
And saw a man who with his gray beard and white hair looked
    quite distinguished.
Approaching, the man greeted him with a bow and addressed
    him as master,
Saying, "You have been so kind as to gather these few lowly
    bones of mine."
    Zhuang Zixiu responded to his greeting in kind and addressed
    him with smile,
Saying, "So then this skeleton is Your Lordship, and Your Lord-
    ship is this skeleton.
I just wanted to ask you from where the work of escaping from
    our shell should start
Since I would like to learn the life-and-death secret of transcend-
    ing the mortal realm."
    The skeleton replied, "A man may live to a hundred years, but
    in the end he must die:
Once you're aware of death, you should delete all foolish thought
    in one stroke.
Only the endless expanse upon death can be counted as joy;
That busy business during your life will never come to an end.
    Those myriad worries without any bounds are all empty—
    what's there to love?
Completely cleansed, the single mind has no hindrance—what
    more could you want?
Don't blame me for these crazy words of mine that go against all
    reason—
Just go on and seek noble rank in that sycophantic crowd in the
    marionette booth!"
    Master Zhuang said, "Skeleton, why don't you return to the
    world of light
So you can display the ambition in your breast and the schemes
    in your belly?"
    The skeleton laughed loudly and answered, "I cannot go there
    again,

The world of light and I have no bond—that's all finished and
  done!
  I've now been a spirit for a few hundreds of years,
I'm free of all pleasure and joy, and free of all sorrow!
Master, you may advise me to return to the world of light,
But I'm afraid that I would eventually fail if I were a man."
  Master Zhuang asked, "What did you accomplish during your
  lifetime?"
And the skeleton replied, "I would like to tell you, but the telling
  fills me with shame.
Once upon a time I managed military and civil affairs as a high
  official with a large salary;
Once upon a time I rode a sleek horse in light furs, enjoying fine
  foods and rare delicacies.
  Once upon a time I had noble sons and fine grandsons, a
  charming wife and beautiful concubines;
Once upon a time I searched for flowers and asked for willows in
  the houses of Chu and the mansions of Qin.[2]
But the accounts of a thousand years—a total mess—are impos-
  sible to clear up,
And in the end, once I had escaped from that sack of skin, my
  bones were exposed.
  I quite regret how I earlier used those three inches of breath in
  a thousand ways!
Happily now all ten thousand affairs have come to an end upon
  one day of death."
Master Zhuang asked, "So what kind of person were you actually
  when alive?"
That skeleton laughed out loud and then again nodded his head:
  "You asked me what kind of man I was, what kind of man was I,
So let me ask you: The skeleton is who? Who is the skeleton?"
Master Zhuang suddenly saw through the skeleton's message,

2. The "houses of Chu and the mansions of Qin" refer to courtesan houses and bor-
dellos. Flowers and willows are common images for courtesans and prostitutes.

As if ghee were poured out on his cranium, the stick hit him
   smack on the head!
   He hurried to ask, "As for escaping this sack of skin—whom
   should I ask for instruction?"
And the skeleton replied, "Ask the Long Mulberry Master for
   details!"[3]
As Master Zhuang thought, "Who can find a Perfected Lord of
   the Way and Its Virtue?"[4]
He wished to ask the skeleton a follow-up question, but the latter
   turned around without looking back.
   As light as could be, he drifted away like a chilly gust of wind,
And even though Master Zhuang was still dreaming, he cried
   out, "Skeleton!"
A moment ago the two parties had been debating,
But suddenly both shape and shadow had disappeared, color and
   form were gone.
   As he was going back, he was filled with doubt as he pondered
   this dreamscape
When from afar he espied a young woman fanning a grave, a
   most elegant posture!

Chapter Two: Fanning the Grave

A skeleton, a pretty face: the two are closely linked—
Who can maintain love and affection for a hundred years?
A red-hot passion had one moment harmonized the zithers,[5]

3. The Long Mulberry Master (Changsangzi) instructed Master Zhuang in immortality techniques.

4. Daode Zhenjun can be translated in a very general sense as "a Perfected Lord of the Way and Its Virtue," as I have done, but many contemporary readers probably will have read this title as a shortened form of Qingxu Daode Zhenjun. According to the widely popular late Ming novel *The Investiture of the Gods* (*Fengshen yanyi*), Qingxu Daode Zhenjun is one of the twelve "golden immortals" below the supreme Daoist deity, Yuanshi Tianzun. His most effective weapon is his Five-Fire Seven-Bird Fan, which can destroy any demon in an instant. Mentioning Qingxu Daode Zhenjun here would point forward to the appearance of the young widow and her fan.

5. Zithers that are tuned in harmony are a common image for a happy marriage.

But there she holds her lute again before your bones are cold.[6]
As sex is only emptiness, so emptiness is sex;
A bond derives from karma, but this karma is no bond.
The bodhisattva Guanyin now sends Dragon Daughter[7] to
the mortal world,
Where she will fan a grave and by that means awaken
Zhuang Zhou from his dream.

Zhuang Zixiu was filled with doubt as he pondered his
dreamscape
When from afar he spied a newly built grave mound, its earth not
yet dry.
A pretty girl dressed in mourning stood by the side of the grave
mound,
And with a gold-speckled fan she was fanning that grave.
Master Zhuang did not grasp the secret design, so he silently
thought,
"Could it be that she fears that the heart of the man in that grave
is not cold?
It's impossible, I'm afraid, to solve this spring-lantern riddle[8]
right at the beginning,
A depressing conundrum—this case really has me depressed here
and now."
When he came closer, he repeatedly wanted to ask, but he
didn't want to meddle,
But then, if he didn't ask, how could he develop his knowledge to
the fullest?

6. In the *Ballad of the Lute* (*Pipa xing*) by the famous Tang poet Bai Juyi (772–846), an aging courtesan, whose husband-patron has left her, once again sings for customers to the accompaniment of the lute.

7. Dragon Daughter (Longnü) is Guanyin's female acolyte. Like her mistress, Dragon Daughter can assume any shape. In other versions of this legend, it is Guanyin herself who manifests herself in the shape of a young widow.

8. In many places in China, riddles were posted on or next to the lanterns displayed at the Lantern Festival of the first full moon of the new year.

So he had no other option but to politely greet her, address her as
    milady,
And say, "Milady, allow me to ask you, why are you fanning this
    grave?
    What is the one in this grave to you and why are you fanning
        like this?
Please be so kind as to tell me the reason behind all of this."
That woman stopped crying and weeping, opened her almond eyes,
And took her time to scrutinize Master Zhuang from head to toe.
    After quite a while she said, "You do not walk the great road,
Why do you have to ask me for my reasons here on this side road?
Why I fan this grave? Of course there's a reason for fanning the
    grave when I'm fanning a grave!
If I am fanning this grave, it's in order that this grave will dry as
    quickly as possible.
    How should I have the ample leisure to engage with you in
        some idle discussion?
Wouldn't I be wasting this fine time and good weather all for no
    purpose?"
Master Zhuang replied, "Milady, if you are willing to tell me
    your reasons,
I promise that this grave mound will dry out on the spot without
    any trouble!"
    The woman said, "Is that true? Will this grave be dry as soon
        as I tell you?"
Master Zhuang nodded his head and said with a smile, "Yes, of
    course!"
But before that woman had said a single sweet word, she first
    shed a tear,
And then said, "Even a man of iron or stone would be moved
    upon hearing my tale!
    The one in this grave is my husband, my partner during his life,
To whom I was tied by a thousand kinds of affection, ten thou-
    sand kinds of love!
We truly hoped for a fine marriage of a hundred years so we
    might grow old together—

Who could have guessed my husband would abandon me and
    descend into the earth.
  Now it would be easy to once again 'tune zithers in harmony,'
But I'm afraid it will be hard 'to paint a good copy of a gourd.'
Moreover, before he died he left me these last words as his
    instructions:
'If you want to remarry you must wait until the earth on my
    grave mound is dry.'
  Because I cannot bear to go against these loving last words of
    my husband,
I therefore have postponed this happy business for these last few
    days.
Sir, do not laugh at me because of my silly passion:
I'm afraid that women constant like me are rather rare!"
  As she was saying this, she handed her fan to the master,
And Zhuang Zixiu made the secret signs, applied the seals, and
    spoke his true words.
With his Five Demon Magic the earth of the grave mound was
    dry as soon as he waved the fan,
And the woman thanked him profusely as her face beamed with
    joy.
  Last night, alas, the lamplight waning and in a cold bed, she
    had laid herself down all alone,
But tomorrow evening her tender jade and warm fragrance will
    share a cushion when sleeping,
So wishing the master all blessings, she respectfully offered him
    the fan as a token of her gratitude,
And said, "I will be off, seeking a new partner, finding another
    marriage."
  Master Zhuang put the fan in his sleeve and went home as he
    had a good laugh:
"This woman had no sense of shame, was deprived of all reason!
She had the nerve to say that during his lifetime their love and
    affection were like fish and water—
If there had been no love or affection, the situation would have
    been too bad for words!"

When he got home, he rapped with the fan on the gate as he
    opened the door,
And when he saw his wife, Madam Tian, he suddenly realized the
    subtle contraption.
When he entered the room, Madam Tian served him his tea and
    saw that the master was very distracted,
So she hastened to ask, "Why do you look so glum and so sor-
    rowed today?"
    Master Zhuang said, "This is driving me mad, oh so mad! This
    is truly driving me mad!
'Most vicious is a woman's heart': on the basis of this experience,
    this statement is true!"
When his wife asked him for his reasons and to tell her what had
    happened,
Master Zhuang recounted the whole story of the woman fanning
    the grave.
    His wife then said, "If I would have been there a moment ago,
I would have shamed her and I would have reviled her to her face!"
She stretched out her hand, grabbed the fan, and tore it to pieces,
She was so furious her powdered face turned sallow, her eyes
    bulged out!
    Master Zhuang reacted, "You shouldn't have torn this family
    heirloom to pieces;
This precedent may later have its use, and you might want to fol-
    low her example.
As long as they are alive all people talk of love and affection,
But once you are dead, each and every one fans the grave."
    His wife wanted to reply, but then she heard her husband cry
    out,
"Oh this pain in my breast! How come my limbs are all soft and
    paralyzed?"
In an instant, the master had attracted a serious and fatal disease;
Very soon he breathed his last, his life tainted by the Yellow
    Springs.
    Despite all seeming deep affection and great love, the ice in her
    bosom warmed,

And soon I fear—secret words and waning passion—the fire she
carried will grow cold.

Chapter Three: Talking Love

So why did Master Zhuang assume illusionary shapes?
He wanted to bring out her hidden feelings through the prince.
The decorated saddle and fine horse were of the best;
Of highest quality were zither, sword, and box of books.
The servant looked exactly like a true and trusted servant;
The book boy was the spitting image of a little book boy.
When thoughts of spring set out to lead one on, seduce one,
Which blossom on the peach will then refuse to show her color?

A handsome prince arrived at the gate and pulled in the reins of
his horse;
He ordered his book boy to knock on the gate and announce his
arrival, without any delay!
"Tell them that a prince of Chu has arrived to pay a visit,
And that he insists on mounting to the hall and seeing the master!"
The little book boy wanted to knock on the gate but saw that
the door stood ajar,
So he sneaked inside and coughed a few times before he opened
his mouth.
He said, "Anybody here? Please report the arrival of a guest from
Chu,
My lord wants to pay a visit, so I have here his card I'd like to
present."
After quite a while, he heard the deeply sad voice of a woman,
saying,
"Master Zhuang passed away yesterday, and today he has been
encoffined.
Since you have so kindly made such a long and wearisome trip, I
should of course ask you to come inside,
But because the corpse is still in the house, I cannot offer proper
hospitality.

Please, young man, convey my greatest respect to your noble
master—

Not only the soul of the deceased will be grateful but I too will
be appreciative."

The little book boy accepted her order and reported what she had
said;

Hearing this, the prince was deeply moved and his tears poured
down.

He dismounted from his horse, and, weeping as he walked, he
called out, "My master!"

In front of the coffin he sadly paid his respects, enumerating the
master's virtues:

"Since my earliest youth I constantly longed to repay your teach-
ing and instruction,

And my longing was such that I did not shrink from this long
trip to visit the master.

Who could have expected that this beam as large as Mount Tai
would be destroyed?[9]

Causing us, the peach trees and plum trees in his yard,[10] to
lament our great loss."

As he was making this speech, the beauty stealthily had a peek
from behind the mourning screen:

Wow! She had once again met her romantic karma from five
hundred years past!

A cap of purple-gold, blue tassels hanging down, and a face so
very handsome!

A silver-white coat, securely fastened around his waist with a yel-
low belt.

Red cloud shoes produce with each step and each move a mild
and harmonious ether,

A gold-speckled fan, each time shaken or waved, calls forth the
breezes of spring.

9. Mount Tai in modern Shandong is the holy Marchmount of the East.
10. This is a common image used to denote disciples and students.

Moreover, his eyes resemble autumn floods free of dust; his
eyebrows resemble the layered greens of distant hills,
Whereas his teeth are as white as the jades from Mount Kun, his
lips as red as the pomegranate of the Fifth Month.
His age was just right—most likely he had only just passed his
capping ceremony.[11]
Who might be the girl who by her virtue in various lives would
become the companion of this passionate lover?
As she was stealthily looking, she heard the prince say, "Allow
me to pay my respect to my teacher's wife."[12]
And the little book boy at his side transmitted his message in very
clear words.
The woman replied, "Since I am wearing mourning, I would not
dare to trouble him so."
But the book boy said, "There's no need to be so modest, since
you are like his own mother."
He stretched out his hand and pulled back the mourning
screen, saying, "Milord, please come inside,
Once you are here, bowing to your teacher's wife is the same as
bowing to the master."
When he had entered her room, the prince kowtowed, and the
beauty responded in kind:
As soon as these two had seen each other, they exchanged furtive
glances.
There in the mourning hall, four eyes were dumbstruck and
two hearts were aglow.
Indeed, "the young man full of desire comes across a maiden filled
with passion."
But because they had barely met, there were so very many
thoughts they could not express,

11. The capping ceremony, when a young man started to put up his long hair and wear
a cap, was held when a boy became an adult.
12. The teacher's wife is addressed more literally as "teacher-mother." A sexual relation
between a student and his teacher's wife would be considered akin to incest.

So they could only stick to the rules of etiquette and exchange a
few questions.

Their conversation finished, the prince announced his depar-
ture, but the beauty asked him to stay,

Saying, "We have here a study that is nice and clean where you
can rest from your travels."

The little book boy chimed in and played along by saying, "That
would truly be marvelous!

Milord just wanted to recuperate from his exertions and take care
of his mount before moving on."

The prince replied, "How could I dare refuse this offer now
you, my teacher's wife, allow me to stay?

Staying here will also make it easier to prepare the sacrificial offer-
ings to be offered to my teacher."

While he was saying "I'm deeply grateful" and went to that
study,

His old servant moved his luggage into the guest room.

Not much later the red sun sank in the west while the round
moon rose,

And the little book boy went back inside to ask for a silver lamp.

When that woman saw the book boy, she immediately told him
to sit down:

Didn't this stir up a full heaven of romance, a limitless
infatuation!

She asked him, "Do you know how old His Lordship may be?"

And the book boy replied, "He was born in a *mao* year, in a *mao*
month, on a *mao* day, and in a *mao* hour."

As soon as she heard these words, the woman was bereft of her
soul:

"How strange! Why are his eight characters exactly the same as
mine?"[13]

---

13. The "eight characters" refer to the four two-character combinations for the hour,
day, month, and year of a person's birth, which determine his or her future. In marriage
negotiations, the eight characters of the two prospective partners are compared in order
to ascertain that the intended marriage will be blessed.

She also asked, "And from which family is the bride of His
    Lordship?"
The book boy replied, "He is not yet engaged, but there is some-
    thing weird.
His Lordship once swore an oath in the presence of his father
    and mother
That he only wanted to marry a woman with the same eight
    characters as himself."
    The woman said, "That our eight characters are the same is a
        rare coincidence,
But even despite this coincidence, it wouldn't work since the
    disparity in wealth cannot be ignored."
The book boy replied, "As long as the eight characters are com-
    pletely the same,
His Lordship doesn't care about noble or lowly and poor or
    destitute.
    If Auntie Zhuang can act as the matchmaker, that would be
        very convenient;[14]
Once we have a matchmaker, I promise that one word of mine
    will clinch the deal."
Because her spring heart was aroused, this woman told him her
    honest desire,
But alas, she mistook a rope of hemp for a red string.[15]
    Suddenly we will once again see in this world of man the ritual
        performed;
A second time we witness the crossing of the two stars in heaven
    above.[16]

14. Auntie Zhuang refers to a female family servant.

15. According to a well-known classical tale from the Tang dynasty (608–906), predes-
tined marriage partners are tied together by the Old Man of the Moon using a red string.

16. Buffalo Boy and Weaving Maiden are two stars (Vega and Altair) separated by
the Heavenly River (Milky Way). They are lovers who are allowed to meet only once a
year, on the night of the seventh day of the Seventh Month, when magpies form a bridge
across the river.

CHAPTER FOUR: SPLITTING THE COFFIN

The book boy transmitted the message, his face all wreathed in a smile;
    The beauty received the good news, and her joy knew no bounds.
The red *luan* danced once again in front of the mandarin-duck mirror;[17]
    Purple swallows would nest all over again on tortoise-shell beams.
Displaying his dashing style to the full, he pursued the Luo maiden;[18]
    Readying herself for clouds and rain, she waited for King Xiang.[19]
Only because the heaven of passion and the ocean of evil deluded
        her true nature
Did she fail to recognize that her new lover was actually her old lover!

    Now tell that the prince quite eagerly agreed to the match:
    That very evening was a lucky hour and good day to enter the
        bridal room.
    The woman moved Master Zhuang's coffin to some other location,
    And in noisy disorder the servant and book boy together helped
        her out.
      In a little while, everything had been arranged in an orderly
        fashion,
    Truly the household was filled with joy: everything came in pairs.
    After a little while, midnight approached and the lucky hour drew
        near,
    So the book boy said, "Let's ask the bride and groom to bow in
        the hall."
      That handsome prince, clad in brocade, a belt of jade, was the
        image of fashion;

17. The *luan* is a phoenix-like bird. Once a captive single *luan* desiring a mate danced in front of a mirror until it died.

18. Once, when crossing the Luo River, the poet Cao Zhi (192–232) had a vision of the river goddess. He describes her seductive charms at length in "Rhapsody on the Goddess of the Luo" (Luoshen fu).

19. When King Xiang of Chu visited Mount Wu, the goddess of the mountain shared his couch in his dream. As she left, she identified herself as the morning clouds and evening rain.

That handsome beauty, in halcyon feathers and pearls, was quite
    heavily made up.
The two of them came together into the hall and bowed to
    Heaven and Earth,
And they silently prayed, "May we be like Liang Hong and Meng
    Guang—the tray lifted as high as the eyebrows!"[20]
    After husband and wife had bowed to each other, exchanged
    the common cup, and finished the ritual,
Their wish was to be granted—in the silence of midnight for the
    first time to taste the crab-apple fragrance!
But suddenly she heard the prince scream and shout, "Too bad!"
And his body collapsed with a crash then and there in the hall.
    The beauty supported him with her hands and asked, "What's
    the matter?"
But she saw that his body was stretched out straight, that his faced
    had turned yellow.
Heavily moaning and with his eyes closed, he was barely
    breathing;
Shivering all over, he clenched his teeth and his hands were
    ice-cold.
    When she asked the book boy whether the prince had earlier
    suffered these symptoms,
The book boy replied, "This is the heart pain from which he
    suffers.
Who could have expected it would manifest itself here today in
    this place—
It just so happens we didn't bring his medicine, so this will soon
    spell his death."
    "What kind of medicine did His Lordship use when earlier he
    suffered this illness?"

---

20. Liang Hong (first century C.E.) lived in retirement. When his bride, Meng Guang,
presented herself to him in all her finery, he ignored her, but when she dressed simply
and brought him his meal, lifting the tray as high as her eyebrows as a sign of respect, he
treated her most affectionately.

Before the book boy had opened his mouth, his tears gushed
   down.
"No other medicine at all but the brains of a living person—
An infusion of that, and his illness is cured, he's healthy again!
   Here this medicine can't be found, so this man cannot be saved.
It must have been determined by his eight characters he'd die
   here."
As he was saying this, he was weeping so much that it seemed he
   was drunk,
But the woman said, "Now don't be so sad, there's something we
   have to discuss.
   Tell me whether the brains of a dead person are any good;
If those can be used, we'll quickly ask someone to find a way."
The book boy said, "Those that are dead less than three days are
   still good,
But I've never heard of a drugstore where they sell human brains."
   But that woman said in her ferocity, "It can't be helped!
In order to save my new husband, I'll have to appeal to my former
   beau."
With the help of the servant and book boy, she set to work
And carried the prince back to the study.
   She told them strictly, "Now guard him well and don't leave his
   side
While I go everywhere to ask someone to find me a brain."
   After she had so deceived the servant and book boy, she went
   back inside,
And once in her room, she took off her long gown and put on a
   short skirt.
At her toilet table she removed hairpins and bracelets, wrapping
   her hair in a white scarf:
Dressed in this light and convenient manner, she was ready for
   murder!
   Once she had found a merciless ax in the kitchen,
She ran as fast as she could to the small mourning chapel.
Lightly she opened the door and then sneaked inside,

And in front of the coffin she silently prayed to her dear deceased
husband:
  "While you were alive, good deeds were your gate, compassion
    your root,
And that's why I dare come to you now to borrow your brains.
Saving a single life surpasses building a seven-story stupa, and you
    also will benefit;
That's why I here by helping my new groom am also helping you."
  With quite some effort she managed to split the coffin's cover
    and lightly tossed it aside,
Then saw how Master Zhuang suddenly sat up, with a smile all
    over his face.
She was so scared that she collapsed on the ground and kowtowed,
    asking, "Don't kill me!"
And Master Zhuang said, "I've recovered from my illness and
    come back to life."
  The woman said, "When I heard you moaning, I came here to
    save you!"
But Master Zhuang replied, "If you want to save me, quickly ask
    someone to find a brain!
'Saving a single life surpasses building a seven-story stupa, and you
    also will benefit.'
'This is the way in which you are helping the new groom and also
    helping the old.'"
  When he said this, she was so ashamed she had no face at all to
    defend her behavior,
And in her desperation, she decided to commit suicide in order to
    find death.
With a white scarf around her neck[21] this woman went off to the
    underworld,
While Master Zhuang found the Way in the *Yellow Courtyard* and
    became an immortal.
  When you search the histories, Master Zhuang never played
    this trick on his wife;

21. This means that she committed suicide by hanging.

This is all a fictional fantasy as performed in the Pear Garden.[22]
Using this fantasy, I wrote a fantastic tale in a fantastic style
In order to awaken you all from the most fantastic dream of all
    eternity.
  Sir, don't love the spring flowers and autumn willows:
Those willow leaves and plum sprigs are dew on grass.
Here in my study I have ten thousand scrolls of the sages,
So I wrote these few lines of extraordinary writing.

Text published by the Wenshengtang in Shengjing in Guangxu 19
(1893)

[Zhang Shouchong, ed., *Manzu shuochang wenxue:*
Zidishu zhenben baizhong, 13–19]

22. Pear Garden has been a designation for the theater ever since the Tang emperor
Xuanzong had actors and actresses trained in the Pear Garden of the palace grounds.

4

One Precious Scroll

Baojuan (precious scrolls) may well constitute the most long-lived and most prolific genre of prosimetric storytelling. The genre's history can be convincingly traced back to the *yinyuan* (tales of causes and circumstances), one of the genres of *bianwen* (transformation text) literature of the ninth and tenth centuries discovered at Dunhuang, while the earliest texts calling themselves precious scrolls date from the fourteenth and fifteenth centuries. In many parts of China (Gansu, Hebei, Zhejiang) the genre is still practiced. In some places, it has even been recognized by the authorities as an "intangible cultural heritage."

Baojuan are religious texts, and under normal circumstances they are performed as a constituent part of a religious ritual. In origin, the precious scrolls are a genre of Buddhist preaching through pious stories and their lessons. From the fifteenth century on, new religions (often designated as "sectarian movements") also used the genre to spread their teaching by composing their own *baojuan*, but that does not alter the fact that the most popular precious scrolls throughout the centuries told well-known Buddhist tales such as the legend of the filial monk Mulian, who saved his mother from hell, and the legend of the pious princess Miaoshan, who achieved enlightenment, saved her father from a debilitating disease, and manifested herself as the bodhisattva Guanyin. Since the genre is often said to have appealed to women in particular, it comes as no surprise that many precious scrolls detail the steadfast piety of devout women who are eventually rewarded for their sufferings. Values that are strongly stressed in these texts are filial piety, strict vegetarianism, and the suppression of desire. From the eighteenth century on, we have many *baojuan* that adapt stories without a strong Buddhist nature, even though as a rule they open with an invocation of the buddhas and bodhisattvas and end with sending them off. By this time, even explicitly Daoist tales could be called *baojuan*.

The Precious Scroll of Master Zhuang's Butterfly Dream and Skeleton (*Zhuangzi diemeng kulou baojuan*) is one such Daoist *baojuan*. It is known from only a manuscript in the collection of the library of the Institute for Chinese Literature of the Academy of Social Sciences, Beijing. It starts with an adaptation of the story of Master Zhuang's meeting with the widow fanning her husband's grave and of his own widow's even stronger desire to be remarried. It also provides an explanation for the troubled relationship between Master Zhuang and his wife that results in her suicide. Master Zhuang's disappointment in human nature results in his decision to roam the world and his subsequent encounter with a skeleton. The precious scroll then includes in Master Zhuang's teachings to the district magistrate (and later also to his wife) a long text said to have been revealed through a planchette by the immortal Liu Qi. This text, which also circulates independently, emerged from one of the many spirit-writing cults that flourished in late imperial China (and continue to flourish in the present day). If earlier adaptations of the legend of Master Zhuang resulted in an urgent plea to reject the world and all its attachments (to begin with, the family), the morality preached to men and women in this spirit-writing text stresses moral life within family and society as the means to transcendence. It has been claimed that precious scrolls and spirit-writing texts are different genres that do not mix, but this quite likely rather late text that has been preserved only in manuscript proves that the rule has its exceptions.

The first part of the text, which narrates the two legends concerning Master Zhuang, is written in an alternation of prose and verse. The sections in verse are written in the standard seven-syllable ballad verse. The spirit-writing text is composed in lines of ten syllables. Such ten-syllable lines, while not uncommon in earlier prosimetric literature, tend to become more and more common over the course of the Qing dynasty (1644–1911), especially in texts from northern China. The ten-syllable lines tend to have a strongly marked tripartite structure of three, three, and four syllables (more rarely three, four, and three syllables), which I have tried to suggest by typographical means in my translation.

The Precious Scroll of Master Zhuang's Butterfly Dream and Skeleton

Newly composed by the Study of Nourishing Nature [Fengcao]

To the tune "Xijiangyue" [West River Moon]:
Status and wealth are a single night's spring dream;
Merits and fame are floating clouds of one moment.
Even your own flesh and blood right before your eyes are not true:
Love and affection turn into enmity, result in hatred!

Don't lock your neck in shackles of gold;
Don't tie your body with chains of jade.
A pure heart, free of desire, transcends the mortal dust,
And sights of pleasure are your due share.

Light and shadow are like an arrow, faster than a shuttle,
But who thinks of reciting Amitabha Buddha's name?
All day long feelings of love fill them with affection;
Wine, sex, money, and rage: these four wear them out.
    It isn't sex that seduces people: they seduce themselves;
It isn't desires that wear them out: they do so themselves.
Constantly occupied by the myriad affairs of this world,
Their hearts are filled with greed and lust without any rest.
    Let me recite the scroll of Master Zhuang of the Zhou:
The fanning of the grave had the wife reopen the coffin.
Outside the city of Luoyang he lamented the skeleton—
He personally preached to us songs in praise of filial piety.

Now tell that during the Warring States period of the Zhou dynasty
there lived a lofty noble by the name of Zhuang Zhou, also known as
Xiu. He hailed from the town of Meng in the state of Song and at one
moment served as a gentleman clerk in this age of the Seven States.

Later he achieved the Way and became known as the Realized Person of Southern Florescence. His teacher was the founder of Daoism. This was Li Er, also known as Boyang. After his mother had carried him for eighty-one years, he was born under a pear tree, and that is why he is called the Old Master. This Master Zhuang had been a white butterfly that was born when chaos first parted. Feeding on the hundred flowers, it had obtained eternal life by practicing self-cultivation. One day, when it was roaming by Jasper Pond and stealing nectar from the flowers of the peaches of longevity, it was killed by the *luan* bird serving in front of the throne of the Queen Mother that caught it in its beak. The butterfly's true spiritual nature was reborn [as Master Zhuang] here in the world below, where he had the good fortune to be fully instructed by the Old Master in the secret message of the five thousand words of the *Classic of the Way and Its Virtue*. Thereupon, he was able to multiply his body and to change his shape; his supernatural powers were large and extensive, and his magical powers were unlimited. When later he visited Qi, Qi's chancellor, Tian Zong, admired his talents and gave him his daughter as wife. Husband and wife lived in harmony and respected each other like guests. Who could have known that King Wei of Chu would want to invite him to become his chancellor? He stubbornly refused the offer and did not accept it. Together with his wife he lived in hiding on Mount Hua, enjoying a free and easy life of liberty.

One day as he walked through the abandoned fields, he came across a beautiful woman who was dressed in the white of mourning. With a fan made of banana leaves, she was fanning her husband's recent grave in order to dry it since she was eager to marry some other man. She said that her husband had been a scholar famous for his teaching and had loved her exceedingly well. But before he had died of consumption, he told her on his deathbed that she should wait until the earth of his grave had dried if she wanted to marry someone else. But now after almost a hundred days, the earth of his grave was still not dry! When Master Zhuang saw this woman so faithless as this, he was truly amazed. On her behalf, he dried the earth of the grave with her fan and then took the fan home with him, where he told his wife what had happened. When his wife heard this story, she reviled that woman as absolutely and totally wrong. When she had reviled her in this way, Master Zhuang heaved a sigh and recited the following four lines:

"Only predestined mutual enemies[1] will be brought together;
When enemies are brought together, when comes the end?
If you know that upon death all love and duty will be gone,
You should do away with attachments while you are alive!"

And he also said,

"While you're alive each and every one declares her love,
But once you are dead, they are all eager to fan your grave.
When painting a dragon or tiger, you can't paint the bones;
I may know hairstyle and face, but I don't know the heart."

When his wife had heard this, she replied to him as follows:

"This type of person is really rarely found in this world.
Even though we may equally belong to the human race,
Smart and intelligent and stupid and foolish are different.
    Don't treat all women of the world with hairpins and skirts
As if they would not be worth even half a hair. As for me,
I fully understand the purport of the Odes and the Rites:
Loyal to a single man all my life, I will never betray him!"
    Hearing this, Zhuang Zhou couldn't suppress a smile:
"Don't make such an excessive claim in such clear words.
In case I would now pass away, how could you ever
Remain such a faithful widow for the rest of your life?
    With your looks like a flower and face like the moon,
How could you keep it up till three or five springtimes?
It is women who have no feeling of morality and duty;
From birth their nature is that of willow floss, of water."
    Upon these words, his wife was filled with angry rage:
"A woman's determination surpasses that of a man—

---

1. Lovers and marriage partners are often considered to be archenemies (*yuanjia*), people who still have to settle a score from a previous life.

Don't mention three years, don't mention five either:
For all my life, till my dying day, I will live all alone!"
   She thereupon snatched the fan from Master Zhuang,
And she tore the fan to shreds, which scattered all over.
"You are presently in good health, you're still alive,
But you haven't deserved such a fine woman like me!"
   Master Zhuang immediately apologized with a smile:
"There is no need at all to fly into such a terrible rage.
Throughout past and present many were loyal and true,
Leaving behind them a fine reputation for all eternity.
   Only if you display the mettle of women like these
Can you be considered a determined and loyal wife."
When by and by more than ten days had passed,
The master contracted an illness that affected his body.
   Time and again, that woman voiced her complaints:
"Why did you go for a walk? And why fan that grave?"
But with every day his illness became more serious
And he started to spit out fresh blood from his mouth.
   Master Zhuang thereupon addressed her as follows:
"My disease is such that very soon I will have to die.
But you have torn that fan of some days ago to pieces—
Otherwise, it could have helped you to fan the grave!"
   His wife immediately replied to him as follows:
"My master, there is no need at all to be worried.
In case you would suffer the unpredictable, I will
Stick to a vegetarian diet, practice self-cultivation.
   During the day I will recite the name of Amitabha,
And at night the Diamond Sutra to save your soul!
If I would ever waver in my chaste determination,
May a cruel death immediately end my rotten life!"
   Master Zhuang thereupon spoke to his wife, saying,
"A couple's attachment may be as deep as the ocean,
But husband and wife are like birds sharing a grove:
When the Great End comes, they fly off and away.
   A man depends on his fame to establish himself;
For a woman chastity surpasses self-cultivation.

Your husband treated you with love and affection,
Please do not ruin my good name and reputation."
     His disease became more serious with every day:
Master Zhuang eventually passed from this world.
The corpse was encoffined and laid out for mourning;
Some monks and priests were hired to save the soul.
     The farmers living behind and in front of the mountain
Also came to mourn him and offer their condolences.
There was also a prince, the king of Chu's third son:
He had traveled a thousand miles to visit the master.

Now tell that Master Zhuang had divided his body and hidden his shape and that his spirit had left his body to manifest a transformation: he had assumed a magical body apart from his body in order to test his wife, Madam Tian. She was actually the green *luan* bird that had been reborn in this world in order to pay back its debt to Master Zhuang. Now today their affinity had come to an end, and their feud would be dissolved as the karma of their earlier lives was paid off. That's why as soon as she saw how exceptionally talented this prince was and what a handsome figure he cut, she immediately abandoned her determination of earlier days and was occupied by the evil notions of lust and love and improper desire. She tried to lead him on in many ways and displayed her love to him a hundred times. The prince rebuffed her repeatedly and his servant warned her off a number of times, but she did not come to her senses at all. In the end she made a scandal of herself and acted against all morality: she even arranged for flowers and candles in the wedding room and the exchange of the wedding toast. But the very moment they were to undo their sashes and take off their clothes, the prince coughed up sputum and complained of a chest pain. Yet even after he had died, she did not show any remorse: she went so far as to open the coffin to take out the brain, concerned only to save her new groom in her desire for the joys of fish and water.[2] Fortunately, Master Zhuang was an immortal, so he was able to return from death and come back to life. Only then did she realize the nature of her mistake, and said with a sigh, "Smart and intelligent all my

2. The expression "fish and water" is a common image for happy sex.

life, I was deluded for just a moment. Earlier I cursed that widow who fanned the grave, but now I have been the wife that opened the coffin. How could I have the face to confront the people of this world?" Eventually she hanged herself from a high rafter and died after committing suicide. What a laugh!

> Master Zhuang now was the one who had the last laugh:
> He encoffined his wife in the casket she'd opened before.
> He thereupon put the torch to their straw-thatched cottage
> And left for the Zhongnan Mountains to practice religion.
>   When the elixir had been completed, his virtue perfected,[3]
> He roamed on clouds and mists to deliver human beings.
> One day he arrived in this manner in the area of Luoyang,
> Where he discovered a skeleton in an abandoned grave.
>   He saved him and that very moment he returned to life:
> A pile of bleached bones had become a man once again!
> But on his left side the skeleton was missing three ribs,
> So these had been replaced with three willow twigs.
>   Once the immortal elixir was placed on the dried bones,
> He grew a skin, acquired flesh, and was filled with energy,
> And then he addressed his benefactor in these words:
> "Now be so kind as to give me my luggage and money!"

Master Zhuang replied, "You were a pile of bleached bones, without any clothes or luggage or umbrella!" But that man said, "That's because you and your acolyte stole my stuff." And he dragged him to the district office of Luoyang. That district magistrate was She Cheng, also known as Kexin. He hailed from Jingzhou in Guangxi and had passed the metropolitan examinations in the *renxu* year. He had just opened the gate to admit claimants. These two people both claimed they had been wronged, and there was no end to their dispute. When the district magistrate heard that Master Zhuang called himself a divine immortal who had turned bleached bones into a man, [he asked,] "What proof do you have?"

---

3. The "elixir" refers to the elixir of immortality.

Master Zhuang replied, "There are three willow twigs that fill out his left side. Now we have come to this pass, it has to be done this way. If I show no humaneness, it's because he lacks all decency." He told the servants to bring some pure water and spat out a mouthful of water on Wu Gui's body. The latter's skin and flesh turned to ashes again, and inside his clothes they found a pile of bleached bones and three willow twigs. Master Zhuang said, "Your Excellency, look at this man! He was originally an evil criminal, and after I had saved him, he has now turned into dried bones once again."

When the district magistrate saw this, he exclaimed in amazement, "You are indeed a divine immortal! Your disciple would like to abandon his office and follow you in order to practice religion." But Master Zhuang replied, "When it comes to practicing religion, it doesn't matter whether you remain a layperson or become a monk. Since ancient times there have been many people who achieved enlightenment as members of society. If you enter on the road of right practice, you have to treat loyalty and filial piety as taught by the Confucians as your root. As an official, you have to exhaust loyalty; as a son, you have to exhaust filial piety. If you make this your basis, entering the Way and practicing religion will be easy! In the Three Teachings, there are no sages and saints, immortals, buddhas and bodhisattvas who were disloyal or unfilial! In our Daoism, there is a major disciple of Patriarch Lü by the name of Liu Qi. He is the Perfected Person for Expanding the Teaching. At the order of his teacher, he descended into the *luan* board[4] in Wu and taught a 'Song Exhorting to Filial Piety,' which is extremely detailed and pertinent. Since ancient times it is said, Lechery is the leader of the ten thousand sins; / Filial piety is the first of the hundred virtues.

> Your Excellency
>> And all you others,
>>> Please lend me your ear and listen:
> The Perfected Person Liu
>> Left us this message
>>> That I will now urge on all of you.

4. The *luan* board is the spirit-writing tablet.

Let's not discuss the present,
       Let's not talk about the past:
              None of that will bring any benefit at all.
There is one thing
       That is extremely important,
              A value you all have to practice.
Now let each of you think
       From where
              You received this physical body:
Who among you
       Did not receive his life
              From his father and his mother?
That body of yours,
       The seed of your parents,
              Originated from one small lump:
One chunk of flesh,
       A mouthful of breath,
              And one drop of blood and seed.
They separately
       Gave these to you
              So this body of yours could be formed,
But how can you
       Consider them as two,
              Separate them from each other?
Now let me tell
       How your parents
              Raised you from this beginning:
For ten months [your mother]
       Carried you in her womb,
              Filled with worry, anxious at heart.
In her belly
       She felt a weight
              Of a hundred pounds, a thousand ounces:
At the moment of birth
       She suffered
              Ten thousand hardships, a thousand pains.

Once you were born,
        Had received your life,
                Your chance of survival was very slim,
And for three years
        She carried you around,
                Taking good care of you in every way.
Cold or warm,
        Fed or hungry:
                Not the slightest mistake was allowed,
And when you fell ill,
        She would blame herself
                For having been careless in your care.
She would far prefer
        To substitute for you
                And suffer your pains with her body—
At such a moment
        She wouldn't dare slacken
                And in the slightest be unconcerned.
She looked after your food,
        She looked after your clothes,
                Happy to go hungry and freezing herself,
And once you grew older,
        She hired a teacher
                To teach you to read books and essays,
And when you had become an adult,
        She invited a matchmaker
                To find you a bride for your marriage,
Hoping that you
        Would revive the family fortune
                And bring glory to your family home.
If you resembled
        A human being only a little,
                Your parents were overfilled with joy,
And if you didn't show progress,
        They were overcome by grief,
                Their innards wracked by great pain.

At the moment of death,
    They didn't close their eyes
        Since they were still worried about you:
This is the way in which
    Your father and mother
        Treated you with love and affection!
To consider it well:
    This body of yours
        Is your parents' branches and leaves:
These branches and leaves
    Have been born from
        Your parents, who are trunk and root.
If you tend them well,
    These roots will give rise
        To flourishing branches and leaves,
And later you yourself
    Will naturally have
        Fine sons and filial grandsons too.
If you in this life
    Enjoy any blessing,
        It's due to your parents' protection;
If you are smart and intelligent,
    If you are capable and skilled,
        It's due to your parents' instruction.
Which single thing,
    Which single quality
        Was not the concern of your parents?
So how could you treat
    Your father and mother
        As outsiders, as strangers and aliens?
Just think of it:
    For every day
        That your body grew and increased,
The physical bodies
    Of your father and mother
        Aged and weakened one more day!

If you do not
      Hurry up and
            Serve them filially as soon as you can,
You will, once
      Your parents have died,
            Regret that you can't do so anymore.
Alas,
      The people of this world
            Do not show any understanding at all,
Because they
      Have darkened their hearts
            And turn their backs on duty and love.
You may have raised them,
      You may have nurtured them,
            But they don't remember that at all;
You may have instructed them,
      You may have found them a bride,
            But to them it all seems so simple.
They do not remember
      That the crow feeds its parents,
            The lamb kneels down to suckle:
You may be a human being,
      But you do not live up to
            Running beasts and flying birds!
Those unfilial acts
      Are way too many
            To allow me to enumerate them,
So I will take
      Only the most common
            And list them for you, so listen.
When your parents
      Ask for something
            That doesn't cost you anything,
You are still too stingy
      To give it to them,
            Valuing money over your parents.

When your parents
    Want something done
        That is easy for you to perform,
You come up with excuses
    And don't want to go,
        Saying that you're unable to do it.
But when you see
    Wealthy and powerful people,
        You flatter them in a hundred ways;
Even if they curse you,
    Even if they beat you,
        You most happily suffer the abuse.
But when your parents
    Curse you but once,
        You talk back to them most angrily,
And if your parents
    Hit you but once,
        You rage at them with bulging eyes.
You love only
    Your wife and concubines,
        Beautiful as flowers, pretty as jade;
You treasure
    Your sons and daughters
        As precious jewels and rare pearls.
When your wife and concubines die,
    Your sons and daughters pass away,
        You weep in a heartrending manner,
But when your parents die,
    You don't shed a tear,
        And you weep without any emotion.
Why don't these people
    Compare
        Wives, concubines, sons, daughters
Together with
    Wealth and glory
        To their father and mother for once?

Heaven will not accept them,
  Earth will not carry them:
    While alive they'll suffer execution,
And upon death
  They will go to hell
    To suffer most gruesome tortures:
Dismembered by saws,
  Burned to ashes by fire,
    Pulverized by millstones and mortars,
They'll be reborn as birds,
  They'll be reborn as beasts,
    And never again as a human being!
So I urge all of you
  To practice filial piety
    For all the rewards it will bring you:
While alive you'll do well,
  Upon death you'll do well,
    And you'll not suffer any hardship.
During your lifetime
  People will respect you
    And you'll be decorated by officials;
You will enjoy wealth,
  You'll enjoy long life,
    And have many sons and grandsons.
At the moment of death
  Immortal maidens and lads
    Will surround you, holding banners,
And escort you
  As you see King Yama,
    Who'll welcome you most friendly.
When your merits are great,
  You can even
    Become an immortal or a buddha;
If your merits are smaller,
  You will be reborn
    To high position and rich income.

Now filial piety
        To your father and mother,
                I tell you, consists of two things,
And these two things
        Definitely are not
                Difficult to do or hard to practice.
The first thing is
        That you must make
                Your father and mother feel at ease,
And the second thing is
        That in their old age
                You must feed your father and mother.
If you are a good person
        And do good deeds,
                You will not bring down any disaster;
By teaching your wife and concubines,
        And teaching your sons and daughters,
                You'll ensure your family's fortune.
If you on your side
        Serve your grandparents
                And feed them in a filial manner,
Then your younger brothers and sisters
        Will on their side
                Treat you with honor and respect.
Make sure that your parents
        Each day they are alive
                Are without a worry for that day,
And one cup of tea
        Or one cup of water
                Will fill their minds with pleasure.
According to your strength
        And depending on your wealth—
                Spare them from hunger and cold;
Support them while they walk
        And make them sit safely,
                Don't leave them alone and lonely.

If they call you,
Answer them quickly
As soon as you hear their request,
And if by chance
They give you an order,
Rise immediately to your feet.
If your parents
Are in the wrong,
Explain it in a gentle manner;
Don't use coarse language,
And don't fly into a rage
So that you anger your parents.
In case your parents
In a moment of passion
Raise their fists and strike you,
You must always
Show a smile on your face—
Never raise your voice in anger!
There are good relatives
Or good friends and neighbors
You can ask to talk them around
So your parents
Will repent of their ways
And come to a different opinion.
And if unfortunately
Both your old parents
At the age of one hundred pass away,
Give them a fine coffin,
Give them a fine shroud,
Build them a sturdy and solid tomb!
Exert all your strength
And consider durability—
Far more important than appearance.
Be filled with sadness
Since in this life
You'll not be able to meet them again.

At each season
>>And on their death day
>>>>Offer the proper prescribed sacrifices,
Regretting that your parents
>>Have departed forever
>>>>And that you'll not see them return.
For a son
>>These actions are
>>>>The duties of filial piety and obedience.
On no account
>>Ignore my words
>>>>As of no concern to you at all!
Alas, in this world
>>There are unfilial people
>>>>Who commit the following mistake:
They say, 'My parents
>>Don't love me at all,
>>>>Despite all the filial piety on my part.'
If you say this,
>>You commit a blunder
>>>>That you cannot explain away.
How can you
>>Competitively
>>>>Compare yourself with your parents?
You may be compared
>>To a grass or weed
>>>>That has been created by Heaven:
Moistened by spring rain,
>>Killed off by autumn frost—
>>>>Who would dare to show anger?
Your parents raised you,
>>So even if they kill you,
>>>>You should still accept your fate:
Throughout this world
>>There is no person
>>>>Who doesn't come from parents!

The most stupid people
>Still understand they must
>>Revere the Buddha, serve the gods,
But you fail to grasp
>That your father and mother
>>Are the highest divinities of all.
Only if you revere them
>Will buddhas and immortals
>>Be pleased by your sacrifices
And from the sky
>Protect and support you,
>>Increasing blessings and longevity.
If you have a son
>And want him to be filial,
>>You have to set an example yourself:
Filiality repays filiality;
>Disobedience repays disobedience—
>>This is a rule that always applies.

To the tune "Langtaosha" [Waves Washing the Sand]:
>In this world there are many people
>Who talk all kinds of nonsense:
>They want to study the Way and practice religion
>But experience no feelings of filial piety—
>What kind of religion is that?

>You are the people's magistrate
>And your age is still young.
>If you're determined to study the Way and practice religion,
>This 'Song of Filial Piety' provides you with guidance—
>Make sure to follow that road!

>Practice only with a proper mind
>As taught by the Sage Confucius.
>Your Excellency, don't look for any other way at all;
>First treat your father and mother really well:
>That's practicing true religion!

The affairs of this world depend on your actions:
You may have the loftiest talents,
But if you treat your father and mother without respect,
You may go to Zhongnan Mountains and study the Way,
But immortals and buddhas won't come!"

Master Zhuang said, "Your Excellency, each and every word of the 'Song of Filial Piety' pierces the bone; each and every phrase penetrates the heart. If people have heard it and still do not repent and filially serve their parents, they are no different from birds and beasts and upon death fall into hell. Even if a thousand buddhas would appear in this world, they would not be able to save them from there!"

Even before he had finished speaking, he saw two servant girls enter from behind the curtain. They greeted him and said, "We two have been ordered by our mistress to ask you, Great Immortal, how a woman should practice religion." Master Zhuang said, "While still at home a woman should filially serve her parents and, following her marriage, a woman should filially serve her parents-in-law and not disobey her husband. As far as threefold obedience and fourfold virtue are concerned, all depends on her true intention and not on the outer traces. That's why the Buddha said that a woman, in practicing religion, will achieve the Good Fruit by way of her eightfold reverence. First, she must revere Heaven and Earth. Second, she must revere the Three Jewels.[5] Third, she must revere the divinities. Fourth, she must revere her father and mother. Fifth, she must revere her parents-in-law. Sixth, she must revere her husband. Seventh, she must revere the poor and indigent, the weak and the old. Eighth, she must revere orphans and widowers, the maimed and the handicapped. Once upon a time, the Perfected Person Liu composed a 'Song to Urge Women on to Filial Piety.' I remember it very well. Indeed: If we would only strictly adhere to the personal teaching of Master Liu, / Each and everyone would be seated in a house of purple-gold.

5. The Three Jewels are the Buddha, the *sangha* (the community of monks and nuns), and the dharma (the teachings of the Buddha).

Today I have here
    A story
        That dates back to ancient times,
I will tell it
    To all of you here,
        So please listen, each and every one!
The Perfected Person Liu
    Was originally a tree,
        Generated by Heaven, fed by Earth:
At the beginning of time
    Heaven and Earth
        Created it by their seed and breath.
Down here on earth
    Was planted
        This one willow tree,
While up in the sky
    Was displayed
        The Willow Asterism.
After some
    Tens of thousands of years,
        His spirit fixed, his breath gathered,
He had the good luck,
    During the Tang dynasty,
        Of meeting with Master Lü Dongbin.[6]
This master
    Took pity on him
        For his sincere study of the Way,
And for that reason
    Delivered him
        So he could become an immortal.
How could it be possible
    That a mere tree
        Would have such a stroke of luck?
Only because

---

6. Here designated by his celestial title, Fuyou Dijun.

His spiritual heart
    Never obscured its original root.
He had no father
    And also no mother,
        So whom did he filially serve?
In the morning he bowed to Heaven,
    At evening he bowed to Earth,
        Repaying them for their favors.
His mind was determined,
    His ambition was fixed,
        He firmly held on to his origin,
And because of his
    Single-minded devotion,
        He moved the sages and deities.
When he met with his master,
    He promptly treated him as
        His stern father and doting mother—
For thousands of years
    He never once slackened
        In his perfect filial piety and respect.
Once he was an immortal,
    His teacher ordered him
        To amass merits to a high degree
And wanted him
    To urge the common people
        To filially serve both their parents.
If there are people
    Who can exhaust filial piety,
        He will come and deliver them—
Whether a man
    Or a woman,
        He will make them immortals!
He has converted
    Many thousands
        Of both male and female persons,
And at present they live

A life of eternal happiness
          On the eastern island of Penglai.
There are also men
          Who have been reborn
                    To high office and noble titles,
And then there are women
          Who have all become
                    Titled ladies of the highest rank.
Because he amassed
          These many merits
                    By urging people to filial piety,
He therefore later
          Was awarded the title of
                    Perfected Lord of Expanded Teaching.
At the behest of his teacher,
          He till this very moment
                    Preaches his sermons to women;
Descending in the *luan* brush,[7]
          He expounds and explains
                    The *Classic Book of Filial Piety*.[8]
Even though you
          May have received
                    The physical body of a woman,
Your father and mother
          Have suffered the same[9]
                    In feeding you and raising you.
While in the womb,
          While still in the belly,
                    The baby's sex cannot be distinguished,
And at your birth
          Your mother suffered

7. The *luan* brush is the spirit-writing tablet.

8. For a study and translation of this text, see Rosemont and Ames, *Chinese Classic of Family Reverence*.

9. The same as in raising a boy.

The same unbearable hardships.
Carrying you in her arms,
Your mother never once said,
'A daughter has no importance.'
Feeding you at her breast,
You mother never
Held back in the least.
You women
Will later
All have that experience,
And once you women
Have had that experience,
It doesn't mean you'll forget.
Who can say
That people don't want
To feed and raise girls?
Your father and mother
Treat their daughters
With even greater care!
Combing your hair
And binding your feet,
They do not shirk effort;
Teaching you how to cook,
Teaching you needlework,
They are so very attentive!
If they are too strict,
They consider that you
Are a temporary guest,[10]
But if they pamper you,
They are also afraid
You may end a failure.
Apart from you for a moment,
They are afraid

10. Because a girl leaves her parents' home upon marriage, her parents have to prepare her well for her life with her parents-in-law and her husband.

That you've lost your honor;
If something goes wrong,
They are afraid
You're hiding something.
When choosing a groom,
They want him to be
A fitting partner in talent and looks;
When selecting a family,
They consider its wealth,
Afraid you might suffer poverty.
Following the engagement,
They fret and worry
How to provide you with a dowry,
But on the day of the wedding,
Despite all their efforts,
You are still not happy at heart.
They can't let you go,
They can't let you stay:
They really have a terrible time:
With a broken heart,
Eyes filled with tears,
They see you off at the gate.
When over there
Husband and wife live in harmony
And parents-in-law are happy at heart,
Then your father and mother
Will show on their face
Quite a glow of satisfaction,
But if something goes wrong,
They'll be filled with vexation
As soon as they learn of the case,
And this will only increase
For the rest of their lives—
Worry and sorrow without end!
From your birth
Your marriage partner

Has been fully predetermined,
So how can you
       Blame your parents
              When things do not work out?
When you have a good life,
       You will thereupon say
              That it's due to your own good fortune,
But when life is hard,
       You will curse your parents
              Because their eyes have been blind;
You will curse your parents
       For marrying you
              To a family that is absolutely wrong,
And your parents-in-law
       You will treat
              As the archenemies you want to kill!
When dealing with your parents-in-law,
       You will say that they are
              The father and mother of someone else,
But when it comes to your own parents,
       You will say again
              That by marrying you left that home.
This would mean
       That you women
              Do not belong to either side,
Which would completely
       Free you from filial piety—
              It doesn't stick to your person at all!
Who would know
       That you women
              Have two sets of father and mother,
And both you have
       To serve filially
              With utmost respect and sincerity.
In the first part of your life
       Your physical body

Is fed and raised by your parents;
In the second part of your life
You rely on your husband
In order to live, till your final day.
Your parents-in-law,
By feeding your husband,
Were actually raising you too.
The heavenly ordained couple
Of husband and wife
Must be counted as one person.
You have always been
The bride of the son
Of your parents-in-law
But were temporarily
Lodged at your mother's place
To grow up into an adult woman,
And only after your marriage
Did you come home
To the place to which you belong:
Your parents-in-law
Actually are
The two parents that gave you life.
In offering tea
And presenting presents,[11]
They incurred many expenditures;
In inviting matchmakers
And entertaining guests,
They undertook much hard work.
They love their son
And love his wife
Without any distinction in kind
Since they hope that you,
Husband and wife,
Will provide for them in old age.

11. Offering tea and presenting presents are two steps in the engagement procedures.

So how is it possible
  That a good lad,
    Who originally was a filial son,
Will not care at all
  For his father and mother
    Once he has been married to you?
Even though you
  May not sow dissension
    Between flesh and blood with your words,
It will be because
  He dotes on you
    And so damages his ambition and energy.
You should therefore
  Speak to your husband
    And explain to him in clearest terms,
'If my parents-in-law
  Brought me here
    To assist and support you, my master,
That was first of all
  Because they wanted me
    To help you in serving your parents,
So how can you,
  Because of me,
    Be remiss in feelings of filial piety?'
This is the way
  In which women
    Should try to speak to their husbands;
This is the way
  To love your husband
    And help him fulfill his filial duties.
How can you
  Flaunt your power
    And treat everyone without respect?
Eventually
  You don't pay
    Any attention to your parents-in-law!

Any money
>   That their son
>   >   Will make, you will hide at your place
To buy clothes
>   And have food
>   >   While keeping that couple in the dark.
Concerned about appearances,
>   You are obsessed
>   >   By the clothes and jewels you'll have,
So when you have cash,
>   You only make plans
>   >   For the profit of your own little family,
Or you have your mother
>   Or younger brother and sister
>   >   Lend the money out to gain interest,
Afraid that when your parents-in-law
>   Get their hands on it,
>   >   His brothers will all divide it evenly.
You say that it was you,
>   Your diligent spinning and weaving,
>   >   Together with your colorful embroidery—
But who could know
>   That by hiding this money
>   >   You're a witch that calls down disaster!
You are unwilling to lend
>   Your parents-in-law
>   >   A single yarn, half a grain of rice;
Among sisters-in-law
>   These trifling matters
>   >   Fill your eyes with a furious hatred.
Abusing your husband,
>   You're 'a chicken that crows at dawn,'
>   >   A woman who wants to be the boss,
And when all matters
>   Mostly go wrong,
>   >   It is all because of your meddling.

Just have a look
    In the temple
        At the hell for pulling out tongues:
The majority there
    Are all women
        Who suffer those atrocious tortures!
And then there are
    Those foul-mouthed women
        Who loudly commandeer their men,
Each day causing
    Their parents-in-law
        To have no moment of peaceful rest.
If her parents-in-law
    Revile her but once,
        She returns to them their curses tenfold;
If they beat her once,
    She immediately threatens
        To wet her pants, hanging from a rope!
This kind of person
    Seeks her own
        Punishments in the underworld courts,
And if she doesn't die,
    She definitely will be
        Struck dead by thunder and lightning!
So I urge you,
    Women in the inner apartments,
        To listen to your parents and obey them:
If they say one thing,
    You do that one thing
        Without displaying any nasty temper.
If you claim
    That taking care
        Of parents is not your responsibility,
Your regret
    Will come too late
        Once you have been married off.

While still at home
  For those many days
    You may have lacked all filial respect,
But now when you're called
  To serve tea or water,
    You'll have to give it all your attention.
In case your husband
  Is traveling abroad
    In order to make some money by trade,
Your old parents-in-law
  Will expect that you
    In his place will take care of their needs.
These old people
  May not need much food,
    But the dishes have to meet their taste,
And their worn clothes
  Have to be carefully washed
    And repaired in a neat and nice manner.
Don't believe
  The words of the vulgar,
    Who argue you'll never be treated fairly—
As a daughter-in-law,
  You are their daughter,
    And they'll not compare you with anyone.
At all times
  Serve them their
    Tea and soup with your own hands, and
Since they have difficulty walking,
  What's the problem
    In supporting them in rising and walking?
If there is something
  That you have bought,
    Think how it might benefit the elderly,
So promptly give it
  To your parents-in-law
    When they ask for it, without any delay!

All that matters is
        That your parents-in-law
                Are pleased with you and happy at heart;
It's none of your business
        If later they give to others
                What earlier they had received from you.
If you respect your husband's brothers,
        Love his sisters, and
                Live in harmony with your sisters-in-law,
Your parents-in-law will be pleased
        Because this daughter-in-law
                Really knows how to be a capable person.
If you help your husband,
        Instruct your children,
                And work hard at the household chores,
Your parents-in-law will be pleased
        Because this daughter-in-law
                Manages to bring glory to their family!
If you filially serve your parents-in-law,
        Your own father and mother
                Will also be pleased with you and happy,
And later,
        When you have a daughter-in-law,
                She will also serve you in a filial manner.
Moreover,
        If you, on behalf of your husband,
                Serve his parents in a most filial manner,
Your husband too
        Will show filial respect
                To his mother-in-law and father-in-law.
I cannot relate in full
        Women's duties
                Of filial piety and of obedience too
But hope that you, milady,
        Will follow this model
                And uphold it in the most careful manner.

Today I've expounded
> Only one-half
>> Of the *Book of Filial Piety for Women*,
But that good breath
> Has already been transmitted to
>> Bodhisattva Guanyin of the Southern Sea.
She summons me
> To give me a reward
>> And to award me the title of buddha,
So let me tell
> That bodhisattva's life
>> As yet a further inspiration to you all.
This bodhisattva
> Was born as
>> The daughter of King Miaozhuang,
But from her birth
> She was determined
>> To devote herself to a life of religion.
When the bodhisattva's father
> Saw that his daughter
>> Loved the Way with all her heart,
He subjected her
> To hundreds of hardships
>> Because he wanted her to marry.
Who could have known
> That this bodhisattva's
>> Mind was as firm as iron and stone:
Her only desire was
> To obtain the Way
>> And then to deliver both her parents.
At a later date
> Her father developed a disease,
>> Evil ulcers covering all of his body,
But this bodhisattva
> Donated her hands and eyes
>> To save her father from his ordeal.

Because of this,
>She moved
>>The Jade Emperor, the god of heaven:
Bathed in a golden light,
>She was seated on a lotus throne,
>>Manifesting myriad transformations.
Her thousand eyes
>Widely observe
>>The ten directions and the three worlds;[12]
Her thousand hands
>Uphold and support
>>The sun, the moon, and the moving stars.
In the school of the Buddha,
>This bodhisattva's
>>Supernatural powers are most extensive;
Throughout eternity
>She manifests her compassion,
>>Saving and delivering people on earth.
If only milady
>Can practice filial piety,
>>There is no need to honor the gods,
And after a hundred years
>You will be able
>>To walk into the gate of the Buddha.

You, milady, and you, servant girls, now listen carefully:
When it comes to practicing religion, it's all in the heart.
A man can by practice become a duke or a marquis,
A woman can by practice become Guanyin herself!
>When born in a rich family, cherish your blessings!
When your blessings are used up, you're still a man.
If you are born in a poor family, a lowly profession,
You didn't tend the field of blessings in earlier lives.
>Your Excellency and milady, please listen carefully:

12. The three worlds of present, past, and future.

In this world there are few who live to a hundred.
From infancy to old age is just like a single dream:
Once in the coffin, the lid is sealed, a tomb erected.
  Even a loving husband and wife can't change places;
Young sons and infant grandsons cannot follow you.
Good fields and fine houses turn into a spring dream;
Embroidered brocade won't cling to your body then.
  Inside the grave, alas, the situation is even worse:
Your seven organs, swelling, turn purple and black.
Blood flows from the corpse as skin and flesh rot
And red and green maggots bore through the bones.
  Once blood and flesh are gone, the skeleton remains:
Each and every one will exhibit this kind of shape,
While your single soul will follow your evil karma
As demon escorts take you in chains to King Yama.
  The Two Judges of Good and Evil examine your deeds;
The Three Corpses[13] report on your actions without fail.
If you practiced the ten virtues, heaven will be yours;
Loyal vassals and filial sons become gods upon death.
  If you practiced in earlier lives, you now enjoy blessing;
But if in this life you stumble, your sins will be heavy.
You may fall into the three pathways of hungry ghosts,
Or you may sink into hell with its unbearable torments.
  In this world there are a million kinds of gradations,
But each will be reborn in accordance with his sins.
Only those who sincerely practiced great filial piety
Ascend, free from karma and sin, to the Pure Land!"

Master Zhuang said, "Your Excellency, 'The sea of suffering stretches endlessly with its waves of karma, / But the bank is there when you turn around, so don't worry.' Husband and wife, you should follow these two songs of filial piety. That is the critical juncture in the practice of religion.

13. The Three Corpses are gods inhabiting the body. They are parasites that cause disease, invite other disease-causing agents into the body, and report their host's crimes and sins to heaven so as to shorten his life span.

Without filial piety, you may practice all you want and blindly refine your body, but you will be unable to realize the Way even if you practice for ten thousand generations." Then Master Zhuang pointed and said, "Over there two immortals are coming this way. You should follow them." When the district magistrate turned around to have a look, he saw only how the Immortal Zhuang rose up into the sky on colored clouds and slowly disappeared. The district magistrate knelt down and kowtowed, but the great immortal never looked back, having left for the Zhongnan Mountains.

Indeed:

> When the whale has freed itself from the golden hook,
> It flaps its tail and wags its head, never to come back!

> The Precious Scroll of Zhuang Zhou has been recited:
> You who live in this world should understand it well.
> Filial piety has always been the root of humaneness,
> And the practice of religion dates back to antiquity.
>   Filial piety is the method of entrance for all practice;
> Don't say that it'll ever be obliterated or annihilated.
> May all of you, having heard this, once you are home
> Serve and please your father and mother most filially.
>   I urge you all to practice virtue and to do good deeds
> So that your sons and grandsons may become officials
> Who will bring peace to country and people and state,
> And establish a reputation that will last for all eternity!

5

One Modern Parody

Lu Xun (pseudonym of Zhou Shuren, 1881–1936) is widely recognized as the greatest writer of modern Chinese literature in the years following the Literary Revolution of 1917 and the May Fourth Movement of 1919. His fame as a writer of fiction is based on two collections of short stories that he published in the 1920s. Many of these stories have a strong autobiographical element and draw on his youth in Shaoxing or his experiences as a teacher in Beijing. After he left Beijing in 1926, he published mostly essays and columns, which were feared for their mordant wit. Throughout the years, he was also extremely productive as a translator. During the final years of his life, when he was living in Shanghai, he returned to the genre of the short story with a collection of retellings of ancient myths and legends, *Gushi xinbian* (*Old Tales Retold*). The last story in that collection "Qisi" (Raising the Dead), is his retelling of the legend of Master Zhuang's encounter with the skeleton.

Lu Xun had, of course, read the *Master Zhuang*, but he also knew the legend of Master Zhuang's encounter with the skeleton, which he may have learned in a number of ways. As a leading scholar of traditional Chinese fiction, Lu Xun would have known the version of the legend in Ding Yaokang's *A Sequel to Plum in the Golden Vase* (*Xu Jinpingmei*). It is very likely that he also knew Wang Yinglin's *Free and Easy Roaming*

(*Xiaoyao you*). He may also have learned of the legend through oral retellings or popular versions that have now been lost. But whereas most earlier versions had condemned the ingratitude of the resurrected skeleton, Lu Xun's version shows great sympathy for the fellow, who is left naked and without a penny when Master Zhuang cannot turn him back into a skeleton, as he begs him to do. In Lu Xun's version, it is Master Zhuang who has become the butt of satire, depicted as a vainglorious intellectual who, for all his fine language, is motivated primarily by self-interest. When the resurrected skeleton in his desperation becomes too demanding in the opinion of Master Zhuang, it is now the latter who does not hesitate to blow an alarm whistle and call a constable to his aid—in that officer of the law only too willing to serve the powers that be, one can easily recognize Confucius, the ultimate bête noir of the modern intellectuals of the May Fourth period.

Even though included in a collection of short stories, Lu Xun's "Raising the Dead" is written as a one-act Western-style play. Late-nineteenth-century problem plays and their realist style of acting had been introduced into China from the early twentieth century onward, and because they lacked music and song were called *huaju* (spoken drama). Lu Xun had translated a number of Western plays. In view of the very detailed stage directions, one wonders to what extent Lu Xun may have envisioned a performance, if only in his mind. In its own day, "Raising the Dead" could, of course, never have been staged. After all, much of the action concerns the doomed attempts of the resurrected skeleton, who comes back to life as naked as the day he was born, to borrow some piece of clothing to cover his shame.

LU XUN

"Raising the Dead"

A large, desolate stretch of land. Everywhere there are grave mounds, but even the biggest ones are no higher than six or seven feet. There are no trees. The field is covered by all kinds of shrubs and weeds, and through those weeds leads a path that has been formed by men and horses. Not far from that road there is a ditch. Houses are to be seen in the distance.

MASTER ZHUANG (*a dark and gaunt complexion, a few graying strands of beard, a Daoist cap, a linen gown; he enters holding a horsewhip*): Ever since my departure from home, I haven't had any water to drink. My thirst is getting worse and worse. To suffer from thirst is really no fun. It would really be much better to turn into a butterfly, but then there are no flowers here either. . . . Hey! There's a pool over there, I'm in luck. (*He runs to the ditch, pushes aside the watercress with his hands, and, scooping the water up in his palms, gulps down more than ten mouthfuls.*) Wow, that was great! Let me slowly walk on. (*While he is walking, he is looking all around him.*) Well there! That's a skull. How did it get there? (*After he has pushed aside the shrubs and weeds, he speaks while tapping the skull.*)

Did you end up this way because out of lust for life and fear of death you acted against all rules and propriety? (*Tap-tap*) Or did you end up this way because you lost your compass and were executed by the sword? (*Tap-tap*) Or did you end up this way because you created a mess and were a shame to your father and mother, wife and son? (*Tap-tap*) Didn't you realize that suicide is the option chosen by the weak? (*Tap-tap-tap!*) Or did you end up this way because you had no food to eat and no clothes to wear? (*Tap-tap*) Or did you end up this way because you had grown old and had to die because your time was up?

(*Tap-tap*) Or . . . Well, it's me who is muddleheaded here, I seem to be putting on a play![1] How could he give me an answer? Fortunately, I'm not that far anymore from the capital of Chu and I don't have to hurry, so let me ask the master of fate, that great divinity, to restore his shape and grow him some flesh. I will talk with him for a while, and then I will let him return to his home village to be reunited with his family members.

(*He puts down his horsewhip; while facing toward the east, he raises both his hands toward Heaven, and at the top of his voice he starts to shout.*)

With utmost sincerity I pay my respects to His Great Heavenly Majesty the Master of Fate! . . .

(*A chill gust of wind and all kinds of* GHOSTS *appear, some with their hair in disarray, some bald, some emaciated, some thick, some male, some female, some young, some old.*)

GHOSTS: Zhuang Zhou, you muddleheaded creature! Even though your beard has grown gray, you still couldn't fathom this. Once you have died, there are no four seasons, and nobody is boss. Heaven and Earth are spring and autumn, and even an emperor doesn't have it so easy. So don't meddle in affairs that are none of your business but hasten on to the capital of Chu to do your own thing. . . .

MASTER ZHUANG: It's you who are the muddleheaded ghosts; even though you have died, you still can't fathom this. You must understand that life is death and death is life, and that a slave is a lord. I am the one who has probed the source of nature and fate. I'm not going to be told what to do by you such small ghosts.

GHOSTS: In that case we'll allow you to make a fool of yourself. . . .

MASTER ZHUANG: I have been invited by a sagely edict of the king of Chu, so I am even less afraid of your tricks!

(*He once again raises his hand toward Heaven and starts to shout in the loudest voice possible.*)

With utmost sincerity I pay my respects to His Great Heavenly Majesty the Master of Fate!

---

1. The play that Lu Xun is thinking of in this instance may well be Shakespeare's *Hamlet*.

Heaven and earth are dark and yellow;
The celestial dome is broad and wide.
The sun and moon: they wax and wane;
Planets and stars are arrayed in rows.[2]
Zhao and Qian and Sun and also Li;
Zhou and Wu and Zheng and Wang.
Feng and Qin and Chu and also Wei;
Jiang and Chen and Han and Yang.[3]

By the authority of the Old Lord of Highest Heaven,[4] hurry as if this were a legal order: I command thee!

(*A clear gust of wind, and that great divinity the* MASTER OF FATE *in a Daoist cap and a linen gown, with a dark and gaunt complexion, and a few graying strands of beard, and holding a horsewhip in his hand, appears in the haze and mist on the eastern side. All the* GHOSTS *have disappeared.*)

MASTER OF FATE: Zhuang Zhou, you are looking for me, so what kind of foolish prank do you want to play this time? You've had plenty of water, why are you still not satisfied?

MASTER ZHUANG: On my way to be received in audience by the king of Chu, I passed by this place and found this skull that still looks like a head. He must have a father and a mother, a wife and a son, but he died out here, which is really too pitiable, too miserable. That is why I implore Your Divinity to restore his shape, give him back his flesh, and allow him to return to life, so he can go back to his home village.

MASTER OF FATE: Ha-ha! You're not serious. Before you have had your fill, you start to meddle in other people's business. You are not serious! This is no joke. Just go on your way and don't seek trouble with me. You must know that "death and life have their fate," so it is difficult for me to arrange matters at will.

---

2. These are the first four lines of the *Text in a Thousand Characters* (*Qianzi wen*), one of the primers in traditional education. The text is composed in rhyming four-syllable lines for easy memorization.

3. These are the first four lines of *The Surnames of the Hundred Families* (*Baijia xing*), another primer. This text is also composed in rhyming four-syllable lines.

4. This is the title of the Old Master as one of the highest gods in the Daoist pantheon.

MASTER ZHUANG: Your Divinity is mistaken. How can we speak of life and death? Once I, Zhuang Zhou, dreamed that I had changed into a butterfly, and I was a butterfly that fluttered about. But when I woke up, I had become Zhuang Zhou, and I was this Zhuang Zhou who's as busy as can be. Until this very day, I have been unable to work out whether it was Zhuang Zhou who in his dream had become a butterfly, or whether it was a butterfly who in his dream became Zhuang Zhou. Seen from this angle, how don't we know that this skeleton right now is very much alive, and that after a so-called return to life he has died? So I implore Your Divinity to do me a small favor and to be somewhat accommodating. As human beings, we have to be flexible, and as a god, one also cannot be too opinionated.

MASTER OF FATE (*with a smile*): As for you, you can talk the talk but you can't walk the walk. You're a human being and no god. . . . Okay, let's try it out!

(*The* MASTER OF FATE *points with the horsewhip to the weeds and disappears in the same instant. A flare of fire emerges from the place to which he had pointed, and out jumps a* MAN.)

THE MAN (*about thirty years old; very tall and with a reddish face, he looks like a peasant. Without a thread on his body, he is stark naked. After rubbing his eyes with his fists, he gathers his wits and then sees* MASTER ZHUANG): Huh?

MASTER ZHUANG: What "huh"? (*Walks toward him with a smile and observes him.*) What were you doing?

THE MAN: *Aiya*, I had fallen asleep. What were you doing? (*Looks around him and starts to scream.*) Damn, where are my pack and my umbrella? (*Looks at his own body.*) Damn it, where are my clothes? (*Squats down.*)

MASTER ZHUANG: Now calm down for a while, don't panic. You have just come back to life. Your possessions, I'm afraid, must have turned to dust a long time ago, or perhaps they were taken away by someone.

THE MAN: What do you mean?

MASTER ZHUANG: Now let me ask you, what is your name and where are you from?

THE MAN: I'm Eldest Son Yang from Yang Family Village. In school I was called Bigong.[5]

MASTER ZHUANG: In that case, what was your business coming here?

THE MAN: I am on my way to visit my in-laws. But I must unwittingly have fallen asleep. (*Becoming agitated.*) Where are my clothes? My pack and my umbrella?

MASTER ZHUANG: Now be calm for a while, don't be so panicky. . . . Let me ask you, in which period did you live?

THE MAN (*stupefied*): What? What do you mean by saying, "In which period did you live?" . . . What about my clothes? . . .

MASTER ZHUANG: Keep quiet! You're so muddleheaded it will be your death! You are concerned only about your own clothes, you are truly an inveterate egotist. You are not yet clear about the concept of "person," so how can you talk about your clothes. So that's why I first of all want to ask you, In which period did you live? . . . Okay, you don't understand that question. (*Thinks for a while.*) So let me ask you then, what happened in your village when, earlier, you were alive?

THE MAN: What happened? Plenty! Yesterday, my little brother's wife got into a fight with our seventh uncle's wife.

MASTER ZHUANG: That's not of sufficient importance.

THE MAN: That's not important enough? . . . Well, Yang Little Three was honored as a filial son. . . .

MASTER ZHUANG: To be honored as a filial son is indeed a very important event. . . . But this is still very hard to track down. . . . (*Thinks for a while.*) Don't you remember any even more important event, because of which everyone was in turmoil?

THE MAN: In turmoil? Sure, sure! That was three or four months ago. Because they wanted to catch the souls of infants to stabilize the foundations of Deer Terrace, everyone was indeed so scared that no chicken or dog was at peace. People hurried to make little amulet sacks that they had these children wear.

MASTER ZHUANG (*surprised*): The Deer Terrace? The Deer Terrace of which period?

5. Bigong is the equivalent of Mustcrap.

THE MAN: That Deer Terrace on which the work was started some months ago!

MASTER ZHUANG: In that case, did you die in the period of King Zhou?[6] This is truly amazing—you have been dead for more than five hundred years!

THE MAN (*getting somewhat angry*): Master, this is our first meeting, you should not make fun of me. All that happened is that I slept here for a while; how can you say I have been dead for more than five hundred years! I have business to attend to; I'm on my way to my in-laws. Now give me back my clothes, my pack, and my umbrella. I don't have the time to play silly games with you.

MASTER ZHUANG: Not so quick! Let me investigate this. How did you fall asleep?

THE MAN: How did I fall asleep? (*Thinks.*) When I arrived here this morning, it seemed as if I heard a thud on my head. Everything went black before my eyes, and I fell asleep.

MASTER ZHUANG: Did it hurt?

THE MAN: It seems it didn't hurt.

MASTER ZHUANG: Hm . . . (*Thinks for a while.*) Ha . . . I understand. It must be the case that at some time in the period of King Zhou of the Shang dynasty you, all by yourself, were walking through this place and ran into robbers who blocked your way. They hit you over the head with their staves, beat you to death, and robbed you of everything you had. At this moment, we are living under the Zhou dynasty, and more than five hundred years have passed, so there is no way to find your clothes. Do you understand?

THE MAN (*looking at* MASTER ZHUANG *with fixed eyes*): I don't understand a word of what you say. Master, if you are willing to stop fooling around, give me back my clothes, my pack, and my umbrella. I have business to attend to, I don't have the time to play silly games with you.

---

6. King Zhou was the last ruler of the Shang dynasty (ca. 1600–1050 B.C.E.). He was renowned for his cruelty. He had stored his jewels and other valuables on Deer Terrace. When his troops were defeated by the armies of King Wu of the Zhou dynasty (traditional dates, 1122–249 B.C.E.), King Zhou committed suicide by burning himself and his possessions on Deer Terrace.

MASTER ZHUANG: This man truly doesn't talk reason. . . .

THE MAN: Who doesn't talk reason? I don't see my belongings, so I grab you on the spot. If I don't demand them from you, from whom should I demand them? (*Rises to his feet.*)

MASTER ZHUANG (*flustered*): Now you listen to me once again. You were actually a skull, and it's because I took pity on you that I asked the master of fate, that great divinity, to bring you back to life. Just think about it: you've been dead for all these many years, so how could your clothes still survive? At present, I don't want any token of gratitude from you. Just sit down for a while and let's talk about the period of King Zhou. . . .

THE MAN: Nonsense! Even an infant of three cannot believe such a tale. And I am thirty-three! (*Starts walking.*) You . . .

MASTER ZHUANG: I truly have that kind of ability. You must have heard about Zhuang Zhou of the Lacquer Grove

THE MAN: I've never heard about him. And even if you had such ability, what fucking use would it have? You've left me here stark naked, so what's the use of bringing me back to life? How do you want me to visit my in-laws? My pack has disappeared too. . . . (*He is about to cry, runs over and grabs* MASTER ZHUANG'*s sleeve.*) I don't believe your nonsense. You're the only one around, so I of course demand my stuff from you. I'll drag you with me to the village head!

MASTER ZHUANG: Calm down, please calm down! My clothes are very old and very much worn, you can't pull at them. Listen to a few words of mine. First of all, you shouldn't be so obsessed by clothes. Clothes are something one can perhaps also do without. Perhaps it is better to have clothes; perhaps it's better not to have clothes. Birds have their feathers and wild animals have their fur, but cucumbers and eggplants are stark naked. This is what is called That side has its advantages and disadvantages, and this side has its advantages and disadvantages. You, of course, cannot say that it is better not to have clothes, but how could you say that it would be better to have clothes? . . .

THE MAN (*getting furious*): Fuck yourself! If you don't give me back my belongings, I will beat you to a pulp. (*Raising one hand as a fist, he grabs* MASTER ZHUANG *with the other.*)

MASTER ZHUANG (*at a loss what to do, trying to shield himself*): Don't dare! Let me go! If not, I will go and invite the master of fate, that great divinity, to return you to death!

THE MAN (*backing off with a sarcastic smile*): Fine, you give me back to death. If not, I want you to return my clothes to me, my umbrella, and my pack. In it I had fifty-two fully round copper coins, one pound and a half of white sugar, two pounds of southern dates . . .

MASTER ZHUANG (*seriously*): You will have no regrets?

THE MAN: Only my wife's kid brother has regrets!

MASTER ZHUANG (*determined*): Then we'll do it that way. Since you are so muddleheaded, I will have to send you back to your origin. (*Changing his expression, he turns toward the east. Raising his two arms toward the sky, he starts to shout at the top of his voice.*)

With utmost sincerity I pay my respects to His Great Heavenly Majesty the Master of Fate!

> Heaven and earth are dark and yellow;
> The celestial dome is broad and wide.
> The sun and moon: they wax and wane;
> Planets and stars are arrayed in rows.
> Zhao and Qian and Sun and also Li;
> Zhou and Wu and Zheng and Wang.
> Feng and Qin and Chu and also Wei;
> Jiang and Chen and Han and Yang.

By the authority of the Old Lord of Highest Heaven, hurry as if this were a legal order: I command thee!

(*There is absolutely no reaction for quite a while.*)

Heaven and earth are dark and yellow!

By the authority of the Old Lord of Highest Heaven: I command thee! . . . I command thee!

(*There is absolutely no reaction for quite a while.*)

(MASTER ZHUANG *looks all around him and slowly drops his arms.*)

THE MAN: Did I die?

MASTER ZHUANG (*dejectedly*): I don't know why, but this time the magic didn't work. . . .

THE MAN (*jumping forward*): In that case, no more nonsense. Give me back my clothes!

MASTER ZHUANG (*stepping backward*): How dare you? You are a barbarian without any understanding of philosophy!

THE MAN (*grabbing him*): You rotten scoundrel, you mastermind of all robbers and thieves! I will first strip off your Daoist gown and then take your horse as payment for my . . .

(MASTER ZHUANG *on the one hand is fending him off and on the other hand as fast as he can takes an alarm whistle from the sleeve of his Daoist gown and frenetically blows it three times. The* MAN *is flabbergasted and slows down his movements. Not much later a* POLICE OFFICER *comes running from somewhere far off.*)

POLICE OFFICER (*shouting while running*): Get hold of him! Don't let him escape! (*When he comes closer, he turns out to be a big fellow from the state of Lu.[7] He is very tall, and he is dressed in uniform. In his hands he holds his stick; his red face is beardless.*) Get hold of him! The bastard!

THE MAN (*once again he has tightly grasped* MASTER ZHUANG): I've got him! The bastard!

(*When the* POLICE OFFICER *arrives out of breath, he grasps* MASTER ZHUANG'*s collar and raises his stick with his other hand. The* MAN *releases his grip, and, slightly bending his body, he covers his private parts with both his hands.*)

MASTER ZHUANG (*pushing back the stick and averting his head*): What's the meaning of this?

POLICE OFFICER: What this should mean? You still are not clear about it?

MASTER ZHUANG (*in a rage*): How is it that I call you and that you arrest me?

POLICE OFFICER: How?

MASTER ZHUANG: I blew the whistle. . . .

POLICE OFFICER: You stole this man's clothes, and you still had the nerve to blow the whistle?

MASTER ZHUANG: I was a traveler passing by on the road when I saw that he had died. But when I saved him, he started to bother me,

---

7. The state of Lu was the home of Confucius, who was renowned for his tall stature.

saying that I had taken his possessions. Just look at me, am I someone who steals?

POLICE OFFICER (*putting away his stick*): "Knowing a man you know his face but not his heart." Who knows. Let's go to the bureau.

MASTER ZHUANG: But that is impossible. I have to hurry on, I am to be received in audience by the king of Chu.

POLICE OFFICER (*startled, releases his grip and scrutinizes* MASTER ZHUANG*'s face*): In that case, you must be the Lacquer . . .

MASTER ZHUANG (*in a better mood once again*): Exactly! I am the Lacquer Grove administrator Zhuang Zhou. How did you know?

POLICE OFFICER: Sir, our bureau chief has mentioned you time and again these last few days. He says that you, sir, are going to make your fortune once you have come to the capital, and that perhaps you would pass by this place. Our bureau chief is also a gentleman in hiding, but he manages this little job on the side. And sir, he very much loves to read your writings. When reading your "Treatise on the Equalization of Things," those lines like "Where there is birth, there must be death; where there is death, there must be birth. Where there is acceptability, there must by unacceptability; where there is unacceptability, there must be acceptability"[8] are written with such force, they are truly superior writings, the best! Sir, you should come to our bureau to rest for a while.

(*The* MAN *is scared and moves back into the shrubs and weeds, where he squats down.*)

MASTER ZHUANG: It is already getting late today, I have to travel on and cannot tarry here any longer. When I come back, I will make sure to pay a visit to your bureau.

(*While he is saying this,* MASTER ZHUANG *starts walking and mounts his horse. The very moment he wants to spur it on, the* MAN *suddenly jumps out of the bushes, runs forward, and grabs the horse by its bit. The* POLICE OFFICER *runs after him and grabs him by his shoulder.*)

MASTER ZHUANG: Why are you still bothering me?

THE MAN: You'll be gone, but I'll have nothing. What do you want me to do? (*Looking at the* POLICE OFFICER.) Mister Officer, please look. . . .

8. *Zhuangzi*, chapter 2. See Zhuangzi, *Complete Works of Chuang Tzu*, 39–40.

POLICE OFFICER (*rubbing behind his ears*): This situation is really difficult to solve. . . . But master . . . in my judgment (*looking at* MASTER ZHUANG), it's still you who is the richer of the two, so give him one piece of clothing so he can cover his shame. . . .

MASTER ZHUANG: That would, of course, be a possibility. Clothes are, in final analysis, not a part of the self. But I will be received in audience this time by the king of Chu. That would be impossible if I was not wearing a gown, and if I were to take off my shirt and wear only my gown, that would also be impossible. . . .

POLICE OFFICER: Yes, you cannot do without them. (*Toward the* MAN.) Let him go!

THE MAN: I'm on my way to see my in-laws. . . .

POLICE OFFICER: Nonsense! If you pester him again, I'll take you to the bureau. (*Raises his stick.*) Get lost!

(*The* MAN *walks backward, and the* POLICE OFFICER *follows him into the shrubs.*)

MASTER ZHUANG: Good-bye!

POLICE OFFICER: Good-bye, sir, have a good trip!

(MASTER ZHUANG, *on horseback, spurs on his horse and rides off. With his hands on his back, the* POLICE OFFICER *watches him as he goes farther and father and disappears in the dust. Then he slowly turns around to go back along the road by which he came.*)

(*The* MAN *suddenly jumps out of the shrubs and pulls the* POLICE OFFICER *by his clothes.*)

POLICE OFFICER: What do you want?

THE MAN: What should I do?

POLICE OFFICER: How should I know?

THE MAN: I wanted to visit my in-laws. . . .

POLICE OFFICER: Then go and visit your in-laws.

THE MAN: But I don't have any clothes.

POLICE OFFICER: So you cannot visit your in-laws without any clothes?

THE MAN: You allowed him to leave. Now you, too, want to get out of here. But you will have to help me out. If I don't ask you, whom should I ask? Just look, how can I go on living like this?

POLICE OFFICER: But I tell you: suicide is the option chosen by the weak.

THE MAN: Then you come up with some solution for me!

POLICE OFFICER (*freeing his lapel*): I don't know any solution for you!

THE MAN (*holding on to the* POLICE OFFICER'*s sleeve*): Then take me with you to the bureau!

POLICE OFFICER (*freeing his sleeve*): How could that be? Stark naked as you are, how can you appear in the street? Let me go.

THE MAN: Then lend me a pair of pants!

POLICE OFFICER: I have only this pair of pants. If I give them to you, I will look ridiculous. (*Pushing him off with all his force.*) Don't bother me! Let go!

THE MAN (*grabbing the* POLICE OFFICER *by the neck*): I absolutely want to go with you.

POLICE OFFICER (*at a loss what to do*): That's impossible!

THE MAN: I will not release you.

POLICE OFFICER: What do you want?

THE MAN: I want you to take me to the bureau.

POLICE OFFICER: This truly is . . . Why would I take you with me? Don't be such a pain in the ass. Let go! If not . . . (*Struggling with all his strength.*)

THE MAN (*holding on to him even tighter*): If not, I cannot visit my in-laws and I cannot go on living. Two pounds of southern dates, one pound and a half of white sugar . . . You allowed him to leave, so you and I will have to fight it out.

POLICE OFFICER (*struggling*): Don't be such a pain in the ass! Let go! Otherwise . . . Otherwise . . . (*While saying this, he has also taken out his whistle and frenetically starts to blow.*)

December 1935

APPENDIX 1

Three Rhapsodies

The anecdote of Master Zhuang coming across a skull and their conversation in a dream was a popular topic with authors of the second and third centuries; we know the names of at least four writers who adapted the theme. For one author, we have only a few lines, not enough to draw any conclusions about the way he developed the story. In the case of Lü An (d. 263), we have only what appears to be a fragment. The piece by Cao Zhi (192–232) may be more or less complete. The only rhapsody on a skull that has a good chance of being preserved in its entirety is the text attributed to Zhang Heng (78–139).

All three texts may elaborate the language but otherwise stay close to the narrative of the anecdote in the *Master Zhuang*. Lü An seems to take issue with the equanimity displayed by the dream apparition of the skull and wants to treat death as a disaster, but the text is too fragmentarily preserved to allow strong conclusions. Cao Zhi allows the dream apparition of the skull to expound at length on its superior pleasures, but in the end he returns to the agnostic attitude of Confucius regarding death: If we do not yet understand life, how could we pretend to understand death? The most original treatment of the theme is provided by Zhang Heng (if he is indeed the author of the text ascribed to him); he comes across not an anonymous skull but that of Master Zhuang, who now himself becomes the spokesman for the transcendent joys of death. But despite his long paean to the return to nothingness, the poet cannot help but cry, and one can only wonder whether he does so because Master Zhuang has died or because he pities him for his delusion. All three poets take care to bury the skull, which would be a superfluous action if they had been convinced by its voice.

These three texts all belong to the genre of *fu* (prose poems/ rhapsodies). This means these texts are declamation pieces, written mostly in rhyming lines of four syllables or of six syllables. The texts are subdivided into stanzas by a switch of rhyme, and they may also include short prose passages, often at the beginning of a new stanza. In the traditional Chinese classification, the *fu* are classified as *wen*, which nowadays is often translated as "prose" but is perhaps better understood as "patterned writings" or belles lettres. This classification excluded, however, the various forms of song. Traditional Chinese literary theory and bibliography did not have a general word corresponding to the modern Western notion of poetry because *shi*, which nowadays is often translated as "poetry," originally referred only to a specific genre of song, just like such later terms as *ci* (lyric) and *qu* (aria). From a formal Western standpoint, the *fu* is therefore best treated as a genre of poetry.

ZHANG HENG

Rhapsody on the Skull

Zhang Pingzi[1] intended
To feast his eyes on the Nine Regions
   And observe transformation in the eight directions.
As the planets turned and the sun traveled,
   Phoenixes soared and dragons raced.
In the south he visited the Vermilion Bank,
   In the north he ascended the Dark Lands;
In the west he passed through the Valley of Dusk,
   And in the east he reached the Supporting Mulberries.[2]
      At that time
It was the season of late autumn,
   And a slight breeze brought a chill.
So he turned the chariot he drove around:
   The left horse soared, the right one whinnied.
He allowed them to graze on the higher fields
   And freely roam about on ridges and hillocks.
Looking around, he saw a skull
   That had been abandoned by the wayside:
Its lower part buried in the damp earth,
   Its upper part covered by glittering frost.

     Zhang Pingzi was saddened and asked him, "Did you
        perhaps
Throw away your life by gobbling up your rations[3]
   So you passed away at an early age?

1. Pingzi is the social name or style of Zhang Heng.
2. These four lines describe journeys to the outer edges of the earth. The sun rises from the Supporting Mulberries at the eastern end of the world.
3. That is, by finishing your supplies before the end of your trip.

Did you flee and die in this place,
  Or come here because you were banished?
Did you possess highest intelligence?
  Or was it perhaps lowest stupidity?
Were you a woman?
  Or were you a male?"

Thereupon, the skull manifested its numinosity, but you could only hear the voice of the spirit, you could not see its shape. The spirit replied,
"I was a man from Song,
  Known as Zhuang Zhou.
My mind roamed beyond all conventions,
  But I could not perfect my own body.
When my life and fate came to their limit,
  I arrived here in this dark dungeon.

But sir, why do you ask me this?" Zhang Pingzi replied,
    "I want to
Appeal to the Five Marchmounts[4]
  And pray to all gods and deities,
That they may resurrect your white bones
  And give you back your four limbs.
We will take your ears om northern *kan*
  And find your eyes in southern *li*;[5]
    We'll have
Eastern *zhen* present you with a pair of feet
  And western *kun* provide you with a belly;[6]
The five organs will be restored
  And the six divinities will return.[7]

---

4. The Five Marchmounts are the holy mountains that dominate the center and the four directions. They were also revered as divinities.

5. *Kan* and *li* are the names of two of the Eight Trigrams. *Kan* represents water; *li* represents fire.

6. *Zhen* and *kun* are the names of two other of the Eight Trigrams. *Zhen* symbolizes thunder; *kun* symbolizes the earth.

7. The six divinities inhabit the human body as the gods of the heart, lungs, liver, kidneys, spleen, and gallbladder.

Would you like that?" The skull replied, "What you
   propose would be too hard!
Death is leisure and rest,
  Life is service and labor.
How can the frozen state of water in winter
   Compare to
   The melting of ice in the springtime?
Are glory and position to the body
   Also not
   Lighter than a speck of dust or a hair?[8]
The blinding sights of flying blades
   Or the work of clerks with tablets and knives
Were a source of shame to Chaofu and Xu You[9]
   And were abandoned by Bocheng Zigao.[10]
Moreover, I have been transformed
   And now roam freely with the Way:
Even Li Zhu cannot see me,
   Even Ziye cannot hear me;[11]
Yao and Shun cannot reward me,
   Jie and Zhou cannot punish me;[12]
Tigers and leopards cannot harm me,
   Swords and lances cannot hurt me.

8. The early philosopher Yang Zhu (fourth century B.C.E.) argued that the preservation of the body was the first priority, and he therefore would not sacrifice a single strand of his hair for the sake of someone else. One of our main sources for the teachings of Yang Zhu are chapters 28 to 31 of the *Master Zhuang*.

9. Both Chaofu and Xu You were hermits who lived during the legendary days of Emperor Yao. When the two of them, on separate occasions, were offered the empire, they indignantly refused the burdensome offer.

10. Bocheng Zigao was one of the feudal lords in the mythic days when Yao and Shun ruled the world. But when Shun ceded the throne to Yu, who would go on to establish the Xia dynasty (ca. 2100–1600 B.C.E.), Bocheng Zigao returned to farming.

11. Li Zhu (also known as Li Lou) was renowned for his keen eyesight; Ziye (also known as Shi Kuang) was known for his sharp hearing.

12. Yao and Shun are perfect rulers from a mythic past. Jie was the evil last king of the Xia dynasty, whereas Zhou was the evil last king of the Shang dynasty (ca. 1600–1050 B.C.E.).

I join in the current of yin and yang,
   I share in the simplicity of the original ether;
I take the process of creation for my father and mother
   And use heaven and earth as my couch and coverlet.
Thunder and lightning serve as my bellows and fan,
   Sun and moon serve as my candle and lamp;
The Celestial River serves as my stream and pond,
   And planets and stars serve as my pearls and jades.
I have united my substance with nature
   And am free of feelings and desires.
When you strain me, I am no purer;
   When you pollute me, I am not troubled.
Without walking, I arrive,
   Without haste, I am gone."

   Thereupon
The voice stopped, the sound ceased,
   And the glare of the spirit disappeared.

   I looked around and decided to depart. I ordered my
      groom
To wrap the skull in a white scarf
   And cover it with the dark earth.
Shedding tears for its sake,
   I poured out a libation by the side of the road.

[Zhao Kuifu, *Lidai fu pingzhu*, 2:716–21; Zhang Heng,
Zhang Heng shiwenji jiaozhu, 247–52]

CAO ZHI

DISCOURSE ON THE SKULL

Master Cao
Roamed on the banks of tanks and ponds,
　　Paced through overgrown and filthy swamps—
Oh so desolate, hidden, and silent:
　　He passed through the dark and scaled the steep.
Looking around, he noticed a skull,
　　All by itself, alone and forlorn.

　　　Leaning on the front bar of his carriage, he questioned the
　　　　skull: "Are you perhaps
An officer who, headband tied and sword in hand, died for his
　　country?
　　Or a soldier who, dressed in armor and holding his weapon,
　　　was slain in battle?
An infant child whose fate came to an end because of a stubborn
　　disease,
　　Or someone who at the end of his life span returned to dark-
　　　ness and gloom?"
Bowing to the remnant skeleton, he heaved a sigh,
　　Pitying the bleached bones for their lack of a soul,
Yet hoped that just as when Master Zhuang went to Chu,
　　It might entrust itself to a dream to communicate its feelings.

Thereupon, [its spirit] suddenly seemed to arrive and vaguely seemed to be present; its shadow appeared, but its face remained hidden as it said with a sharp voice, "Sir, from where may you be? You not only have taken the trouble to visit me but also have shown sympathy for my decaying remains, and not sparing the sounds you bestow on me, you comfort me with your words. But while you may be well versed in elocution, you do not yet penetrate the feelings of the other world or know the discourse on life and death.

Now death is spoken of as returning, and returning here means returning to the Way. As for the Way, the body
> Takes pride in having no shape
>> So it can move and change with Transformation:
> Yin and yang cannot effect any change,
>> The four seasons cannot cause any harm.

> For that reason
> It permeates the realm of the infinitesimal
>> And pervades the hall of the unfathomable;
> Gaze, and you cannot see its form;
>> Listen, and you cannot hear its voice.
> Scoop from it, and it will not grow empty;
>> Pour into it, and it will never be full.
> No strong storm is able to make it wither;
>> No soft breeze is able to make it flourish.
> Apply pressure, and it will not flow;
>> Let it freeze, and it will never stop.

> Empty and pure, hidden and submerged,
>> It is coterminous with the Way:
> Undisturbed, it sleeps forever—
>> No pleasure is greater than this!"
>> Master Cao replied, "Let me
> Report to the emperor on high
>> And pray to the gods and deities
> To let the master of fate rescind his registers
>> So your bones and shape can be returned to you."

The skull thereupon heaved a heavy sigh and lamented with wide-open sockets: "Too bad! How come you are so obtuse? Once upon a time the master of great simplicity was so unkind as to burden me without any reason with a shape and to torture me with life. Now I have had the good fortune to die, so I have been able to return to my true self. Why are you so in love with weary toil, whereas I am in love with untrammeled ease? Please leave, and I will return to Grand Emptiness." That was the end of his words, the last to be heard, and the glare of his soul disappeared like a mist. Turning around, Master Cao gave orders to go back. He thereupon ordered his groom to dust the skull with a black fly whisk and cover it with a white kerchief. Next they placed it out of sight by the side of the road, covered it with red earth, and hid it under green branches.

> Now the different situations of existence and nonbeing
>   Have been set out in detail by Xuanni,[13]
> So how can an empty reply, a spirit's manifestation,
>   Declare the absolute equality of death and life?

[Cao Zhi, *Cao Zhi ji jiaozhu*, 524–28]

13. Xuanni is one of the names for Confucius. The reference is most likely to *Lunyu*, XI.12: "Jilu asked how the spirits of the dead and the gods should be served. The Master said, 'You are not able even to serve man. How can you serve the spirits?' 'May I ask about death?' 'You do not understand life. How can you understand death?'" (adapted from Confucius, *Analects*, 107).

LÜ AN

Rhapsody on the Skull

Deeply grieved and filled by sorrow,
   I then roamed through my old village,
Where I came across a skull
    That was lying by the wayside.
       I thereupon
Looked down and up, and heaved a sigh
   As I addressed the blue vault of the sky:
"Who is this person
    Whose life was cut short?
His body is dissolving in the open field,
    His bones lie exposed in this wilderness.
       I will
Dress you in seasonal clothes,
    Gift you with the proper attire,
And in an inner and outer coffin
    Move you to a room of darkness."

       Thereupon
The skull seemed to be shaken;
    The spirit was moved and reacted.
As if there and yet as if not there—
    I vaguely discerned a shape.
A friendly expression and fair skin
. . .

"Long ago, because I lacked virtue,
    I transgressed against Highest Heaven,
And when I arrived to roam in this place,
    Heaven robbed me of my years.

As a result,
All of my skin dissolved and disappeared,
   And my white bones were scattered all over.
My four limbs were destroyed and hidden by the rampant weeds;
   My lonely soul is overcome by sadness at the Yellow Springs.[14]
But who is born must return to Transformation,
   Every bright morning reverts to dusk.
If we research this up above and here below,
   There's no creature that departs from this rule."

   Thereupon, I
Was moved by his bitter suffering,
   But sneered at what he expounded.
"Because of your terrible hardship
   As shape and spirit are torn apart,
      I now
Will house you in the solid earth,
   So it may be your eternal location:
We will have to go our different ways,
   From now on we will be separated."

[Ji, *Ji Kang ji jiaozhu*, 431]

14. The name Yellow Springs refers to the underworld, the realm of the dead.

APPENDIX 2
Twenty-One Lyrics

The use of the image of the skeleton both as a metonym for death and as a metaphor for a lack of enlightenment as it was developed in their preaching by Wang Chongyang and other early patriarchs of Quanzhen Daoism in the twelfth century continued to enjoy considerable popularity in later moralistic publications and was enthusiastically taken up by the sectarian authors of the fifteenth and sixteenth centuries. The most conspicuous use of this image is in the "Twenty-One Pure Sound Lyrics Lamenting the World and Alerting the Frivolous," which appears as an appendix in some editions of *The Book of Nonactivism in Lamentation for the World* (*Tanshi wuwei juan*),[1] one of the precious scrolls written by Luo Qing (second part of the fifteenth century), who most likely was also the author of the "Twenty-One Lyrics."

Luo Qing, who hailed from Shandong, was of a humble background. He was a religious seeker throughout his life and recorded his search for truth (which ultimately has to be found within one's own nature, which is identical with the ultimate) in a set of five precious scrolls that are collectively known as the "Five Books in Six Volumes." In various editions and adaptations, they have continued to circulate and inspire believers.

1. First printed in 1601, *Tanshi wuwei juan* was reprinted in 1678, 1882, and 1919.

Luo Qing's teachings are often associated with the belief in the Eternal Mother, even though the figure of the Eternal Mother is much more clearly present in later sectarian precious scrolls. According to the belief in the Eternal Mother, we humans are her children, who have strayed from their original hometown; in order to call us back to our true nature, the Eternal Mother has sent down (or manifested herself as) a sequence of teachers and deities (the most recent of whom are the patriarchs of the new religions). Again, ultimately that original hometown and true nature will be found within oneself. As long as we as human beings fail to achieve that mystical insight, however, we will be walking corpses and moving skeletons as long as we are alive, and upon our death (which may come any moment), our bodies will decay into skeletons while our souls will be subjected to the endless sufferings of punishments in hell and the unending chain of transmigration powered by karma.

The text of the "Twenty-One Pure Sound Lyrics" consists of a short prose sermon followed by the twenty-one songs. Lyrics lamenting the physical skeleton (as shown in a painting?) and addressing the unenlightened listeners as skeletons alternate with lyrics that sing the joy of transcendent enlightenment. These latter lyrics compare the ultimate substance of our being to a dazzling light and a golden body that will freely manifest itself upon death of the physical body.

LUO QING

Twenty-One Pure Sound Lyrics Lamenting the World and Alerting the Frivolous

The empty flowers before your eyes you wrongly take as true;
Out of the blue you make distinctions, fixing near and distant.
When fame and profit have no limit, hardship has no limit,
But light and shadow have a limit and so has your life.

I lament this skeleton, this skeleton of seven feet! By nature it tended to the stingy desire for money and treasure, but when it breathed out, it could not be sure it would also breathe in. You men and women of the ten directions, don't blame me—who of you understands that bitter advice is the best medicine? This skeleton is a dead skeleton, but panting and gasping with wide-open eyes, you are living skeletons! In the *Water Repentance*, the lord of heaven Indra became a firefly.[2] In the *Precious Repentance of Emperor Wu of the Liang*, his consort Lady Chi became a snake.[3] In the *Glance Collection*, the lord of heaven of the upper region

---

2. The *Water Repentance* refers to the *Compassion Water Repentance* (*Cibei shuichan*) by the Tang-dynasty monk Zhixuan (812–883). This is a liturgy for a Buddhist penitential ritual seeking the generation of merit for the participants and the transfer of that merit to others, especially deceased relatives. Such liturgies, which contained long lists of the sins that human beings would have committed during their innumerable lives and stressed the inevitable dire punishments, were quite popular in traditional China. For a general description of such liturgies in the sixteenth and seventeenth centuries, see Zürcher, "Buddhist *chanhui* and Christian Confession," 106–16.

3. The *Precious Repentance of Emperor of Wu of the Liang* (*Liang huang baochan*) is another liturgy for a Buddhist penitential ritual. Lady Chi, the consort of Emperor Wu of the Liang dynasty (502–556), was reborn as a snake because of the jealousy she had manifested as empress. Legend has it that when Emperor Wu was informed of her fate, he instituted the repentance liturgy that carries his name. See Chappell, "*Precious Scroll of the Liang Emperor*."

became a fish.[4] In one precious scroll, monks and priests upon losing their footing become ants, and in another precious scroll women and girls stumble and fall among the "winter criers."[5] You men and women of the ten directions have all come together, but of the ten persons who seek the Way, nine persons will retreat. Those who will not retreat are true and substantial, and in the moment of danger they will emit a blazing light. Those who retreat from the Way are foolish and stupid and will eternally be reborn in one of the four classes of living beings without any possibility of release.

A gatha reads,

> With every breath our human life expects Impermanence;
> We see with our own eyes the sun that sets behind the hills.
> If strength gives out on Treasure Hill,[6] you turn your head in vain:
> Once you have lost your human shape, you'll never get it back.[7]

This bitter advice is the truth, these are no idle words. Fake and fake! When one day such a skeleton has died, the other skeletons will weep sadly, overcome by fear.

> Skeleton, I lament you:
> You gathered a family capital and amassed a fortune:
> You constructed a brick hall and a tile-covered dwelling.
> You walked along main street, you stood on main street;
> Competing for fame and profit, you bragged of your skills.

---

4. The *Glance Collection* refers to *The Great Canon at One Glance Collection* (*Dazang yilan ji*), a short summary of Buddhist teachings.

5. "Winter criers" is my translation of *hanhaochong* (literally, "insects that cry in the cold"). One source describes the creatures as a kind of large bat, another as "a bird that cries at night seeking dawn; in the summer months it is covered by feathers, but in the winter it goes naked and cries both day and night, and that why it is called a 'winter crier.'"

6. Those who hear the truth but do not convert are compared to people who enter a storehouse filled with jewels but return empty-handed because they cannot make up their minds as to which treasure to take.

7. It will be impossible to be reborn as a human being for ten thousand kalpas.

O skeletons,
If today unannounced Impermanence arrived,
O skeletons,
That brick hall you constructed,
That brick hall and tile-covered dwelling, you couldn't take them
    along!

Skeleton, I lament you:
Because you never strove for *samadhi*:
Whoever learns the good news so bright and majestic
Will emit a blazing light that permeates heaven and earth:
It cannot be increased, it cannot be diminished;
It cannot be polluted, it cannot be purified.
You ready-made skeletons,
If one day unannounced Impermanence arrives,
O skeletons,
You'll be unable to regain that golden body for eternal kalpas!

Skeleton, I lament you:
Your mother carried you for ten long months,[8]
And who were you when you had been born?
You became you only when you grew up, became an adult!
You ate fine food and wore fine clothes—
A bag of blood and pus, a ghostly skeleton!
O skeletons,
If one day unannounced Impermanence arrives,
O skeletons,
Let me ask you,
Where will your food, your clothes, your glory and wealth have gone?

Skeleton, I lament you:
You practiced self-cultivation believing in form[9] and so made a
    foolish mistake.

---

8. In China, a pregnancy is said to last for ten months, since the gestation period is
counted from the month of conception to the month of birth.
   9. This is a reference to Daoist techniques of self-cultivation that seek physical longev-
ity and an eternal life in the flesh.

"Emptiness is identical to phenomena; phenomena are emptiness,"[10]
So practicing self-cultivation believing in form doesn't enlighten
    the mind,
And self-cultivation relying on an illusion is making a foolish
    mistake:
All forms that may exist are insubstantial and deluding.
O skeletons,
If one day unannounced Impermanence arrives,
O skeletons,
You willingly will suffer bitter hardship,
Bitter hardship as all turns out to be empty.

Skeleton, I lament you:
I don't know whether you are a priest's skeleton or a layman's
    skeleton,
Whether you are a prime minister or a royal prince,
Whether you are a man's skeleton or a woman's skeleton—
For all your glory and wealth, you've turned into a skeleton.
The scenery of a hundred years is like snapping your fingers.
O skeletons,
If one day unannounced Impermanence arrives,
O skeletons,
I ask you where is your realized person,[11]
Where oh where is your realized person?

O skeletons, I lament you:
I lament you so much it is killing me, this lament is killing!
When Impermanence arrives, you'll all end up like this.
So hurry and hasten and find a way of escape!
Entrust yourself to an enlightened teacher to seek a way of escape.
Pleasure without limit is originally your origin,

---

10. This is a line from the Heart Sutra, a very short and extremely popular wisdom
text. For translations and discussions, see, for example, "Heart Sutra (Xin jing)," in *Ways
with Words*, ed. Yu et al., 113–45.

11. The "realized person" is one who has achieved insight into the eternal truth of his
or her own nature.

You'll be freed forever from the Three Disasters and Eight Dangers.[12]
O skeletons,
If one day unannounced Impermanence arrives,
O skeletons,
Only in this way you'll be fine,
For all eternal kalpas you'll be fine forever!

O skeletons, please listen:
Each and everyone is bound to turn into a skeleton.
Men and women are bound to turn into skeletons,
Princes and ministers are bound to turn into skeletons,
Heroes and champions are bound to turn into skeletons.
The scenery of a hundred years is like snapping your fingers.
O skeletons,
If one day unannounced Impermanence arrives,
O skeletons,
You'll be carried to overgrown suburbs,
To overgrown suburbs where you're bound to turn into a skeleton.

O skeletons, please listen:
I manifest a golden body—congregation, please listen.
When the ears hear sounds and colors, a bright light appears;
When the eyes see blue and yellow, you manifest a golden body.
When the nose smells fragrant and foul, a bright light appears;
When the mouth discusses all things, you manifest a golden body.
O skeletons,
If today unannounced Impermanence arrives,
O skeletons,
You'll drop this skeleton
And manifest a golden body in all directions!

12. The Three Disasters refer to death by the sword, during a pestilence, or from a famine. During the end of a kalpa, the Three Disasters refer to fire, water, and wind. The Eight Dangers refer to the conditions that make it difficult to see the Buddha or hear his teachings: when one is in hell; when one is a hungry ghost; when one is reborn as an animal; when one lives on the northern continent, where all is pleasure; when one is reborn as a god in one of the long-life heavens; when one is deaf, blind, or dumb; when one is an agnostic philosopher; and when one is born in the intermediate period between the life of the Buddha and his successor.

O skeletons, I lament you:
To obtain a human shape is something exceedingly rare,
It may be compared to dredging a needle from the ocean.
But by killing living beings, you again create evil karma;
In the underworld courts of hell you can't dispute the facts.
The scenery of a hundred years is like snapping your fingers.
O skeletons,
If today unannounced Impermanence arrives,
O skeletons,
Once you've lost your human shape,
A human shape will be hard to acquire again.

O skeletons, I lament you:
Each and everyone has an indestructible body;
Without coming or going, it shines through eternity.
Transcending the Buddha and Ancestor, it has no name;
It doesn't care for monk or layman, it doesn't need practice.
Throughout heaven and earth it emits a bright light.
O skeletons,
If today unannounced Impermanence arrives,
O skeletons,
If you used your time wrongly,
You will fall and sink and drown for eternal kalpas.

Skeleton, I lament you:
You fought over fame and profit, displaying your tricks;
Abandoning sons and daughters, you were dragged here.
Those pampered boys and girls you loved so dearly—
Today you accompany mounds of earth in the wilds.
When called, you don't react; when beaten, you feel no pain.
Your fight over fame and profit has turned into emptiness.
O skeletons,
If today unannounced Impermanence arrives,
O skeletons,
Merit and fame that cover the world,
Even that merit and fame will turn into emptiness.

O skeletons, I lament you:
The ten emperors, the Yama lords, gnash their teeth;
The registers of the Ten Kings provide a clear record.[13]
When yakshas arrive and evil ghosts arrest you,
You'll lose your human shape forever, without a change,
You'll suffer on trees of swords and mountains of knives.
O skeletons,
If today unannounced Impermanence arrives,
O skeletons,
If your strength failed on Treasure Mountain,
If your strength failed, your conversion was in vain!

O skeletons,
If there's karma, you will meet despite a thousand miles,
But without karma, you'll fail to do so even face-to-face.
You may sleep together, sit together, cohabitate in joy,
O skeletons,
But don't know who next year will still be here.
The fight over fame and profit is foolish ignorance;
Impermanence, so life and death, turns all into ashes.
This morning you and I may be united in pleasure,
O skeletons,
But you don't know who next year,
Who next year will still be here.

O skeletons, I lament you:
In this world of light you may for a moment have cheated your
        way,
But great glory, wealth, and status are only a bubble on the water.
This one sack of pus and blood is not strong and solid at all,
So how can you escape from Impermanence, life and death?
At the moment of danger, of life and death, the parting is painful.

---

13. The Ten Kings (also designated as the ten emperors) are the judges in the ten courts of the underworld, through which all souls have to pass after death. King Yama is the highest judge of them all, but at times all ten judges are addressed as Yama lords.

O skeletons,
Following this parting,
Who knows where you will enter another shell?

O skeletons, I lament you:
This lament is killing me, this lament is killing.
Each and everyone so foolish and ignorant, hard to convert.
Dear gentlemen, quickly repent of what you've done before;
If your repentance comes too late, you'll fall into transmigration.
If today unannounced Impermanence arrives,
O skeletons,
If you have used this life wrongly,
You'll never again acquire [a human shape] for eternal kalpas.

O skeletons, I lament you:
Never born, never annihilated, free from life and death;
No additions, no detractions: ready-made from the beginning.
No pollution, no purification, requiring no practice at all.
And if one day unannounced the four elements disperse,
O skeletons,
Throughout the worlds of the ten directions,
Throughout these worlds you'll manifest your golden body.

O skeletons, please listen:
From before the first division you had your nature;
From the before the Three Teachings,[14] you had your nature.
From before monk and layman, you had your nature;
From before precepts and rules, you had your nature.
O skeletons,
Those without wisdom will retreat,
But those who are intelligent will do great.

O skeletons, please listen:
When I mention your original nature, it is a provisional name;
Originally it is without name and can freely do as it pleases.

14. The Three Teachings are Confucianism, Daoism, and Buddhism.

In truth, there is no origin that serves as feet.
Who would dare to forcefully impose a name on emptiness?
Casually opening up the eye without name
Surpasses practicing for eighty thousand stretches.
O skeletons,
If one day unannounced the four states disintegrate,[15]
Then throughout the worlds of the ten directions,
Throughout those worlds you will manifest your golden body.

O skeletons, I lament you:
Your original appearance is a limitless body,
The ten million worlds are only a mote of dust.
The worlds in the ten directions provide no obstacle;
Without any obstacle, it is free to do as it pleases.
If one day unannounced Impermanence arrives,
O skeletons,
[Your body] will resemble an empty flower,
And filled with pleasure you will be your own master.

O skeletons, now all listen:
You enjoy the finest foods, a hundred delicacies;
You enjoy brick halls and tile-covered dwellings.
You enjoy covered couches and sitting cushions;
You enjoy coverlets of the ten kinds of brocade.
O skeletons,
When you are carried to the overgrown suburbs,
You will join the earthen mounds in those overgrown suburbs.

Skeleton, I lament you:
Today you have become a ghost with bared fangs:
Your flesh has turned into dust and soil and earth;
Your bones have turned into this ghostly skeleton.
You may have laughed at those who fought over fame and profit,
But today you have turned into a ghostly skeleton.

15. The "four states" refer to birth, being, decay, and death.

O skeletons,
How I lament those so very smart,
Those so very smart and intelligent people!

[Appended to (Luo Qing,) *Tanshi wuwei juan,*
in *Baojuan chuji,* ed. Zhang Xishun, 1:543–71]

APPENDIX 3

Ten Skeletons

In the introduction, I drew a parallel between, on the one hand, Master Zhuang's laments on the skeleton in which he questions the skeleton about his identity when alive and ends up listing all possible crafts and professions in society from high to low and, on the other, the late medieval European pictorial and textual tradition of the dance of death, in which representatives of each status and craft are invited by death in the shape of a decomposing corpse or skeleton to follow him. We find an even closer parallel to this European textual tradition of the dance of death in "The Ten Skeletons," an anonymous poem of unknown date that was published as an appendix in the 1899 printing of the *Precious Scroll on the Emperor of the Liang Dynasty* (*Liang huang baojuan*).

While the title of the song promises ten kinds of skeletons (and the author introduces himself in the final stanza as the eleventh skeleton), and while the song is made up of ten stanzas, it actually includes only eight stanzas that introduce one social type that is urged to cut its attachment to this world and convert to a life of religious practice in order to achieve enlightenment and escape the fate of an abandoned skeleton out in the wild. In the final stanza, the ultimate aim of a life of religious practice is identified with rebirth in the Pure Land in the Western Paradise of Amitabha Buddha.

The Ten Skeletons

I'm growing old, advanced in years—my heart is filled with sorrow
Since unavoidably this human life will reach its exit.
Old age, I find to my regret, does no one any good,
So I advise you, dashing heroes, make a bold decision.
There comes a day when unannounced Impermanence arrives—
A skeleton is what you will become once you have died.

The people of the highest sort are not inclined to practice;
They order slaves and maids around, they live in quite a style.
Their rooms are filled with pretty wives and gorgeous concubines;
Their gardens, groves, and fields and lands cover a thousand hills.
Pillars and beams are carved and painted in extensive mansions—
A skeleton is what they will become once they have died.

The people of the middling sort are not inclined to practice:
The loans they every day extend, these occupy their minds!
At home, their gold and silver fill their coffers and their boxes,
And wine and meat to their delight do never leave their throat.
They are well versed in go and chess, calligraphy and painting;
The furnishings that they have bought are all the latest style.
They're unrestrained in seeking pleasure to their heart's content—
A skeleton is what they will become once they have died.

The people of the lowest sort are not inclined to practice—
Three meals of tea and rice a day are far beyond their means.
Supported by a bamboo stave and carrying a jug,
They beg for food out in the streets, crying by day and night.
By night, they rest in some pavilion without any blanket,
Their bodies shivering from cold—a pain beyond control!
For their three meals throughout the day, they must rely on
        others—
A skeleton is what they will become once they have died.

Old ladies, eighty years of age, are not inclined to practice,
As with their sons and grandsons, they are having a good time.
They're busy, oh so busy, managing the household budget—
Their waist is bent, their back is curved, their hair has all gone
    white.
They still believe, despite old age, that they will live forever,
Not knowing that their warrant has been issued by King Yama.
There is a day when unannounced Impermanence arrives—
A skeleton is what they will become once they have died.

Young women in the prime of youth are not inclined to practice:
Day in, day out they put on powder, daub on fragrant oil.
Their eyes and eyebrows are so clear, a wonder to behold;
The red and green of skirt and jacket have been rightly matched.
With faces filled with spring's allure, they're everybody's darlings;
They have the looks of a Xi Shi,[1] displaying quite some style.
But even though they well may be as pretty as a flower,
A skeleton is what they will become once they have died.

Court ministers and bureaucrats are not inclined to practice:
In purple coats with belts of jade, they are the dukes and nobles.
Their honor guards in all their colors fill the crowds with fear
And terrify the country folks, so each is sick with worry.
Local elites and magistrates pay their respect to them
As if they were divinities, as if they were immortals!
They have no clue a day will come that they will fall from
    power—
A skeleton is what they will become once they are dead.

The generals engaged in war are not inclined to practice;
With bow and arrows in their hands, they plan and scheme for
    battle,

---

1. Xi Shi was the most beautiful maiden in the ancient state of Yue. When King Goujian of Yue set out to destroy the rival state of Wu, he had Xi Shi trained in all the arts of seduction and sent her as a present to the king of Wu. The king of Wu was indeed bewitched by the beauty of Xi Shi and in his infatuation neglected his duties, whereupon Goujian destroyed his kingdom.

And when they have subdued the south, they will subdue the
      north—
Their minds are set on rank and pay; they seek a noble title.
"Throughout the ages emperors have fought over the world,
And it was we who were appointed captains of the army."
When killing people, they will kill them in the millions—
A skeleton is what they will become once they are dead.

Those younger guys of twenty years are not inclined to practice;
While training in the martial arts, they flash their dashing style.
Their greatest joy is cursing others, beating people up,
And while they fight, they strain their voices, even curse their
      neighbors!
There comes a day when unannounced good fortune will escape,
And they will suffer in some prison, overcome by sorrow.
They may well be the greatest heroes, the most stalwart fellows—
A skeleton is what they will become once they have died.

Now I am done with my lament over ten skeletons,
I face them filled with sorrow—the eleventh skeleton!
    A lack of prior practice will result in present hardship:
You have no reason to complain to Heaven and to Earth.
The wealthy people practiced goodness in some prior life;
The poor refused to practice in their lives up to the present.
    Imagine how you're bound to suffer if you do not practice—
I urge you to start practice early to avoid such sorrow.
Now if today you hear this message and don't turn around,
You do deserve to burn in boiling oil upon your death.
    But if you follow the good Way as quickly as you can,
This skeleton you'll shed while rising to the Western Heaven.
The utmost joy of that Pure Land is great beyond description,
You will enjoy eternal life: a hundred million years!

> [Liang huang baojuan (1899), in *Zhongguo zongjiao*,
>   ed. Pu, appendix, 2:42a–44a]

CHARACTER LIST

An Lushan　安祿山

"Ba Yu minjian fashi—kulou zhenyan
　(Tan kulou)"　巴渝民间法事—
　骷髏真言（叹骷髏）
Bai Jin　白金
Bai Juyi　白居易
"Baigu"　白骨
Baijia xing　百家姓
baojuan　寶卷
baqi zidi　八旗子弟
Beihai　北海
bianwen　變文
Bocheng Zigao　伯成子高
Bo Yi　伯夷

Cao Cao　曹操
Cao Pi　曹丕
Cao Zhi　曹植
Changsangzi　長桑子
"Chao Tianzi"　朝天子
Chaofu　巢父
Chen Kui　陳奎

Chen Tuan　陳搏
Chen Yiqiu　陳一球
chenzi　襯字
Chi (Lady)　郗
chou　丑
Chu　楚
chuanqi　傳奇
Chuci　楚辭
Chunqiu　春秋
Chunshuzhai　春樹齋
ci　詞
Cibei shuichan　慈悲水懺
cihua　詞話
Cilin zhaiyan　詞林摘艷
Cui (Judge)　崔
"Cui yanei baiyao zhaohuo"　催衙內
　白鷂招禍

da xian　大限
Dafo dingguangju tuoluoni jing　大佛
　頂廣聚陀羅尼經
Daode jing　道德經
daoqing　道情

Daoqing shizhong　道情十種
Dazang yilan ji　大藏一覽集
Deng Tong　鄧通
"Deshengling"　得勝令
Ding Yaokang　丁耀亢
"Dongwujin"　東武近
Dou E yuan　竇娥冤
Du Hui　杜蕙
Du Kang　杜康
Du Yingtao　杜穎陶
dujuan　杜鵑

Fan Juqing　范巨卿
Fan Kuai　樊噲
Fan Li　范蠡
Fei Changfang　費長房
Feng Menglong　馮夢龍
Fengshen yanyi　封神演義
fu　賦
"Fu banmian nü kulou"　賦半面女
　　骷髏
Fuyou Dijun　孚佑帝君

Gao Xingjian　高行健
Gelian huaying　隔簾花影
Gou Jian　句踐
"Gu meijiu"　沽美酒
Gu mingjia zaju　古明家雜劇
Guan Hanqing　關漢卿
Guan Yu　關羽
Guan Zhong　管仲
Guangcheng　廣成
Guanyin　觀音
Guben xiqu congkan sanji　古本戲曲
　　叢刊三集
guci　鼓詞
Guiguzi　鬼谷子
"Guizhixiang"　桂枝香
Guo Degang　郭德纲
Guo Xiang　郭象
Gupen ge Zhuangzi tan kulou　鼓盆
　　歌莊子嘆骷髏

Gushi huapu　顧氏畫譜
Gushi xinbian　故事新編

Han Xiangzi　韓湘子
*Han Xiangzi jiudu Wengong daoq-
　　ing*　韓湘子九度文公道情
Han Xiangzi zhuan　韓香子傳
Han Xin　韓信
hanhaochong　寒號蟲
He Zhizhang　賀知章
Honglou meng　紅樓夢
huaben　話本
huaju　話劇
Huang Gongwang　黃公望
Huang Tingjian　黃庭堅
Huangting jing　黃庭經
"Huangying'er"　黃鶯兒
Hudie meng　蝴蝶夢
Hui Shi　惠施

Ji Kang　嵇康
Jia Rui　賈瑞
Jie　桀
Jin Bao　金堡
jing　淨
Jingshi tongyan　警世通言
Jingu qiguan　今古奇觀
Jingyang　景陽
"Jinshanghua"　錦上花
Jinwu meng　金屋夢
jiu se cai qi　酒色財氣
Jiude song　酒德頌
Jiuge　九歌
Ju Lian　居廉
juan　卷

kan　坎
Kong Fangxiong　孔方兄
Kong Rong　孔融
Kūkai　空海
Kulou baojuan　骷髏寶卷
Kulou ge　骷髏歌

Kulou huanxi tu　骷髏幻戲圖
"Kulou tan"　骷髏嘆
Kulou yeche tu　骷髏拽車圖
"Kulou zhenyan"　骷髏真言
kun　坤

"Langtaosha"　浪淘沙
laosheng　老生
li　吏
li　離
Li Bai　李白
Li Chunfeng　李淳風
Li Dan　李聃
"Li Daoren dubu Yunmen"　李道人
　　獨步雲門
Li Fuyan　李復言
Li Gongzuo　李公佐
Li Kang　李康
Li Lou　離婁
Li Shouqing　李壽卿
Li Song　李嵩
Li Zhu　離朱
Liang Dong　良棟
Liang Hong　梁鴻
Liang huang baochan　梁皇保懺
Liang huang baojuan　梁皇寶卷
"Liangjing fu"　兩京賦
Liezi　列子
Ling Mengchu　凌蒙初
Ling Zhe　靈輒
lingtai　靈台
liqu　里曲
Liu Bang　劉邦
Liu Bei　劉備
Liu Hongsheng　劉鴻聲
Liu Kun　劉琨
Liu Ling　劉伶
Liu Qi　柳棨
Liu Xiu　劉秀
"Liuxian wenhua yichan—xiaoshun
　　tongsu ge"　柳仙文化遺产—孝
　　順通俗歌

Longnü　龍女
Lü An　呂安
Lü Dongbin　呂洞賓
Lü Jingru　呂敬儒
Lu Jinzhi　陸進之
"Lu sheng"　盧生
Lu Xun　魯迅
luan　鸞
Luo Lilang　羅李郎
Luo Pin　羅聘
Luo Qing　羅清
"Luoshen fu"　洛神賦

ma　馬
Ma Danyang　馬丹陽
Ma Yu　馬鈺
Maiwangguan　脈望館
"Mantingfang"　滿庭芳
Meng　蒙
Meng Guang　孟光
Meng Jiangnü　孟姜女
menghanyao　蒙汗藥
"Mengyi"　夢異
Miaoshan　妙善
Miaozhuang　妙莊
Mingcheng　冥城
mo　末
"Mo yu'er"　摸魚兒
Mulian　目連

Namo Amituo fo　南無阿彌陀佛
Namo Guanshiyin pusa　南無觀世
　　音菩薩
Nanhua zhenjing　南華真經
"Nanke taishou zhuan"　南柯太守傳
"Nankezi"　南柯子
Ningzhai　寧齋
niu　牛

Pang Juan　龐涓
peng　鵬
Peng Yue　彭越

Penglai　蓬萊
pin　品
Pinang ji　皮囊記
Pingzi　平子
Pipa xing　琵琶行
Pu Songling　蒲松齡

Qi Biaojia　祁彪佳
Qianche tu　牽車圖
Qianyan zhong zuo kulou　錢眼中
　坐骷髏
Qianzi wen　千字文
Qiaogu qiujin　敲骨求金
"Qiaopai'er"　橋牌兒
Qin Gui　秦檜
"Qingjiangyin"　清江引
Qingliangshan　清凉扇
Qinglongsi　青龍寺
Qingming　清明
Qingxu Daode Zhenjun　清虛道德
　真君
qinshu　琴書
"Qinyuanchun"　秦園春
"Qisi"　起死
Qiu Chuji　丘處機
qu　曲
Quanzhen　全真
Quhai zongmu tiyao　曲海總目提要

sanqu　散曲
Sha Heshang　沙和尚
Shancai Longnü baojuan　善才龍女
　寶卷
Shangqing　上清
"Shanpoyang"　山坡羊
Shen Tai　沈泰
sheng　生
Sheng Ming zaju erji　盛明雜劇二集
"Shenzui dongfeng"　沈醉東風
shi　詩
Shi Chong　石崇
Shi Jiu Jingxian　史九敬先

Shi Kuang　師曠
Shi Pang　石龐
Shiji　史記
"Shuahai'er"　耍孩兒
Shun　舜
shuo　說
si　絲
si　思
Si da chi　四大癡
"Si jiake"　思佳客
Siku quanshu　四庫全書
Sima Qian　司馬遷
Simi tu　四迷圖
siming　司命
Sishengyuan　四聲猿
song　頌
Song Ci　宋慈
Su Shi　蘇軾
Su Wu　蘇武
Sun Bin　孫臏
Sun Feng　孫鳳
Sunshi shuhua chao　孫氏書畫抄

Taiping geci　太平歌詞
Taizong　太宗
Tan Chuduan　譚處端
"Tan kulou"　嘆骷髏
Tanshi wuwei juan　嘆世無為卷
Tao Qian　陶潛
Tao Zhu　陶朱
"Taoyuan yi guren"　桃源憶故人
"Ti hua kulou"　題畫骷髏
"Ti kulou tu"　題骷髏圖
Tian Wen　田文
Tianshi　天史
tongbao　通寶

wai　外
Wang Chongyang　王重陽
Wang Fanzhi　王梵志
Wang Kai　王愷
Wang Mang　王莽

Wang Xifeng   王熙鳳
Wang Yinglin   王應遴
Wanmin simo tu   萬民四末圖
Wei Zhongxian   魏忠賢
wen   文
Wu Gui   武貴
Wu Wenying   吳文英
Wu Zhen   吳鎮

Xi Chu Bawang   西楚霸王
Xi Shi   西施
Xiang Yu   項羽
xiangsheng   相聲
xiaosheng   小生
Xiaoyao you   逍遙遊
Xie Guo   謝國
"Xijiangyue"   西江月
"Xijiangyue ci"   西江月詞
*Xinbian zengbu pinglin: Zhuangzi tan
    kulou nanbei ciqu*   新編增補評
    林莊子嘆骷髏南北詞曲
Xingshi hengyan   醒世恆言
"Xinshuiling"   新水令
xiong   凶
Xiongnu   匈奴
Xiyou ji   西遊記
Xiyuan lu   洗冤錄
Xizi   西子
Xizi ji   西子記
Xu Jia   徐甲
Xu Jinpingmei   續金瓶梅
Xu Wei   徐渭
Xu You   許由
Xuanni   宣尼
Xuanyuan   軒轅
Xuanzang   玄藏
Xue kulou danao Baihuating   血骷髏
    大鬧百花停

Yan Ling   嚴陵
Yan Zhuang   演莊
Yan Zhuang xindiao   演莊新調

"Yan'er luo"   雁兒落
Yang   楊
Yang Erzeng   楊而曾
Yang Guozhong   楊國忠
Yang Xi   楊羲
Yang Xiong   揚雄
Yang Zhu   楊朱
yangge   秧歌
Yangtai   陽台
Yao   堯
Yecao   野草
Yecheng Laoren   冶城老人
yin   陰
Yingzhou   瀛洲
yinyuan   因緣
Yonglegong   永樂宮
Yu   禹
Yuan Hua   袁華
Yuan Tianzhen   袁天罡
yuanben   院本
yuanjia   冤家
Yuanqu xuan   元曲選
Yuanshi Tianzun   元始天尊
Yue Fei   岳飛
Yuefu wanxiangxin   樂府萬象新
yugu   漁鼓
yugu   愚鼓
Yunlai Daoren   雲來道人
yunyu   雲雨

zaju   雜劇
zan   贊
Zang Maoxun   臧懋循
"Zaoluopao"   皂羅袍
Zhaijin qiyin   摘錦奇音
Zhang Cong   張聰
Zhang Cong   張從
Zhang Daqian   張大千
Zhang Fei   張飛
Zhang Guobin   張國賓
Zhang Han   張翰
Zhang Heng   張衡

BIBLIOGRAPHY

Aarne, Antti, and Stith Thompson. *The Types of Folktales: A Classification and Bibliography*. 2nd rev. ed. Helsinki: Suomalainen Tiedeakatemia, 1973.

Baltrušaitis, Jurgis. *Le moyen âge fantastique: Antiquités et exotismes dans l'art gothique.* Paris: Flammarion, 1981.

Berkson, Mark. "Death in the *Zhuangzi*: Mind, Nature, and the Art of Forgetting." In *Mortality in Traditional Chinese Thought*, edited by Amy Olberding and Philip J. Ivanhoe, 191–224. Albany: State University of New York Press, 2012.

Boltz, Judith Magee. "Singing to the Spirits of the Dead: A Daoist Ritual of Salvation." In *Harmony and Counterpoint: Ritual Music in Chinese Context*, edited by Evelyn S. Rawski and Rubie S. Watson, 177–225. Stanford, Calif.: Stanford University Press, 1996.

——. *A Survey of Taoist Literature, Tenth to Seventeenth Centuries.* Berkeley: Institute of East Asian Studies and Center for Chinese Studies, University of California, 1987.

Brakel-Papenhuyzen, C. "The Tale of the Skull: An Islamic Description of Hell in Javanese." *Bijdragen tot de Taal-, Land- en Volkenkunde* 158, no. 1 (2002): 1–19.

Campany, Robert Ford. *To Live as Long as Heaven and Earth: A Translation and Study of Ge Hong's "Traditions of Divine Transcendents."* Berkeley: University of California Press, 2002.

Cao Xueqin. *The Story of the Stone.* Vol. 1, *The Golden Days.* Translated by David Hawkes. Harmondsworth: Penguin, 1973.

Cao Xueqin 曹雪芹 and Gao E 高鹗. *Honglou meng* 红楼梦. Beijing: Renmin wenxue chubanshe, 1982.

Cao Zhi 曹植. *Cao Zhi ji jiaozhu* 曹植集校注. Annotated by Zhao Youwen 趙幼文. Reprint, Taipei: Ming wen, 1985.

Chai Junwei 柴俊为, ed. *Jingju da xikao* 京剧大戏考. Shanghai: Xuelin chubanshe, 2004.

Chappell, David W. "The *Precious Scroll of the Liang Emperor*: Buddhist and Daoist Repentance to Save the Dead." In *Going Forth: Visions of Buddhist Vinaya; Essays Presented in Honor of Professor Stanley Weinstein*, edited by William M. Bodiford, 40–67. Honolulu: University of Hawai'i Press, 2005.

Che Xilun 车锡伦. "Daoqing kao" 道情考. *Xiju yanjiu* 70 (2006): 218–38.

Che Xilun 車錫倫, comp. *Zhongguo baojuan zongmu* 中國寶卷總目. Beijing: Beijing Yanshan chubanshe, 2000.

Chen Tsu-wen. "*Hamlet* and *The Butterfly Dream*." *Tamkang Review* 6, no. 2; 7, no. 1 (1975–1976): 287–302.

Chen Yuan 陳垣, comp. *Daojia jinshi lüe* 道家金石略. Beijing: Wenwu chubanshe, 1988.

Clark, James M. *The Dance of Death in the Middle Ages and the Renaissance*. Glasgow: Jackson, 1950.

Confucius. *The Analects*. Translated by D. C. Lau. Harmondsworth: Penguin, 1979.

Daozang 道藏. 1,120 fascicles. Shanghai: Hanfenlou, 1923–1926.

Dekker, Ton, Jurjen van der Kooi, and Theo Meder. *Van Aladdin tot Zwaan kleef aan: Lexicon van sprookjes; Ontstaan, ontwikkeling, variaties*. Nijmegen: SUN, 1997.

Ding Ruomu 丁若木. "'Xingxing han, pinang chepo, bianshi kulou': Cong Wu Zhen hua kulou shuoqi" 惺惺汉, 皮囊扯破, 便是骷髅—从吴镇画骷髅说起. *Zongjiaoxue yanjiu*, no. 1 (1996): 41–47.

Ding Yaokang 丁耀亢. "Southern Window Dream." Translated by Wilt L. Idema. *Renditions* 69 (2008): 20–33.

——. *Xu Jinpingmei* 續金瓶梅. Original woodblock edition. In *Guben xiaoshuo jicheng*, 43:1–4. Shanghai: Shanghai guji chubanshe, 1990.

Dudbridge, Glen. *The Legend of Miaoshan*. Oxford: Oxford University Press, 2004.

Dudink, Adrian. "Lubelli's *Wanmin simo tu* (*Picture of the Four Last Things of All People*), ca. 1683." *Sino-Western Cultural Relations Journal* 28 (2006): 1–17.

Eirakukyū hekiga 永樂宮壁畫. Kyoto: Binobi, 1981.

Eskildsen, Stephen. *The Teachings and Practices of the Early Quanzhen Taoist Masters*. Albany: SUNY Press, 2004.

Faure, Bernard. *The Rhetoric of Immediacy: A Cultural Critique of Chan/Zen Buddhism*. Princeton, N.J.: Princeton University Press, 1991.

Feng Menglong 冯梦龙, comp. *Jingshi tongyan xinzhu quanben* 警世通言新注全本. Annotated by Wu Shuyin 吴书荫. Beijing: Shiyue wenyi chubanshe, 1994.

——, comp. *Stories to Awaken the World*. Vol. 3 of *A Ming Dynasty Collection*. Translated by Shuhui Yang and Yunqin Yang. Seattle: University of Washington Press, 2009.

——, comp. *Stories to Caution the World*. Vol. 2 of *A Ming Dynasty Collection*. Translated by Shuhui Yang and Yunqin Yang. Seattle: University of Washington Press, 2005.

——, comp. *Xingshi hengyan xinzhu quanben* 醒世恒言新注全本. Annotated by Zhang Minggao 张明高. Beijing: Shiyue wenyi chubanshe, 1994.

Fu Xihua 傅惜華. *Mingdai chuanqi quanmu* 明代傳奇全目. Beijing: Renmin wenxue chubanshe, 1959.

——. *Mingdai zaju quanmu* 明代雜劇全目. Beijing: Zuojia chubanshe, 1958.

——. *Yuandai zaju quanmu* 元代雜劇全目. Beijing: Zuojia chubanshe, 1957.

Gamble, Sidney D. *Chinese Village Plays from the Ting Hsien Region (Yang Ke Hsüan).* Amsterdam: Philo Press, 1970.

Garber, Marjorie. *Shakespeare After All.* New York: Anchor Books, 2005.

Gertsman, Elina. *The Dance of Death in the Middle Ages: Image, Text, Performance.* Turnhout, Belgium: Brepols, 2010.

Giès, Jacques. *Les arts de l'Asie centrale: La collection Paul Pelliot du Musée national des arts asiatiques; Guimet.* Vol. 1. Paris: Réunion des Musées Nationaux, 1995.

Graham, A. C. *Disputers of the Tao: Philosophical Argument in Ancient China.* Chicago: Open Court, 1989.

Gu Fu 顧復. *Pingsheng zhuangguan* 平生壯觀. 4 vols. Shanghai: Shanghai renmin meishu chubanshe, 1962.

Guo Jingrui 郭精銳 et al., eds. *Che wangfu quben tiyao* 車王府曲本提要. Guangzhou: Zhongshan daxue chubanshe, 1989.

Guo Yingde 郭英德. *Ming Qing chuanqi zonglu* 明清传奇综录. Shijiazhuang: Hebei jiaoyu chubanshe, 1997.

Hanan, Patrick. *The Chinese Short Story: Studies in Dating, Authorship, and Composition.* Cambridge, Mass.: Harvard University Press, 1973.

——. "The *Yün-men chuan*: From *Chantefable* to Short Story." *Bulletin of the School of Oriental and African Studies* 36, no. 2 (1973): 299–308.

Hansen, William. *Ariadne's Thread: A Guide to International Tales Found in Classical Literature.* Ithaca, N.Y.: Cornell University Press, 2002.

Harrison, Ann Tukey, ed. *The Danse Macabre of Women: Ms. fr. 955 of the Bibliothèque Nationale.* With a chapter by Sandra L. Hindman. Kent, Ohio: Kent State University Press, 1994.

Hawkes, David. *Ch'u tz'u: The Songs of the South; An Ancient Chinese Anthology.* Oxford: Oxford University Press, 1959.

Henschen, Folke. *The Human Skull: A Cultural History.* London: Thames & Hudson, 1965.

Hong, Jeehee. "Theatricalizing Death and Society in *The Skeleton's Illusory Performance* by Li Song." *Art Bulletin* 93, no. 1 (2011): 60–78.

Hu, Siao-chen. "In the Name of Correctness: Ding Yaokang's *Xu Jin Ping Mei* as a Reading of *Jin Ping Mei*." In *Snakes' Legs: Sequels, Continuations, Rewritings, and Chinese Fiction,* edited by Martin W. Huang, 75–97. Honolulu: University of Hawai'i Press, 2004.

Hurvitz, Leon, trans. *Scripture of the Lotus Blossom of the Fine Dharma.* Translated from the Chinese of Kumārajīva. New York: Columbia University Press, 1976.

Idema, Wilt. L. *The Dramatic Oeuvre of Chu Yu-tun (1379–1439).* Leiden: Brill, 1985.

——. "Free and Easy Wanderings: Lu Xun's 'Resurrecting the Dead' and Its Precursors." *Chinese Literature: Essays, Articles, Reviews* 34 (2012): 15–29.

——. *Personal Salvation and Filial Piety: Two Precious Scroll Narratives of Guanyin and Her Acolytes.* Honolulu: University of Hawai'i Press, 2008.

——. "Prosimetric and Verse Narrative." In *The Cambridge History of Chinese Literature.* Vol. 2, *From 1375,* edited by Kang-i Sun Chang and Stephen Owen, 343–412. Cambridge: Cambridge University Press, 2010.

——. "Skulls and Skeletons in Art and on Stage." In *Conflict and Accommodation in Early Modern East Asia: Essays in Honour of Erik Zürcher,* edited by Leonard Blussé and Harriet T. Zurndorfer, 191–215. Leiden: Brill, 1993.

Idema, Wilt, and Stephen H. West. *Chinese Theater, 1100–1450: A Source Book.* Wiesbaden: Steiner, 1982.

Ikkyū Sōjun. "Ikkyū's Skeletons." Translated by R. H. Blyth. *Eastern Buddhist* 6, no. 1 (1973): 111–25.

Ji Kang 嵇康. *Ji Kang ji jiaozhu* 嵇康集校注. Annotated by Dai Mingyang 戴明揚. Beijing: Renmin wenxue chubanshe, 1962.

Jiang Kebin 姜克濱. "Huangdan yu yinyu de chonggou—lun *Gushi xinbian* 'Qisi'" 荒诞与隐喻的重构—论故事新编起死. *Shenyang shifan daxue xuebao,* no. 4 (2010): 84–87.

——. "Shilun *Zhuangzi tan kulou* gushi zhi shanbian" 试论庄子叹骷髅故事之嬗变. *Beijing huagong daxue xuebao (shehui kexueban),* no. 2 (2010): 29–33.

Jiang Kun 姜昆 and Ni Zhongzhi 倪钟之. *Zhongguo quyi tongshi* 中国曲艺通史. Beijing: Renmin wenxue chubanshe, 2005.

Johnson, Dale R. *Yuan Music Dramas: Studies in Prosody and Structure and a Complete Catalogue of Northern Arias in the Dramatic Style.* Ann Arbor: Center for Chinese Studies, University of Michigan, 1980.

Jordan, David K., and Daniel L. Overmyer. *The Flying Phoenix: Aspects of Chinese Sectarianism in Taiwan.* Princeton, N.J.: Princeton University Press, 1986.

Kang Baocheng 康保成. "Bushuo 'Kulou huanxi tu'—jianshuo 'kulou,' 'kuilei' ji qi yu fojiao guanxi" 补说骷髅幻戏图兼说骷髅傀儡及其与佛教关系. *Xueshu yanjiu,* no. 11 (2003): 127–29.

——. "'Gulou ge' de zhenwei yu yuanyuan xintan" 骷髅格的真伪与渊源新探. *Wenxue yichan,* no. 2 (2003): 99–106.

——. "Sha Heshang de kulou xianglian: Cong toulu chongbai dao mizong yishi" 沙和尚的骷髅项链从头颅崇拜到密宗仪式, *Henan daxue xuebao,* no. 1 (2004): 75–78.

Klein, Esther. "Were There 'Inner Chapters' in the Warring States? A New Examination of Evidence About the *Zhuangzi.*" *T'oung Pao* 96 (2010): 299–369.

Komjathy, Louis. *Cultivating Perfection: Mysticism and Self-Transformation in Early Quanzhen Daoism.* Leiden: Brill, 2007.

Kurtz, Léonard P. *The Dance of Death and the Macabre Spirit in European Literature.* 1934. Reprint, Geneva: Slatkine, 1975.

Laing, Ellen Johnston. "Li Sung and Some Aspects of Southern Sung Figure Painting." *Artibus Asiae* 37, nos. 1–2 (1975): 5–38.

Lan Liming 藍立蓂, ed. *Huijiao xiangzhu Guan Hanqing ji* 彙校詳注關漢卿集. 3 vols. Beijing: Zhonghua shuju, 2006.

Laufer, Berthold. "Origins of Our Dance of Death." *Open Court* 22 (1908): 597–604.

——. *Use of Human Skulls and Bones in Tibet.* Chicago: Museum of Natural History, 1923.

Lei Jingxuan 雷競璇. *Kunqu Hudiemeng: Yibu chuantongxi de zaixian* 崑劇蝴蝶夢一部傳統戲的再現. Hong Kong: Oxford University Press, 2005.

Lévy, André. *Inventaire analytique et critique du conte chinois en langue vulgaire.* Part 1, vol. 1. Paris: Collège de France, Institut des hautes études chinoises, 1979.

Li E 厲鶚. *Nan Song yuanhua lu* 南宋院畫錄. In *Huashi congshu* 畫史叢書, compiled by Yu Anlan 于安瀾. Shanghai: Shanghai renmin meishu chubanshe, 1963.

Li Fengshi 李逢時 [Jiubiao 九標] et al. *Si da chi* 四大癡. Late Ming woodblock edition. Harvard-Yenching Library, Harvard College Library, Cambridge, Mass.

Li Fushun 李福順. "Li Song he ta de 'Kulou huanxi tu'" 李嵩和他的骷髏幻戲图. *Duoyun*, no. 3 (1981): 165–68, 150.

Liezi. *The Book of Lieh-tzu.* Translated by A. C. Graham. London: Murray, 1960.

Liu, Siyuan. "Theatre Reform as Censorship: Censoring Traditional Theatre in China in the Early 1950s." *Theatre Journal* 61, no. 3 (2009): 387–406.

Liu Guangmin 刘光民. *Gudai shuochang bianti xipian* 古代说唱辨体析篇. Beijing: Shoudu shifan daxue chubanshe, 1996.

Loewe, Michael, ed. *Early Chinese Texts: A Bibliographical Guide.* Berkeley: Society for the Study of Early China and Institute of East Asian Studies, University of California, 1993.

Lou Siun [Lu Xun]. *Contes anciens à notre manière.* Translated by Li Tche-houa. Paris: Gallimard, 1959.

Lu Hsun [Lu Xun]. *A Brief History of Chinese Fiction.* Translated by Yang Hsien-yi and Gladys Yang. Beijing: Foreign Languages Press, 1959.

——. *Old Tales Retold.* Translated by Yang Hsien-yi and Gladys Yang. Beijing: Foreign Languages Press, 1961.

Lu Xun 鲁迅. *Lu Xun xiaoshuo ji* 鲁迅小說集. Beijing: Renmin wenxue chubanshe, 1964.

——. *The Real Story of Ah-Q and Other Tales of China: The Complete Fiction of Lu Xun.* Translated by Julia Lovell. New York: Penguin, 2009.

Lüders, Else, and Heinrich Lüders. *Buddhistische Märchen aus dem alten Indien.* Düsseldorf: Diederichs, 1981.

Ma Yu 馬鈺. *Danyang shenguangcan* 丹陽神光燦. Vol. 791 of the *Daozang.*

——. *Dongxuan jinyu ji* 洞玄金玉集. Vols. 789–790 of the *Daozang.*

——. *Jianwu ji* 漸悟集. Vol. 786 of the *Daozang.*

Mair, Victor. "The *Zhuangzi* and Its Impact." In *Daoism Handbook*, edited by Livia Kohn, 30–52. Leiden: Brill, 2000.

Marsone, Pierre. *Wang Chongyang (1113–1170) et la fondation du Quanzhen: Ascètes taoïstes et alchimie intérieure*. Paris: Collège de France, Institut des hautes études chinoises, 2010.

Meng Yuanlao 孟元老. *Dongjing menghua lu* 東京夢華錄. Annotated by Deng Zhicheng 鄧之誠. Reprint, Hong Kong: Shangwu yinshuguan, 1961.

Meng Yuanlao et al. *Dongjing menghua lu (wai si zhong)* 東京夢華錄外四種. Beijing: Zhonghua shuju, 1962.

Minghe yuyin 鳴鶴餘音. Vols. 744–745 of the *Daozang*.

Motsch, Monika. *Mit Bambusrohr und Ahle: Von Qian Zhongshus "Guanzhuibian" zu einer neubetrachtung Du Fus*. Frankfurt: Lang, 1994.

Mu Soeng. *The Diamond Sutra: Transforming the Way We Perceive the World*. Boston: Wisdom Publications, 2000.

Nappi, Carla. *The Monkey and the Inkpot: Natural History and Its Transformation in Early Modern China*. Cambridge, Mass.: Harvard University Press, 2009.

Nitti, Patrizia, ed. *C'est la vie! Vanités de Pompéi à Damien Hirst*. Paris: Flammarion, 2010.

Ono Shihei 小野四平. "Dōjō ni tsuite" 道情について. In *Chūgoku kinsei ni okeru tampen shōsetsu no kenkyū* 中国近世における短篇小說の研究, 288–309. Tokyo: Hyōronsha, 1979.

Ouyang Xun 歐陽詢, comp. *Yiwen leiju* 藝文類聚. Edited by Wang Shaoying 汪紹楹. Beijing: Zhonghua shuju, 1965.

Overmyer, Daniel L. *Precious Volumes: An Introduction to Chinese Sectarian Scriptures from the Sixteenth and Seventeenth Centuries*. Cambridge, Mass.: Harvard University Asia Center, 1999.

Owen, Stephen. *Remembrances: The Experience of the Past in Classical Chinese Literature*. Cambridge, Mass.: Harvard University Press, 1986.

Pennacchietti, Fabrizio A. *Three Mirrors for Two Biblical Ladies: Susanna and the Queen of Sheba in the Eyes of Jews, Christians, and Muslims*. Piscataway, N.J.: Gorgias Press, 2006.

Picard, François. "Le chant du squelette (Kulou ge)." *Journal asiatique* 292 (2004): 382–412.

Pregadio, Fabrizio, ed. *The Encyclopedia of Taoism*. 2 vols. London: Routledge, 2008.

Pregadio, Fabrizio, and Lowell Skarr. "Inner Alchemy." In *Daoism Handbook*, edited by Livia Kohn, 464–97. Leiden: Brill, 2000.

Pu Wenqi 濮文起, ed. *Zhongguo zongjiao lishi wenxian jicheng: Minjian baojuan* 中國宗教歷史文獻集成民間寶卷. 20 vols. Hefei: Huangshan shushe, 2005.

Qi Biaojia 祁彪佳. *Yuanshan tang Ming qupin jupin jiaolu* 遠山堂明曲品劇品校錄. Edited by Huang Shang 黃裳. Shanghai: Shanghai chuban gongsi, 1955.

Qian Decang 錢德蒼, comp. *Zhuibaiqiu* 綴白裘. 6 vols. Beijing: Zhonghua shuju, 2005.

Qian Zhongshu 錢鍾書. *Guanzhui bian* 管錐篇. 4 vols. Beijing: Zhonghua shuju, 1979.

Qing Menggu Che wangfu cang zidishu 清蒙古车王府藏子弟书. 2 vols. Beijing: Guoji wenhua chuban gongsi, 1994.

Quan Qing ci 全清词. Beijing: Zhonghua shuju, 1994.

Rabinovitch, Judith N., and Timothy R. Bradstock, trans. and eds. *Dance of the Butterflies: Chinese Poetry from the Japanese Court Tradition*. Ithaca, N.Y.: East Asia Program, Cornell University, 2005.

Red Pine. *The Diamond Sutra: Text and Commentaries*. Washington, D.C.: Counterpoint, 2001.

Ren Guangwei 任光伟. "'Shuahai'er' zonghengkao" 耍孩児纵横考. In *"Xiqu yishu" ershinian jinian wenji Xiqu wenxue, xiqushi yanjiu juan* 戏曲艺术二十年纪念文集 戏曲文学戏曲史卷, 395–418. Beijing: Zhongguo xiju chubanshe, 2000.

Rosemont, Henry, Jr., and Roger T. Ames. *The Chinese Classic of Family Reverence: A Philosophical Translation of the "Xiaojing."* Honolulu: University of Hawai'i Press, 2009.

Sanford, James H. "The Abominable Tachikawa Skull Ritual." *Monumenta Nipponica* 46, no. 1 (1991): 1–20.

——. "The Nine Faces of Death: 'Su Tung-po's' *Kuzō-shi*." *Eastern Buddhist* 22, no. 2 (1988): 54–77.

——. *Zen-Man Ikkyū*. Chico, Calif.: Scholars Press, 1981.

Sawada Mizuho 澤田瑞穗. "Dōjō ni tsuite" 道情について. *Chūgoku bungaku geppō* 44 (1938): 117–23.

Scott, A. C. *Traditional Chinese Plays*. Vol. 1. Madison: University of Wisconsin Press, 1970.

Shen Tai 沈泰, ed. *Sheng Ming zaju erji* 盛明雜劇二集. Reprint, Beijing: Zhongguo xiju chubanshe, 1958.

Shen Xiping 申喜萍. "Shixi daojiao dui Zhongguo huihua de yingxiang" 试析道教对 中国绘画的影响. *Yishu tansuo*, no. 4 (2004): 68–72.

Shi Honglei 史宏蕾 and Yi Bao 伊宝. "Shanxi Jishan Qinglongsi yaodian bihua de minsu fengge tezheng" 山西稷山青龙寺腰殿壁画的民俗风格特征. *Meishu daguan*, no. 3 (2009): 76–77.

Sima Qian 司馬遷. *Shiji* 史記. 10 vols. Beijing: Zhonghua shuju, 1959.

Sui Shusen 隋樹森, comp. *Quan Yuan sanqu* 全元散曲. 2 vols. Beijing: Zhonghua shuju, 1964.

Sun Fuxuan 孙福轩. "Daoqing kaoshi" 道情考释. *Daojiao luntan*, no. 2 (2005): 17–22.

Sung Tz'u [Song Ci]. *The Washing Away of Wrongs: Forensic Medicine in Thirteenth-Century China*. Translated by Brian E. McKnight. Ann Arbor: Center for Chinese Studies, University of Michigan, 1981.

Suzuki, Daisetz Teitarō, trans. *The Lankavatara Sutra: A Mahayana Text*. Reprint, Taipei: SMC Publishing, 1991.

Tan Chuduan 譚處端. *Shuiyun ji* 水雲集. Vol. 798 of the *Daozang*.

Tang Guizhang 唐圭璋, comp. *Quan Jin Yuan ci* 全金元詞. 2 vols. Beijing: Zhonghua shuju, 1979.

Tottoli, R. "The Story of Jesus and the Skull in Arabic Literature: The Emergence and Growth of a Religious Tradition." *Jerusalem Studies in Arabic and Islam* 28 (2003): 225–59.

Uther, Hans-Jörg. *The Types of International Folktales: A Classification and Bibliography, Based on the System of Antti Aarne and Stith Thompson.* 3 vols. Helsinki: Suomalainen Tiedeakatemia, 2004.

Wagner, Rudolf G. *The Contemporary Chinese Historical Drama: Four Studies.* Berkeley: University of California Press, 1990.

Waley, Arthur. *Chinese Poems.* London: Unwin Paperbacks, 1982.

Wang, Eugene Y. *Shaping the Lotus Sutra: Buddhist Visual Culture in Medieval China.* Seattle: University of Washington Press, 2005.

[Wang Jilie 王季烈, ed.] *Guben Yuan Ming zaju* 孤本元明雜劇. Reprint. Beijing: Zhongguo xiju chubanshe, 1958.

Wang Kui 王夔. "Mingkan xiqu sanchu *Zhou Zhuangzi tan kulou* xintan" 明刊戏曲散出周庄子叹骷髅新探. *Anhui daxue xuebao*, no. 1 (2005): 121–25.

Wang Liqi 王利器. *Yuan Ming Qing sandai jinhui xiaoshuo xiqu shiliao* 元明清三代禁毁小说戏曲史料. Rev. ed. Shanghai: Shanghai guji chubanshe, 1981.

Wang Senran 王森然. *Zhongguo jumu cidian* 中国剧目辞典. Shijiazhuang: Hebei jiaoyu chubanshe, 1997.

Wang Weiyi 王惟一. *Tongren yuxue zhenzhi tujing* 銅人腧穴針灸途經. In *Zhenzhi mingzhu jicheng* 针灸明著集成, edited by Huang Longxiang 黄龙祥, 166–215. Beijing: Huaxia chubanshe, 1997.

Wang Yinglin 王應遴. *Yan Zhuang xindiao* 衍莊新調. In *Wang Yinglin zaji* 王應遴雜集. Original woodblock edition of ca. 1620 held at the Naikaku Bunko, Tokyo.

Wang Zhe 王嚞. *Chongyang quanzhen ji* 重陽全真集. Vols. 793–796 of the *Daozang*.

Wilhelm, Helmut. "On Chuang-Tzu Plays from the Yüan Store." *Literature East and West* 17, nos. 2–4 (1973): 244–52.

Wilson, Liz. *Charming Cadavers: Horrific Figurations of the Feminine in Indian Buddhist Hagiographic Literature.* Chicago: University of Chicago Press, 1996.

Wood, Frances, and Mark Barnard. *The Diamond Sutra: The Story of the World's Earliest Dated Printed Book.* London: British Library, 2010.

[Wu Cheng'en.] *The Journey to the West.* Translated by Anthony Wu. 4 vols. Chicago: University of Chicago Press, 1977–1983.

Wu Xiaohong 毌小红 et al., eds. *Shanxi luogu* 山西罗鼓. Taiyuan: Shanxi renmin chubanshe, 1991.

Wu Yimin 武艺民. *Zhongguo daoqing yishu gailun* 中国道情艺术概论. Taiyuan: Shanxi guji chubanshe, 1997.

Wu Zhefu 吳哲夫, ed. *Zhonghua wuqiannian wenwu jikan: Songhua pian* 中華五千年文物集刊宋畫篇 IV. Taipei: Zhonghua wuqiannian wenwu jikan bianji weiyuanhui, 1981.

Xiangmeng Ciren 香夢詞人. *Zhuangzi qiwen yanyi* 庄子奇文演義. Shanghai: Dadong shuju, 1918.

Xie Boyang 謝伯陽, comp. *Quan Ming sanqu* 全明散曲. 5 vols. Jinan: Qi Lu shushe, 1993.

Xu Fuming 徐扶明. "Kunqu *Hudie meng* de lailong qumai" 昆劇蝴蝶梦的来龙去脉. *Yishu baijia*, no. 4 (1993): 96–103.

Xu Jingbo 徐静波. "Guanshiyin pusa kaoshu" 观世音菩萨考述. In *Guanyin pusa quanshu* 观音菩萨全书, 226–65. Shenyang: Chunfeng wenyi chubanshe, 1987.

Xu Zhenhui 徐振辉. "*Honglou meng* de xing yu ai" 红楼梦的性与爱. *Shuwu*, no. 4 (2002): 42–44.

Xu Zifang 徐子方. *Ming zaju yanjiu* 明雜劇研究. Taipei: Wenjin chubanshe, 1998.

Yang, Richard F. S. trans. *Four Plays of the Yuan Drama*. Taipei: China Post, 1972.

Yang Erzeng. *The Story of Han Xiangzi: The Alchemical Adventures of a Daoist Immortal*. Translated by Philip Clart. Seattle: University of Washington Press, 2007.

Yang Xiu 杨休. "Li Song 'Simi tu' chukao" 李嵩四谜图初考. *Sichuan wenwu*, no. 5 (2008): 69–71.

Yangjiafu yanyi 楊家府演義. Shanghai: Shanghai guji chubanshe, 1980.

Yangjiajiang yanyi 楊家將演義. Beijing: Baowentang, 1980.

Yao, Ted. "Quanzhen—Complete Perfection." In *Daoism Handbook*, edited by Livia Kohn, 567–93. Leiden: Brill, 2000.

Ye Dejun 葉德均. *Song Yuan Ming jiangchang wenxue* 宋元明講唱文學. Shanghai: Gudian wenxue chubanshe, 1957.

Yi Ruofen 衣若芬. "Kulou huanxi: Zhongguo wenxue yu tuxiang zhong de shengming yishi" 骷髏幻戲—中國文學與圖象中旳生命意識. *Zhongguo wenzhe yanjiu jikan* 26 (2005): 73–125.

Yong You. *The Diamond Sutra in Chinese Culture*. Los Angeles: Buddha's Light Publishing, 2010.

Yongle gong 永乐宫. Beijing: Renmin meishu chubanshe, 1964.

Yü, Chün-fang. *Kuanyin: The Chinese Transformation of Avalokiteśvara*. New York: Columbia University Press, 2001.

Yu, Pauline, Peter Bol, Stephen Owen, and Willard Peterson, eds. *Ways with Words: Writing About Reading Texts from Early China*. Berkeley: University of California Press, 2000.

Yuan dianzhang 元典章. Taipei: Wenhai chubanshe, 1964.

Yuefu wanxiangxin 樂府萬象新. In *Haiwai guben wan-Ming xiju xuanji sanzhong* 海外孤本晚明戲劇選集三種, edited by Li Fuqing 李福清 and Li Ping 李平, 319–644. Shanghai: Shanghai guji chubanshe, 1993.

Yunmen zhuan 雲門傳. National Library of Peiping Rare Books Collection Microfilms, no. 2699.

Zeng Bairong 曾白融, ed. *Jingju jumu cidian* 京剧剧目辞典. Beijing: Zhongguo xiju chubanshe, 1989.

Zeng Yongyi 曾永義. *Ming zaju gailun* 明雜劇概論. Taipei: Xuehai chubanshe, 1979.

Zhaijin qiyin 摘錦奇音. In *Shanben xiqu congkan* 善本戲曲叢刊, edited by Wang Qiugui 王秋桂, vol. 3. Taipei: Xuesheng shuju, 1984.

Zhan Renzhong 詹仁中. "Shitan daoqing" 試谈道情. *Quyi yishu luncong* 7 (1988): 52–57.

Zhang Heng 張衡. *Zhang Heng shiwenji jiaozhu* 張衡詩文集校注. Annotated by Zhang Zhenze 張震澤. Shanghai: Shanghai guji chubanshe, 1986.

Zhang Shasha 張莎莎. "'Kulou' yixiang zhong de zhengzhi yuyan: 'Zhuangzi tan kulou' yu Zhang Heng *Kulou fu*, Cao Zhi *Kuloushuo* de bijiao" 骷髏意象中的政治寓言庄子叹骷髏与张衡骷髏赋曹植骷髏说的比較. *Leshan shifan xueyuan xuebao* 27, no. 4 (2012): 38–39.

Zhang Shouchong 张寿崇, ed. *Manzu shuochang wenxue: Zidishu zhenben baizhong* 满族说唱文学子弟书珍本百种. Beijing: Minzu chubanshe, 2000.

Zhang Xishun 張希舜, ed. *Baojuan chuji* 寶卷初集. 40 vols. Taiyuan: Shanxi renmin chubanshe, 1994.

Zhang Zehong 张泽洪. "Daojiao chang daoqing suojian de Lao Zhuang sixiang: Yi *Zhuangzi tan kulou* daoqing wei zhongxin" 道教唱道情所见的老庄思想以庄子叹骷髏道情为中心. In *Quanzhendao yu Lao-Zhuang xue guoji xueshu yantaohui lunwenji* 全真道与老庄学国际学术研讨会论文集, edited by Xiong Tieji 熊铁基 and Mai Zifei 麦子飞, 558–75. Wuhan: Huazhong shifan daxue chubanshe, 2009.

——. *Daojiao chang daoqing yu Zhongguo minjian wenhua yanjiu* 道教唱道情与中国民间文化研究. Beijing: Renmin chubanshe, 2011.

Zhao Guangya 赵光亚. "Lu Xun xiaoshuo *Qisi* de wenti xuanze yu chonggou" 鲁迅小说起死的文体选择与重构. *Nanjing shifan daxue wenxueyuan xuebao*, no. 1 (2012): 62–67.

Zhao Jingshen 赵景深. "Sichuan zhuqin *Sanguozhi* xu" 四川竹琴三国志序. In *Quyi luncong* 曲艺丛谈, 227–31. Beijing: Zhongguo quyi chubanshe, 1982.

Zhao Jingshen 趙景深. *Yuanren zaju gouchen* 元人雜劇鈎沉. Shanghai: Shanghai guji chubanshe, 1956.

Zhao Kuifu 赵逵夫, ed. *Lidai fu pingzhu* 历代赋评注. Chengdu: Ba Shu shushe, 2010.

Zheng Qian 鄭騫. *Beiqu taoshi huilu xiangjie* 北曲套式彙錄詳解. Taipei: Yiwen yinshuguan, 1973.

Zheng Xie 鄭燮. *Chêng Pan-ch'iao: Selected Poems, Calligraphy, Paintings and Seal Engravings*. Translated by Anthony Cheung and Paul Gurofsky. Hong Kong: Joint Publishing, 1987.

Zheng Zhenduo 鄭振鐸, comp. *Zhongguo gudai banhua congkan* 中國古代版畫叢刊. 4 vols. Shanghai: Shanghai guji chubanshe, 1988.

Zhou Chunyi 周純一. "Taiping geci yanjiu, shang" 太平歌詞研究上. *Minsu quyi*, no. 60 (1989): 102–27.

——. "Taiping geci yanjiu, xia" 太平歌詞研究下. *Minsu quyi*, no. 61 (1989): 116–27.

Zhu Xiyuan 朱希元. "Yongle gong bihua tiji luwen" 永乐宫壁画题记录文. *Wenwu*, August 1963, 65–78.

Zhuang Shen 莊申. "Luo Pin yu qi *Guiqu tu*—jian lun Zhongguo guihua zhi yuanliu" 羅聘與其鬼趣圖—兼論中國鬼畫之源流. *Zhongyang yanjiusuo Lishi yuyan yanjiusuo jikan* 44, no. 3 (1972): 403–34.

Zhuangzi. *Chuang-tzu: The Seven Inner Chapters and Other Writings from the Book Chuang-tzu*. Translated by A. C. Graham. London: Allen & Unwin, 1981.

———. *The Complete Works of Chuang Tzu*. Translated by Burton Watson. New York: Columbia University Press, 1970

Zürcher, Erik. "Buddhist *chanhui* and Christian Confession in Seventeenth-Century China." In *Forgive Us Our Sins: Confession in Late Ming and Early Qing China*, edited by Nicolas Standaert and Ad Dudink, 103–28. Sankt Augustin: Monumenta Serica Institute, 2006.

INDEX

Page numbers in italics refer to illustrations in the text.

TRANSLATIONS FROM THE ASIAN CLASSICS

Twenty Plays of the Nō Theatre, ed. Donald Keene. Also in paperback ed. 1970

Chūshingura: The Treasury of Loyal Retainers, tr. Donald Keene. Also in paperback ed. 1971; rev. ed. 1997

The Zen Master Hakuin: Selected Writings, tr. Philip B. Yampolsky 1971

Chinese Rhyme-Prose: Poems in the Fu Form from the Han and Six Dynasties Periods, tr. Burton Watson. Also in paperback ed. 1971

Kūkai: Major Works, tr. Yoshito S. Hakeda. Also in paperback ed. 1972

The Old Man Who Does as He Pleases: Selections from the Poetry and Prose of Lu Yu, tr. Burton Watson 1973

The Lion's Roar of Queen Śrīmālā, tr. Alex and Hideko Wayman 1974

Courtier and Commoner in Ancient China: Selections from the History of the Former Han by Pan Ku, tr. Burton Watson. Also in paperback ed. 1974

Japanese Literature in Chinese, vol. 1: *Poetry and Prose in Chinese by Japanese Writers of the Early Period*, tr. Burton Watson 1975

Japanese Literature in Chinese, vol. 2: *Poetry and Prose in Chinese by Japanese Writers of the Later Period*, tr. Burton Watson 1976

Love Song of the Dark Lord: Jayadeva's Gītagovinda, tr. Barbara Stoler Miller. Also in paperback ed. Cloth ed. includes critical text of the Sanskrit. 1977; rev. ed. 1997

Ryōkan: Zen Monk-Poet of Japan, tr. Burton Watson 1977

Calming the Mind and Discerning the Real: From the Lam rim chen mo of Tsoṇ-kha-pa, tr. Alex Wayman 1978

The Hermit and the Love-Thief: Sanskrit Poems of Bhartrihari and Bilhaṇa, tr. Barbara Stoler Miller 1978

The Lute: Kao Ming's P'i-p'a chi, tr. Jean Mulligan. Also in paperback ed. 1980

A Chronicle of Gods and Sovereigns: Jinnō Shōtōki of Kitabatake Chikafusa, tr. H. Paul Varley 1980

Among the Flowers: The Hua-chien chi, tr. Lois Fusek 1982

Grass Hill: Poems and Prose by the Japanese Monk Gensei, tr. Burton Watson 1983

Doctors, Diviners, and Magicians of Ancient China: Biographies of Fang-shih, tr. Kenneth J. DeWoskin. Also in paperback ed. 1983

Theater of Memory: The Plays of Kālidāsa, ed. Barbara Stoler Miller. Also in paperback ed. 1984

The Columbia Book of Chinese Poetry: From Early Times to the Thirteenth Century, ed. and tr. Burton Watson. Also in paperback ed. 1984

Poems of Love and War: From the Eight Anthologies and the Ten Long Poems of Classical Tamil, tr. A. K. Ramanujan. Also in paperback ed. 1985

The Bhagavad Gita: Krishna's Counsel in Time of War, tr. Barbara Stoler Miller 1986

The Columbia Book of Later Chinese Poetry, ed. and tr. Jonathan Chaves. Also in paperback ed. 1986

The Tso Chuan: Selections from China's Oldest Narrative History, tr. Burton Watson 1989

Waiting for the Wind: Thirty-six Poets of Japan's Late Medieval Age, tr. Steven Carter 1989

Selected Writings of Nichiren, ed. Philip B. Yampolsky 1990

Saigyō, Poems of a Mountain Home, tr. Burton Watson 1990

The Book of Lieh Tzu: A Classic of the Tao, tr. A. C. Graham. Morningside ed. 1990

The Tale of an Anklet: An Epic of South India—The Cilappatikāram of Iḷaṅkō Aṭikaḷ, tr. R. Parthasarathy 1993

Waiting for the Dawn: A Plan for the Prince, tr. with introduction by Wm. Theodore de Bary 1993

Yoshitsune and the Thousand Cherry Trees: A Masterpiece of the Eighteenth-Century Japanese Puppet Theater, tr., annotated, and with introduction by Stanleigh H. Jones, Jr. 1993

The Lotus Sutra, tr. Burton Watson. Also in paperback ed. 1993

The Classic of Changes: A New Translation of the I Ching as Interpreted by Wang Bi, tr. Richard John Lynn 1994

Beyond Spring: Tz'u Poems of the Sung Dynasty, tr. Julie Landau 1994

The Columbia Anthology of Traditional Chinese Literature, ed. Victor H. Mair 1994

Scenes for Mandarins: The Elite Theater of the Ming, tr. Cyril Birch 1995

Letters of Nichiren, ed. Philip B. Yampolsky; tr. Burton Watson et al. 1996

Unforgotten Dreams: Poems by the Zen Monk Shōtetsu, tr. Steven D. Carter 1997

The Vimalakirti Sutra, tr. Burton Watson 1997

Japanese and Chinese Poems to Sing: The Wakan rōei shū, tr. J. Thomas Rimer and Jonathan Chaves 1997

Breeze Through Bamboo: Kanshi of Ema Saikō, tr. Hiroaki Sato 1998

A Tower for the Summer Heat, by Li Yu, tr. Patrick Hanan 1998

Traditional Japanese Theater: An Anthology of Plays, by Karen Brazell 1998

The Original Analects: Sayings of Confucius and His Successors (0479–0249), by E. Bruce Brooks and A. Taeko Brooks 1998

The Classic of the Way and Virtue: A New Translation of the Tao-te ching of Laozi as Interpreted by Wang Bi, tr. Richard John Lynn 1999

The Four Hundred Songs of War and Wisdom: An Anthology of Poems from Classical Tamil, The Puṟanāṉūṟu, ed. and tr. George L. Hart and Hank Heifetz 1999

Original Tao: Inward Training (Nei-yeh) *and the Foundations of Taoist Mysticism,* by Harold D. Roth 1999

Po Chü-i: Selected Poems, tr. Burton Watson 2000

Lao Tzu's Tao Te Ching: A Translation of the Startling New Documents Found at Guodian, by Robert G. Henricks 2000

The Shorter Columbia Anthology of Traditional Chinese Literature, ed. Victor H. Mair 2000

Mistress and Maid (Jiaohongji), by Meng Chengshun, tr. Cyril Birch 2001

Chikamatsu: Five Late Plays, tr. and ed. C. Andrew Gerstle 2001

The Essential Lotus: Selections from the Lotus Sutra, tr. Burton Watson 2002

Early Modern Japanese Literature: An Anthology, 1600–1900, ed. Haruo Shirane 2002; abridged 2008

The Columbia Anthology of Traditional Korean Poetry, ed. Peter H. Lee 2002

The Sound of the Kiss, or The Story That Must Never Be Told: Pingali Suranna's Kalapurnodayamu, tr. Vecheru Narayana Rao and David Shulman 2003

The Selected Poems of Du Fu, tr. Burton Watson 2003

Far Beyond the Field: Haiku by Japanese Women, tr. Makoto Ueda 2003

Just Living: Poems and Prose by the Japanese Monk Tonna, ed. and tr. Steven D. Carter 2003

Han Feizi: Basic Writings, tr. Burton Watson 2003

Mozi: Basic Writings, tr. Burton Watson 2003

Xunzi: Basic Writings, tr. Burton Watson 2003

Zhuangzi: Basic Writings, tr. Burton Watson 2003

The Awakening of Faith, Attributed to Aśvaghosha, tr. Yoshito S. Hakeda, introduction by Ryuichi Abe 2005

The Tales of the Heike, tr. Burton Watson, ed. Haruo Shirane 2006

Tales of Moonlight and Rain, by Ueda Akinari, tr. with introduction by Anthony H. Chambers 2007

Traditional Japanese Literature: An Anthology, Beginnings to 1600, ed. Haruo Shirane 2007

The Philosophy of Qi, by Kaibara Ekken, tr. Mary Evelyn Tucker 2007

The Analects of Confucius, tr. Burton Watson 2007

The Art of War: Sun Zi's Military Methods, tr. Victor Mair 2007

One Hundred Poets, One Poem Each: A Translation of the Ogura Hyakunin Isshu, tr. Peter McMillan 2008

Zeami: Performance Notes, tr. Tom Hare 2008

Zongmi on Chan, tr. Jeffrey Lyle Broughton 2009

Scripture of the Lotus Blossom of the Fine Dharma, rev. ed., tr. Leon Hurvitz, preface and introduction by Stephen R. Teiser 2009

Mencius, tr. Irene Bloom, ed. with an introduction by Philip J. Ivanhoe 2009

Clouds Thick, Whereabouts Unknown: Poems by Zen Monks of China, Charles Egan 2010

The Mozi: A Complete Translation, tr. Ian Johnston 2010

The Huainanzi: A Guide to the Theory and Practice of Government in Early Han China, by Liu An, tr. John S. Major, Sarah A. Queen, Andrew Seth Meyer, and Harold D. Roth, with Michael Puett and Judson Murray 2010

The Demon at Agi Bridge and Other Japanese Tales, tr. Burton Watson, ed. with introduction by Haruo Shirane 2011

Haiku Before Haiku: From the Renga Masters to Bashō, tr. with introduction by Steven D. Carter 2011

The Columbia Anthology of Chinese Folk and Popular Literature, ed. Victor H. Mair and Mark Bender 2011

Tamil Love Poetry: The Five Hundred Short Poems of the Aiṅkuṟunūṟu, tr. and ed. Martha Ann Selby 2011

The Teachings of Master Wuzhu: Zen and Religion of No-Religion, by Wendi L. Adamek 2011

The Essential Huainanzi, by Liu An, tr. John S. Major, Sarah A. Queen, Andrew Seth Meyer, and Harold D. Roth 2012

The Dao of the Military: Liu An's Art of War, tr. Andrew Seth Meyer 2012